The Economic Crisis in Social and Institutional Context

This book explores the foundations of the current economic crisis. Offering a heterodox approach to interpretation it examines the policies implemented before and during the crisis, and the main institutions that shaped the model of advanced economies, particularly in the last two decades.

The first part of the book provides a theoretical analysis of the crisis. The roots of the 'great recession' are divided into fundamentals with origins in financial liberalization, financial innovation and income distribution, and complementary or contributory factors such as the international imbalances, the monetary policy and the role of credit rating agencies. Part II suggests various paths to recovery while emphasizing that it will be necessary to develop alternative strategies for sustainable economic recovery and growth. These strategies will require genuine political support and a new 'great European vision' to address major issues concerning the EU such as unemployment, structural regional differences and federalism.

Drawing on various schools of thought, this book explains the complexities of the crisis through a wider evolutionary-institutional and heterodox framework.

Sebastiano Fadda is Professor of Economics and Director of the Research Center ASTRIL at the Department of Economics, University Roma Tre, Italy.

Pasquale Tridico is Professor of Economic Policy and Jean Monnet Chair at the Department of Economics, University Roma Tre, Italy.

Routledge Advances in Heterodox Economics

Edited by

Wolfram Elsner

University of Bremen

and

Peter Kriesler

University of New South Wales

Over the past two decades, the intellectual agendas of heterodox economists have taken a decidedly pluralist turn. Leading thinkers have begun to move beyond the established paradigms of Austrian, feminist, institutional-evolutionary, Marxian, Post Keynesian, radical, social and Sraffian economics – opening up new lines of analysis, criticism and dialogue among dissenting schools of thought. This cross-fertilization of ideas is creating a new generation of scholarship in which novel combinations of heterodox ideas are being brought to bear on important contemporary and historical problems.

Routledge Advances in Heterodox Economics aims to promote this new scholarship by publishing innovative books in heterodox economic theory, policy, philosophy, intellectual history, institutional history and pedagogy. Syntheses or critical engagement of two or more heterodox traditions are especially encouraged.

1 **Ontology and Economics**
Tony Lawson and his critics
Edited by Edward Fullbrook

2 **Currencies, Capital Flows and Crises**
A post Keynesian analysis of exchange rate determination
John T. Harvey

3 **Radical Economics and Labor**
Frederic Lee and Jon Bekken

4 **A History of Heterodox Economics**
Challenging the mainstream in the twentieth century
Frederic Lee

5 **Heterodox Macroeconomics**
Edited by Jonathan P. Goldstein and Michael G. Hillard

6 **The Marginal Productivity Theory of Distribution**
A critical history
John Pullen

7 **Informal Work in Developed Nations**
Edited by Enrico A. Marcelli, Colin C. Williams and Pascale Jossart

8 **The Foundations of Non-Equilibrium Economics**
The principle of circular and cumulative causation
Edited by Sebastian Berger

9 **The Handbook of Pluralist Economics Education**
Edited by Jack Reardon

10 **The Coming of Age of Information Technologies and the Path of Transformational Growth**
A long run perspective on the 2000s recession
Davide Gualerzi

11 **Cultural Economics and Theory**
The evolutionary economics of David Hamilton
William M. Dugger, William Waller, David Hamilton, and Glen Atkinson

12 **The Cultural and Political Economy of Recovery**
Social learning in a post-disaster environment
Emily Chamlee-Wright

13 **The Foundations of Institutional Economics**
K. William Kapp
Edited by Sebastian Berger and Rolf Steppacher

14 **Alternative Theories of Competition**
Edited by Jamee K. Moudud, Cyrus Bina and Patrick L. Mason

15 **In Defense of Post-Keynesian and Heterodox Economics**
Responses to their critics
Edited by Frederic S. Lee and Marc Lavoie

16 **The US Economy and Neoliberalism**
Alternative strategies and policies
Edited by Nikolaos Karagiannis, Zagros Madjd-Sadjadi and Swapan Sen

17 **Technological Change and Network Effects in Growth Regimes**
Exploring the microfoundations of economic growth
Torsten Heinrich

18 **The Foundations of Evolutionary Institutional Economics**
Generic institutionalism
Manuel Wäckerle

19 **Re-Thinking Economics**
Exploring the work of Pierre Bourdieu
Edited by Asimina Christoforou and Michael Lainé

20 **Networks of Institutions**
Institutional emergence, social structure and national systems of policies
Shuanping Dai

21 **An Ecosystem Approach to Economic Stabilization**
Escaping the neoliberal wilderness
Rodrick Wallace

22 **The Economic Crisis in Social and Institutional Context**
Theories, policies and exit strategies
Edited by Sebastiano Fadda and Pasquale Tridico

This series was previously published by The University of Michigan Press and the following books are available (please contact UMP for more information):

Economics in Real Time
A theoretical reconstruction
John McDermott

Liberating Economics
Feminist perspectives on families, work, and globalization
Drucilla K. Barker and Susan F. Feiner

Socialism After Hayek
Theodore A. Burczak

Future Directions for Heterodox Economics
Edited by John T. Harvey and Robert F. Garnett, Jr.

Are Worker Rights Human Rights?
Richard P. McIntyre

The Economic Crisis in Social and Institutional Context

Theories, policies and exit strategies

Edited by Sebastiano Fadda and Pasquale Tridico

Routledge
Taylor & Francis Group
LONDON AND NEW YORK

First published 2015
by Routledge
2 Park Square, Milton Park, Abingdon, Oxon OX14 4RN

and by Routledge
711 Third Avenue, New York, NY 10017

Routledge is an imprint of the Taylor & Francis Group, an informa business

British Library Cataloguing in Publication Data
A catalogue record for this book is available from the British Library

Library of Congress Cataloging in Publication Data
The economic crisis in social and institutional context: theories, policies and exit strategies/[edited by] Sebastiano Fadda.
pages cm.
Includes bibliographical references and index.
1. Recessions. 2. Financial crises. 3. Economic development.
4. Economic policy. 5. Global Financial Crisis, 2008–2009.
I. Fadda, Sebastiano.
HB3711.E424 2015
330.9'0511–dc23 2014036829

ISBN: 978-1-138-80559-0 (hbk)
ISBN: 978-1-315-75219-8 (ebk)

Typeset in Times New Roman
by Wearset Ltd, Boldon, Tyne and Wear

Contents

Figures

Tables

Contributors

Editors

Sebastiano Fadda is Professor of Economics and Director of the Research Center ASTRIL at the Department of Economics, University Roma Tre, Italy, where he teaches Advanced Labour Economics and Economic Growth. He is the director of a two-year Master's degree course (Labour Market, Industrial Relations and Welfare Systems). He has worked extensively on institutions, economic development and labour economics issues. He is the author of many journal articles and books on these issues, including two edited books with Routledge (*Financial Crisis, Labour Markets and Institutions*, 2013; *Institutions and Development after the Financial Crisis*, 2013).

Pasquale Tridico is Professor of Economic Policy and Jean Monnet Chair at the Department of Economics, University Roma Tre, Italy, where he lectures in Labour Economics, European Labour Market and Development Economics. He is General Secretary of the EAEPE (European Association for Evolutionary Political Economy). In the academic year 2010–2011 he was a Fulbright Research Scholar at the New York University. He is the author of several books and articles on institutional economics, labour markets, varieties of capitalism and financial crisis, including three edited books with Routledge (*Financial Crisis, Labour Markets and Institutions*, 2013; *Institutions and Development after the Financial Crisis*, 2013; *Economic Policy and the Financial Crisis*, 2014). He is also the author of *Institutions, Human Development and Economic Growth in Transition Economies* (Palgrave, 2011).

Contributors

Philip Arestis, University of Cambridge, UK.

Vincent Duwicquet, CLERSE, University of Lille 1, France.

Wolfram Elsner, University of Bremen, Germany.

Sebastiano Fadda, University Roma Tre, Italy.

John Groenewegen, Delft University.

Elias Karakitsos, Global Economic Research.

Maria Lissowska, Warsaw School of Economics and European Commission.

Jacques Mazier, CEPN, University Paris 13.

Pascal Petit, CEPN, University Paris 13.

Jamel Saadaoui, BETA, University of Strasbourg.

Malcolm Sawyer, University of Leeds.

Ngai-Ling Sum, Lancaster University.

Pasquale Tridico, University Roma Tre.

Jacek Wallusch, Institute of Cliometrics and Transition Studies.

Beata Woźniak-Jęchorek, Poznan University of Economics.

Brigitte Young, University of Muenster.

Acknowledgements

This book is a collection of papers presented at the EAEPE (European Association for Evolutionary Political Economy) Summer School held at the University Roma Tre, in Italy, 1–5 July 2013. The Summer School's main theme was 'Social and institutional context of the crisis'. Authors elaborated policies, institutions and exit strategies from the crisis. We wish to thank all the participants at the Summer School, students and professors, who were a source of great inspiration.

About the book

The aim of this book is to explore both the foundations of the current economic crisis, offering a heterodox approach to interpret the crisis, and the policies implemented during the crisis and before, along with the main institutions which shaped the model of advanced economies in the last two decades in particular. The book is divided in two parts. In the first part a theoretical analysis to interpret the crisis is put forward. The main interpretation here is that in the current socio-economic systems the understanding of the causes and remedies of a crisis is a complex issue in which the level of actors, the level of private governance, the level of public governance and the level of social values need to be addressed in an interdependent, systemic, evolutionary way. In this context, the origins of the 'great recession' are divided into fundamentals (which originate in the financial liberalization, financial innovation and income distribution) and complementary or contributory factors (such as the international imbalances, the monetary policy and the role of credit rating agencies). In the second part, we show, through a range of different examples, empirical evidences, varieties of capitalism and of political economy frameworks, observed policy options and discourse analysis that there are several ways to go out from the crisis, to develop alternative strategies for sustainable economic recovery and growth. These strategies need first of all genuine political support, and, as far as the European Union is concerned, a new scheme of governance, a new 'great European vision' which would address the major EU issues such as unemployment, structural regional differences and federalism.

The advantage of this analysis is connected with its complexity and with the multi-task attempts and scientific three purposes of the book. First of all the attempt to explain the crisis through a wider evolutionary-institutional and heterodox approach, which is not at all based on a single school of thought, but quite multi-disciplinary and complex. Second, the attempt to propose alternative development strategies. Third, the attempt to propose a critical review of the current political economy paradigm in which advanced economies are inserted.

Introduction

Sebastiano Fadda and Pasquale Tridico

This book focuses on the current financial and economic crisis that advanced economies in particular have been suffering in the past seven years at least since 2007. It has the objective to explore both the foundations of the economic crisis, offering a heterodox approach to interpret the crisis, and the policies implemented during the crisis and before, along with the main institutions which shaped the model of advanced economies in the last two decades in particular. The book offers also an exit perspective explored through case studies, and development strategies.

The book is divided into two parts. The first part has the broad ambition to show that the current financial and economic crisis can be considered a systemic crisis, and it involves politics, social values and economics. In general, the origins of the 'great recession' are found in the financial liberalization, financial innovation and distributional effects. The contributory factors were: international imbalances; monetary policy; the role of credit rating agencies. The book reviews the changes in the structure of the financial sector associated with financialization, and argues that those changes have made for a financial system more prone to crisis. It is argued that those changes may have tended to reduce the rate of growth. In this context, the financial and economic crisis appears also as a crisis of dramatic over-accumulation, favoured by the emerging and circulation, during the booming period of financial innovation, of fictitious capital at a global level.

In Europe, economic difficulties are deepened by strong philosophical differences based on economic doctrines that are conditioned by a legacy of national Varieties of Capitalism. On the one side, there is the German ordoliberal doctrine which hails from the late nineteenth century, which is an anti-Keynesian, supply side export-led, monetarist rule-based model, and on the other a demand-led Keynesian doctrine. The first seems to dominate due to the veto that Germany is able to play within the EU and within the Eurozone in particular. These ordoliberal policies, and in particular the supply side policies in place in the past 15–20 years in the EU, worsened the position of Mediterranean economies. The reforms of the labour market, with the introduction of labour flexibility, the neoliberal policies adopted following both the Washington Consensus at international level and the Maastricht Treaty at European level, along with other policies introduced in parallel, such as retrenchment of welfare state and privatization of public goods, had cumulative negative consequences on the inequality, on the consumption, on the aggregate demand, on the labour productivity and on the GDP dynamics.

The second part is more policy oriented. First of all it criticizes the attempt to implement in Europe structural reforms aiming at reducing social expenditure. We argue that neither the budget constraint, nor the globalization process, nor the efficiency issue are to be considered valid reasons why the welfare state should be reduced. While a deep restructuring of the welfare system seems necessary in order to improve its effectiveness and its response to the changing social needs, the restructuring efforts should focus on increasing productivity and reducing the unit costs of welfare services.

We present a collection of stylized facts about economic and institutional convergence/divergence in Eurozone countries in the period 2007–2011, from a Varieties of Capitalism perspective. The aim is to show a sort of 'Germanization' of macroeconomic policies in the Eurozone as reflected in the Fiscal Compact which do not seem to solve problems, in particular in Mediterranean economies. In fact, it will be argued that the diversity in the Eurozone has costs and advantages respectively for countries whether they are confronted with an overvalued or undervalued euro. In order to overcome these problems, we propose a budgetary federalism, based on long-term investment programmes with an enlarged political support.

Another focus of this second part of the book will be the damages, in particular in post-transition countries (new member states of the European Union), created by extreme financialization, where growing inequality and poverty together with consumerism may be indicated as a reason of rapidly growing debt, mostly in the form of consumer credits. Indebtedness enabled by foreign financing amplified the possibilities to consume, but, when easy credit disappeared, deepened recession. Recovery strategies here can be offered only by demand side policies. It emerges also clearly that differentiated strategies are needed in Europe, in particular when one adds the new EU member states' perspective. Finally, it is interesting to look at the cultural political economy approach to examine the current discourses and practices of crisis recovery. This would allow to see the inconsistencies of political leadership and the tensions which arise between reality and rhetorical discourses.

The structure of the book

The book is structured in two parts. In the first part ('Crisis interpretation: A heterodox approach) the authors try to give alternative explanations of the crisis and of the contradictions of the financial capitalism model which was embraced by most of the advanced economies in the last two to three decades. In Chapter 1 John Groenewegen argues that all scientific knowledge is formulated in models of the real world. In applying concepts, theories and models inevitably choices are made: in representing the real world the scientist isolates vertically and horizontally such that reality becomes 'manageable'. These choices are not arbitrary. On the contrary: the debate among scientists is about the relevancy of specific models for on the one hand the research questions one is interested in (what causes the economic crisis?) and on the other hand about the resemblance of the assumptions in the models with the conditions in the real world. Groenewegen distinguishes two schools of thought in institutional economics: one based on the methodological principles of neoclassical economics (NIE) and the other based on alternative principles (OIE). On the basis of that markets and the actors are modelled and consideration about consequences and causes of the crisis vary.

In Chapter 2 Philip Arestis and Elias Karakitsos discuss the causes of the 'great recession' and the policy implications. They concentrate on the financial liberalization and income redistribution, which produced the new financial engineering rooted in the USA, which led to an extraordinary mispricing of risk. The new financial engineering practice led to the growth of collateralized debt instruments, especially so collateralized mortgages, essentially through the parallel banking sector in the USA. When that market collapsed the 'great recession' emerged. The authors distinguish between the main factors and the contributory factors of the crisis. Then they turn to economic policy implications with a number of very interesting proposals for countries or groups of countries, and the European Union in particular.

In Chapter 3 Malcolm Sawyer discusses the characteristics of a sustainable development model. An ecologically sustainable growth path, he argues, has many prerequisites: amongst those would be the construction of a financial system which is itself sustainable and which is consistent with the funding of investment which supports a sustainable growth path. The financial system has often been viewed as something of a driver for economic growth, and as such lower and sustainable growth requires some taming of the financial system. The first part of his chapter discusses the relationships between financialization, growth of the financial sector and growth of economic activity. It is particularly concerned with whether indeed the financial system fosters growth, and whether more recently the relationship between financial growth and economic growth has changed. The second is based on the argument that there is not a general shortage of finance for investment particularly in a slower growth era, and that much more attention should be paid to ensuring that the direction of finance is towards environmentally friendly and 'green' investment. It cannot be expected that a financial system will ensure such a direction of finance, and that measures will be needed in terms of regulation and restructuring the financial system to aid the redirection of finance.

In Chapter 4 Wolfram Elsner puts forward an interesting Marxian explanation of the crisis. He explores the crisis and some implications against the Marxian profit rate (PR). The PR helps in explaining a number of phenomena often considered disparate. The focus is on integrating exploded fictitious capital in the PR and to estimate a corrected PR. Elsner estimates global fictitious capital and calculates a conventional and a corrected PR for Germany. The corrected PR has reached a historical low under neoliberalism, in spite of an increase in profit masses and profit shares in GDP, between one-half and one-fifth of the conventional PR (for post-WWII USA and UK, and post-1991 Germany, respectively). In contrast to the conventional PR, it also has further decreased. The financial crisis thus appears to be a crisis of dramatic over-accumulation. The consequences include reinforced redistribution and a run for transformation into real values (resources-/land-grabbing). The redistribution requirements for a 'usual' PR appear inconsistent even with formal democracy.

In Chapter 5 Brigitte Young confronts the different ideas on the basis of which the Eurozone crisis was managed. In particular she compares the German ordoliberalism models versus the post-Keynesian model and she argues that the inability of European member states of the Eurozone to arrive at a coordinated reform agenda for the Euro crisis is not due to failures of individual leaders, but rather due to philosophical differences based on economic doctrines that are conditioned by a legacy of national Varieties of Capitalism. On the one side, there is the German ordoliberal doctrine which hails from the late nineteenth century which is an anti-Keynesian, supply side export-led, monetarist rule-based model, and on the other a demand-led Keynesian model. The author tries to demonstrate how economic ideas of ordoliberalism have become agenda setters and actors using these ideas have become veto players in preventing an alternative discourse and practice, i.e. non-austerity at the Euro level. In the present Euro crisis resolution scenario, the influence of ordoliberalism is most evident in the institutions such as the German Bundesbank and the Federal Ministry of Finance with its focus on price stability. This argument differs from more traditional explanations which cite geopolitical factors such as Germany becoming a more normal nation, to the hypothesis of Germany being a 'reluctant Hegemon' (*The Economist*), to subjective factors such that Angela Merkel has little connection to the European idea (Tony Judt).

In Chapter 6 Pasquale Tridico compares the economic crisis and the decline which is occurring in Italy with the crisis in France and Germany. The current global economic crisis, which also Italy fell into in 2008, represents just the last step of a long declining path for the Italian economy which began in the 1990s, or to be more precise in 1992 and 1993. This was not the case for France and Germany. In particular, the author argues, the reasons which explain the long Italian decline, and partly also the deeper recession today, as well as the lack of recovery from the current crisis, can be found in the past reforms of the labour market. We focus on the labour flexibility introduced in the last 15 years, which had, along with other policies introduced in parallel, cumulative negative consequences on the inequality, on the consumption, on the aggregate demand, on the labour productivity and finally on the GDP dynamics. These policies were possible within the neoliberal model inaugurated in Italy with the adhesion to the Washington Consensus doctrine, and the changes introduced by the Maastricht Treaty.

In the second part of the book ('Exit perspectives and development strategies') the authors advance possible solutions, alternative models and empirical analysis on the basis of which good policies and institutions could be designed.

In Chapter 7 Sebastiano Fadda argues that a deep restructuring of the welfare system is necessary in order to improve its effectiveness and its response to changing social needs. However, restructuring efforts should focus on increasing productivity and reducing the unit costs of welfare services. In fact, neither the budget constraint, nor the globalization process, nor the efficiency issues are to be considered valid reasons as to why the welfare state should be reduced. Unfortunately, widespread ideological preferences and perverse resistance against unit cost reduction seem to be supporting the trend towards a reduction in social expenditures through a substantial downsizing, if not the full dismantling, of the welfare state.

In Chapter 8 Vincent Duwicquet, Jacques Mazier, Pascal Petit and Jamel Saadaoui discuss the future of the euro. The Euro crisis, they argue, illustrates the deficiencies of adjustment mechanisms in a monetary union characterized by a large heterogeneity. Exchange rate adjustments being impossible, few alternative mechanisms are available. Nevertheless, fiscal policy could play an active role. In a federal state like the USA its stabilization coefficient is around 20 per cent. But there is no equivalent in the European case. Well-integrated capital markets, with portfolio diversification and intra-zone credit, have been proposed as a powerful adjustment mechanism by the 'international risk sharing' approach. Intra-zone credit and capital income from international portfolios would have stabilization coefficients around 20–30 per cent each. These results have been used during the 2000s by proponents of liberal economic policies in the EU to promote deeper financial integration without having to develop a federal budget. However, the theoretical basis and the results, the authors conclude, appear highly questionable.

In Chapter 9 Maria Lissowska discusses the role of credit to households as an element speeding up consumption to unsustainable levels and thus contributing to the run up to financial crisis of 2008. She provides an overview of the literature indicating different underpinnings of the crisis. This chapter analyses the particular case of post-transition countries where increase of household debt was very fast and underpinned by rising income inequalities, suspicious consumption and availability of credit. However, a similar process of cumulating of household debt took place in Western European countries, while the initial debt level was higher and mortgage credit constituted its prevailing part. The chapter then points out the differentiated degree of deleveraging of households and its reasons across countries. It confirms that increase of lending to households should be very prudent to avoid further risk of non-performing loans and over-indebted consumers, by the spiral of broadening risk margins and the negative selection of more and more risky borrowers.

In Chapter 10 Jacek Wallusch and Beata Woźniak-Jęchorek argue that the labour market policy in unified Europe operates in an extremely diversified environment. Persistent unemployment has structural characteristics, which ultimately depend on the institutional arrangement regarding unemployment benefits and employment protection. The relationship between unemployment and labour market institutions, however, goes much deeper and concerns norms, habits, traditions and culture. The aim of this chapter is to trace the impact of real wage and selected institutional variables (Kaitz index, gender gap, tax wedge and union density) on the unemployment rate in the old and new EU countries. The authors' estimations show that both magnitude and the direction of unemployment rate responses differ in old and new EU economies. These conclusions seem to be particularly important from the perspective of creating recommendations for EU Labour Market Policy.

Finally, in Chapter 11 Ngai-Ling Sum discusses the cultural political economy (CPE) roots of the crisis recovery. In particular she applies a cultural political approach to examine the 'BRIC' (Brazil, Russia, India and China) cases. During crises, economic and political actors search for and/or construct objects of 'growth' and 'hope' that may secure recovery. She examines three overlapping stages in the (re-)making of the 'BRIC' as an object of 'hope', starting with its invention after the 9/11 attacks. Then she examines how 'BRIC' discourses were recontextualized in the Sinophone world, focusing on how China's 'growth' was supported by a vast stimulus package following the 2008 global financial crisis. This package posed serious fiscal challenges, especially for regional-local authorities. It intensified land-based accumulation, inflated the 'property bubble', stimulated land clearance/dispossession, local government debt and social unrest. Finally, she summarizes the main lessons of this CPE-inspired analysis of the 'BRIC' imaginaries and the Chinese case and considers alternative imaginaries.

Part I

Crisis interpretation

A heterodox approach

1 Economic crisis and the explanatory power of (institutional) economics

John Groenewegen

Introduction

In a scientific discipline specific research questions are formulated, which have to be answered in a well-defined way concerning logical reasoning, theory formation and testing. The reality, as science attempts to understand, is multidimensional, complex, full of interdependencies, feedback loops, different groups of actors with different motivations, interests, power and values. Moreover, the reality is dynamic due to creative acts of actors, interaction between actors, changes in physical structures, in preferences, values, norms and (shared) mental maps. Science tries to understand, explain and in the end predict the complex, dynamic reality by means of frameworks, theories and models.[1] In short: by means of abstractions of the reality.

Economists analyse the world and its events, like an economic crisis, on the basis of models, of abstractions. Economists, like all scientists, construct representations of the real world and apply the insights based on these 'scientific realities' in their analyses of the causes of the event and in formulating policy recommendations about how to prevent it from happening again.

In this chapter I will first elaborate on the different scientific realities that exist within (institutional) economics. It will be explained that the different 'representations' of reality need to connect to a 'target' reality in order to have relevant explanatory power. In the next sections I will discuss how first mainstream economics (neoclassical and new institutional economics) represents economic reality and how in general causes of a crisis are identified and remedied. Second I will do the same for the alternative school of original institutional economics. It is the subject of hot scientific debates which school of thought provides the most relevant representation of the target reality and which one has most explanatory power in relation to events like economic crisis and their solutions.

1 Different representations of the economic crisis

The real world is a complex phenomenon human beings cannot directly comprehend through their senses: they structure the complex reality according to certain categories about which they have found out over time that the connectedness of the categories with the reality is sufficient for not being constantly surprised by events in the real world.[2] So the scientist can be presented as an agent who makes a model, a representation, of the real world, that should more or less resemble the real world. In discussing representations (concepts, theories, models) it seems useful to distinguish between the natural world and the social world. Natural scientists make representations of the physical or biological nature in order to discover how nature really is, how the natural world works, to discover what exists (ontology). With models in which scientists create their 'scientific realities' they isolate, exclude in their models elements from the real world in order to make 'logical reasoning and calculations' possible. Scientists make concepts, or constructs (Schütz 1953), that represent variables of the real world and with reasoning and calculations they arrive at hypotheses about patterns and laws that would exist in the real world out there. The hypothesis about atoms, molecules, particles and genes and how they are connected and cause specific events are tested by means of prototypes, mathematical models and simulations. The tests can lead to adaptations of the prototype and when everything works well the Voyager, or the Soyuz, can be constructed. It can also be that the tests continue to go wrong and then the scientific knowledge or the calculations have to be adapted; theory then has to be adapted into a better representation of reality. In this way the natural scientist is after discovering the 'Truth' about the natural reality, how it is ordered according to its laws and regularities. Following the philosophy of pragmatism I would say that abduction (qualitative induction), deduction and (quantitative) induction are and should be part of such a scientific approach.[3]

Social scientists, like economists, also model the social world using concepts, theories and models. The difference with the natural world would be the human being as a thinking volitional actor, who decides and behaves in a different way than molecules do, which complicates the construction of a scientific reality. In the social domain actors are present that differ from molecules and atoms: they think, make choices and decide. In order to make a social system function, coordination between actors is necessary, which is done through institutions, like norms, laws and regulations.

How do these sciences go about with the reality of an economic crisis?

Searle (2005) explains how human beings construct the social reality by imposing 'status functions' on the natural world: X (the natural world of physical beings in a building of steel and concrete) becomes Y (the institutionalized world of Wall Street) in context C (2008 with a specific political American setting and specific shared mental models). Similar to the natural scientists, the social scientists work with constructs, but now the constructs of the actors in the social domain are added. Actors in the world of Wall Street act on the basis of constructs. Firms like Lehman Brothers, government actors and representatives of interest groups, they all apply abstractions, representations of the world they think they live in. A social scientist trying to understand that social world in order to design institutions, makes a 'construct of the constructs' the actors apply (Schultz 1937; Groenewegen 2014).

Value sensitive design[4]

The world of values connects well to the world of institutions in the sense that values are also social constructions about for instance the incomes actors in the financial world should earn in comparison to the actors in the supervising institutions who are controlling them. Or the values about what is morally acceptable behaviour in selling mortgages to starters on the housing market (Correljé and Groenewegen 2009; Correljé *et al.* forthcoming). Similar to institutions, values and norms are 'socially constructed' and can be changed by human beings, albeit at a different speed and in a different way than institutions like laws and regulations.

The characterization of different representations in economics

In models of the real world researchers isolate purposefully from parts of reality and create a so-called scientific reality. One of the big questions scientists face in for instance understanding and explaining economic crisis and have disagreement about is the right way and the right degree of abstraction in relation to the reality. How abstract can the rationality of actors be modelled? How complex can the institutional and social environment in which they operate be modelled? How detailed should the interaction among actors be modelled? Below we discuss how in economics the modelling is done in different ways and how consequently economic reality and the causes and remedies of the economic crisis are differently represented. Before doing so we close this paragraph with a summary of the elements involved in building models. Mäki (2011, p. 2) depicts model representation as a multi faceted process, in which

> Agent A
> uses multi-component object M as
> a representative of (actual or possible) target R
> for purpose **P**,
> addressing audience **E**,
> at least potentially prompting genuine issues of relevant resemblance between M and R to arise;
> describing M and drawing inferences about M and R in terms of one or more model descriptions **D**;
> and applies commentary **C** to identify and coordinate the other components.

With building the model M the scientist makes isolations in the real world R, the target reality, in a vertical or horizontal way. Necessarily the model leaves parts of reality, and so potential explanatory variables of the crisis, out of the representation. The model is designed with a specific purpose P, a specific research question, for a specific issue to be understood and solved. (Groenewegen and Vromen 1996). Furthermore the model is made to address a specific audience like scientific colleagues, to test a specific hypothesis, or to advise politicians.

Both P and E guide scientists in the way they model the real world, in what they take on board and what they isolate from. The selection of what is inside and outside the model, what is endogenous and what is exogenous, is done with a specific purpose but also for a specific audience. This can be a scientific audience of colleagues or opponents or a more policy oriented audience of politicians. The point is that the choice of audience has an impact on the way of isolating, on the way of choosing the representation. The political belief of self-regulating markets that since the ideology of Reagan and Thatcher have dominated the political scene has for instance a large impact on economic modelling. When the audience is first of all the academic colleagues, which is mostly the case, then scientists have a drive to isolate in such a way that the purpose of 'elegant, rigorous modelling' is fulfilled with description D in which mathematics and diagrams dominate over 'analytical narratives'. In commentary C scientists make clear what the role of other not modelled components would be. In the commentary the scientist should explain how the model connects to the real world, what has been left out and why, what consequently the limitations of the model are. However, this part of the process of modelling is often more implicit than explicit. In economics much attention is on the formal modelling and the claim 'then would be that economists may have been excessively and uncritically constrained by considerations of formal tractability rather than empirical adequacy, and this has imposed serious limitations on how they view the world' (Mäki 2011, p. 5).

Crucial is the relevant resemblance between M and R: the model should resemble reality in a relevant way, i.e. relevant in relation to P and E. Groenewegen and Vromen (1996) made also explicit in that respect the importance of the connection of the assumptions in the model and the conditions in reality. When for instance the model assumes a selection based on anonymous competition and the conditions in reality are of a protected monopoly, then the model and reality do not resemble each other in a relevant way. For another research question, or under other conditions in the target reality the model might be a good representation.

Important is the claim that the model should sufficiently connect to the real target world: there should be resemblance between the model and reality so the causes of for instance the crisis are included in the model.

In the following we will discuss how different schools of (institutional) economics model the real world by discussing the research questions the models are supposed to answer and the conditions of the reality the models include and exclude. We will show how actors are modelled, in what kind of structures they operate and how in those scientific realities the actors are constrained and enabled by their environmental structures. For our purpose we consider the broad distinction between only two schools of economics, mainstream economics (neoclassical and New Institutional Economics) and the alternative (Original Institutional Economics), as appropriate.

2 Mainstream economics and the crisis

In this section[5] we explain the foundations of the model mainstream economics makes as a representation of the economic reality to be explained. We will claim that the foundations of New Institutional Economics are similar to NCE and that is why we consider it appropriate to put both NCE and NIE under the label of mainstream economics. This in contrast to the alternative of Original Institutional Economics we will discuss below.

Neoclassical economics

How does NCE represent the target reality? What is the nature of the reality and how can we best acquire knowledge about it? We will first briefly address these ontological and epistemological questions in such a way that we understand how NCE models the target world and how consequently the economic crisis is explained.

Broadly speaking neoclassical economics is modelled after the way physics models the natural world. First it adheres to the philosophy of positivism:[6] science aims at the discovery of universal causal laws, which represent in an objective way the relationship between variables in a reality, which is knowable to all scientists in the same objective way.[7] The aim of science is to reveal the Truth, which is hidden in the objects of the reality around us. In theories, like for instance a theory to explain the differences between interest rates different countries have to pay for their loans, a distinction is made between dependent (the rise of interest rate for government loans) and the independent variables (exogenous variables like the budget deficit of the government), which cause the changes in the differences in the rates between countries. The causal relationship is formulated in a (universal) law to be tested in an objective way by (other) researchers, who will use the same objective method of deductive analysis.[8] Based on validated laws a discipline like economics is able to make predictions, which would hold anytime anywhere (but only if the assumptions stated at the beginning of the deduction are true).

In the vision of a positivist the world that is scientifically of interest only consists of empirical phenomena, which can be observed through our senses (August Comte). Later in the 1930s the Vienna Circle turned that vision into a theory of knowledge: knowledge can only be based on direct, so-called pre-theoretical observation. Facts are so-called brute facts and from them scientists can logically derive deductions, which are to be tested in reality.[9]

The second pillar of NCE is its methodological individualism.

In the standard neoclassical model individual consumers are assumed to decide on the basis of their utility function: the subjective value. The utility of a good or service is the capability to satisfy individual wants and the value of an object is what the individual ascribes to it because of her preferences. Given her preferences, the consumer is assumed to maximize her utility through her demand in the market. Individual producers determine what they offer in the market, taking into consideration the profits they collect at a given market price. The aggregate demand of all individual consumers, in confrontation with the aggregate supply, results in a certain amount of goods traded at the equilibrium price.

The preferences are given for the economist: the individual is the starting point of the analysis and her preferences are exogenous. This approach, based on individual utility functions, allows for individuals having moral preferences, like acting in the interests of others (Becker 1996). Yet, that is outside the domain of economic inquiry. In that sense economics is a 'value-free' science: it does not study and evaluate the subjective values as such, but takes the 'revealed preferences' as a given.

The actors in NCE are modelled with specific characteristics of rationality (which makes an *ex ante* calculation of optimal combinations possible) and rules of behaviour (they maximize utility and profit and minimize costs). The *homo economicus* is a fully informed actor, who is positioned in a well-defined environment of a specific market structure (for instance a perfectly competitive market, or a monopoly). This environment is analytically considered a static given; exogenous to the model. In applying the Methodology of the Scientific Research Programme on NCE, Latsis (1976) identified the hard core, protective belt and heuristics of neoclassical economics. He concluded that the core models are all of a 'single-exit structure'; given the characteristics of the actors and the situation, logically they have no other option than to calculate and to 'choose' the one optimal solution, which is the one theory predicts.[10]

To sum up: neoclassical theory adheres to the positive-normative dichotomy, that separates facts ('what is') from values ('what ought to be'). The wants and subjective valuation of actors are exogenously given, i.e. objective facts for the scientific researcher. A normative analysis of those facts cannot and should not be part of the economists' scientific inquiry: the positive and the normative should be carefully separated and then, it is claimed, economics is a value-free science. A related tenet to this separation is the claim that the facts are objectively accessible through our senses. The facts economics is studying are 'brute facts', i.e. they are in no way constructed by the theoretical concepts used (see below for details).

Economists present their discipline as a value-free science in the sense that they do not normatively appraise the subjective values of the actors and in the sense that in their scientific investigation they have objectively access to the facts.

Nevertheless neoclassical economics applies at least two values: one is about the supremacy of subjective values over collective values and the second one is about the supremacy of the market mechanism. An important value judgement of NCE about the market is it being the most adequate coordination mechanism to connect demand and supply and to incentivize efficient behaviour both in a static and a dynamic sense.

The market and crisis

The design issue in NCE focuses on efficient market structures. NCE adherents are convinced of one thing: competition will bring the best outcome possible for society, whatever that may be. A well-functioning market will reveal the outcomes over time, and prices will reflect the aggregated preferences of the consumers and the optimal combinations of the production factors.

When a number of specific conditions concerning the market structure and formal competition law is fulfilled, the individual suppliers in the market will be put under the pressure of competition, resulting in a search for the most efficient combinations of scarce resources to offer the individual consumers products and services at the lowest price possible to fulfil their subjective values. Moreover, the market will also push participants to innovate both in products, production processes and governance structures, in order to stay ahead of competitors. So, subjective values are central and the market is the most effective and efficient means to realize that end. Note that in NCE the introduction of the market and its competitive nature does not tell us anything about the specific outcomes the market will bring us. Which services will be offered, at what prices, which values of whom will be fulfilled is unknown.

In NCE this conviction has led to a description of the ideal type of a competitive market with many independently operating suppliers and many consumers as the reference model and to a corresponding competition policy. All market actors should have equal access rights to the market and to the relevant objective information. All private institutional arrangements like vertically integrated firms, strategic alliances or acquisitions and public interventions other than based on competition law, are considered 'anti-competitive', because they reduce the number of market participants, and their independent behaviour and private choices. Firms are production functions and the market is a 'signalling device', in which prices objectively signal consumers and producers what the scarcities are and when these have changed due to exogenous shocks.

Also the consumers in the mainstream market economy are assumed to serve the functioning of the market economy well; the right consumer behaviour is to switch to another product, or supplier, when price and quality differences indicate so.

The universal rules of the (competitive) game described above and the corresponding rights and norms of consumers and producers in the market are part of the so-called deontological ethical rules that embed the neoclassical market and that should be enforced by legal measures to make the market function properly (Van Staveren 2007).

So based on two value judgements – the subjective value is what counts and the market is the best institution to realize subjective values – neoclassical economics considers the right design and implementation of the market as the main task of an economist. Consequently, when the economy is in crisis the cause is to be found in a bad design of markets and the remedy is in correcting those mistakes. This can be a matter of power asymmetry, abuse of power, a matter of information asymmetry, a lack of information or insufficient rules about the correct behaviour of the economic actors.

New Institutional Economics

Since the mid 1970s the school of New Institutional Economics (NIE) developed strongly with Nobel laureates like Ronald Coase, Douglass North and Elinor Ostrom and Oliver Williamson. Earlier Nobel laureates like Friedrich von Hayek, Kenneth Arrow and Herbert Simon are also often considered to be institutionally oriented economists (Williamson 1975). The NIE addresses questions that were not part of NCE, such as why do institutions like property rights and firms exist? What is the role of values and norms in society? What is the impact of differences in the institutional environments on the allocation of goods and services? In short: why do institutions exist and why do they matter? In addressing such questions, NIE introduced additional attributes to the economic actor: bounded rationality and opportunistic behaviour. The first is about the limited capacity of actors to capture all relevant information and to calculate the optimal outcome, or to make a complete contract in which all eventualities are taken care of. The second is about the possibility that actors abuse asymmetry of information, by providing misleading information to others or even cheat them. The actors are positioned in complex and uncertain environments implying that they are not able, as in NCE, to eliminate all uncertainties through complete contracting. Hence, to govern their transactions in an efficient way, the actors create institutional arrangements like vertically integrated firms, long-term contracts and branch associations. Maintaining the value-free philosophical and methodological characteristics of NCE,[11] NIE explains that institutional arrangements exist because they are efficient as they minimize transaction costs.

Expanding the world of NCE, Williamson (1975) showed how all kinds of private governance structures were not meant only to build up market power, but that they were also aimed to reduce transaction costs. Hence they should not be forbidden by competition law; the subtitle of his book was 'Analysis and Antitrust Implications'. Private ordering of markets serves efficiency, not only to be calculated as a minimization of production costs as in neoclassical economics, but also as a minimization of transaction costs.

NIE introduced another economic vision on private and public institutional arrangements and in Williamson (1979) a range of efficient governance structures was discussed. Each of these governance structures can be efficient to coordinate specific types of transactions, depending on the degree of asset specificity of the good or service transacted. When the investments are very specific then the investment is worthless when the transaction is ended. The degree of asset specificity has implications for the possibility of opportunistic behaviour and therefore for the need of safeguards. When transactions have a low asset specificity then the 'ideal' traditional market contract is most efficient. Indeed, the danger of potential opportunism is absent because of the high level of competition and high substitutability between the competitors.

When asset specificity increases safeguards are to be built into the contract, e.g. through long-term contracting, and so-called 'hybrid' governance structures, in which contracts are combined with organizational structures that limit the autonomy of the actors. So, the efficient governance structure moves from market to the hierarchy of the vertically integrated firm. Subsequently, Williamson moved from there into the public sphere of regulation and state owned enterprises ('public bureau'), because at even higher levels of asset specificity and uncertainty public governance of regulation and state owned enterprises are required to allow transactions taking place.

Hence, the design issue in NIE is about 'getting the institutions right' at the level of the formal institutions and 'getting the governance structures right' at the level of the institutional arrangements (for details see Williamson 1998, Figure 1.1). Although Williamson gave most of his attention to level 3 many of the economists that work in the domain of NIE also apply transaction costs insights to design issues at the level of the formal institutions. Spiller (2013) for instance has demonstrated how the cost of regulation in the form of 'public contracting' in situations of governmental and third party opportunism can be analysed and how institutions can be designed to minimize opportunistic behaviour.

The market and the crisis

NIE, at least the Williamsonian branch, connects perfectly to NCE: the same type of optimization questions, the same type of modelling actors and their environments, and the same type of philosophical foundations about facts and values, make NIE the other school of the broad category of mainstream economics. The model M, the purpose P, the audience E, result in a relevant resemblance of M and R, that make NCE and NIE similar kinds of modelling. Consequently the explanations of the crisis and the remedies are much alike: 'get the institutions right and get the institutional arrangements right' and then the selection mechanism of markets will produce the best outcome possible. If the system is not working properly the cause should be in not having the 'institutions right'.

3 Original Institutional Economics and the crisis

In the USA at the end of the nineteenth century Thorstein Veblen was a well-known institutional economist, who was highly critical of neoclassical economics (Veblen 1899, 1904). In his opinion NCE was too formal and abstract, too static and wrongly based on the theoretical assumption of individual actors that are disconnected from their institutional environment. Until around 1945 an influential group of institutional economists dominated the development of the discipline in the USA. Wesley Mitchell (1927), John R. Commons (1931, 1934) and Clarence Ayres (1944) joined Veblen in his criticism of NCE and underlined the importance of including institutions in the economic explanation (see Gruchy 1972 for details). The work of those institutional economists is called Original

Institutional Economics (OIE). With respect to values the OIE developed the so-called social theory of value: values are not considered to be exogenous to the economy and only based in the individual preferences, but are constituted in a process of interaction between individuals, in which pre-existing values play a structuring role. This fundamental difference between the subjective theory (NCE and NIE) on the one hand, and the social theory of value (OIE)[12] on the other (Tool 1986), reflects a number of other differences, like the attributes and motivations of actors, the structures that embed actors and the interaction between actors and structures.

According to OIE, the economy, first of all, is an evolving system, in which actors of a different nature (political, economic, social) with different interests and capabilities and with different degrees of power take decisions. They act, react, follow, initiate ... choose. In doing so, these actors are constrained and enabled by structures such as technology, formal and informal institutions and their own 'mental maps' (Denzau and North 1994). In the evolving economy actors, structures and values are mutually constituted. The nature of economic reality is one of change and the core research question economics should pose is first of all about understanding that change.

A second important difference between NCE and NIE on the one hand and OIE on the other, is about the nature and role of markets as allocation mechanisms. Above we explained how markets are conceptualized according to the subjectivist theory of value: markets are neutral and prices should reflect subjective values. Intervention from 'outside' is allowed to make either markets function properly or when constraints are needed for exogenous (moral) reasons. In line with the social theory of value, OIE approaches markets and non-market allocation mechanisms differently. First, the question about society's collective values is asked: what *ought* to be and what is the end? Then the actual situation is characterized and analysed; the *is*. If there is a gap between the ought and the is, the question is raised how the gap should be repaired. When (intrinsic) values (and their related instrumental values and policy objectives) do not match with the actual performance of the economy, how then to intervene? An important starting point of OIE analysis is normative: what are the values of societies to design for (the 'ought', the 'end') and when these are compared with the 'is', what then to do about the gap?[13]

In order to understand the role of individual and collective actors in the process of change, OIE considers a deep understanding of the drivers and motivations of actors of utmost importance. Institutionalists want to know about the 'why', so in case another outcome is desired, they have to know how behaviour could be changed, by means of what kind of interventions. Instincts, habits and customs are seen as important drivers and motivations for human decisions. Habits for instance are dispositions of actors that have evolved over long periods of time and form the basis of many of actors' decisions. It would be a misunderstanding, however, to consider habits as mechanically repeated behaviour: 'habits of thought' form the foundation of much of our behaviour and contain past beliefs and experiences, but at the same time human actors have a large capacity to deliberate and to choose; they are also 'volitional' (Commons 1934; Bromley 2006). Moreover, actors are well able to identify habits, to analyse how they influence behaviour and to evaluate whether the habits contribute to realizing the desired consequences of actions, or not. If not, then actors can make existing habits and their consequences explicit, and start a process of deliberation in an attempt to change habits (Hodgson 2004; Bromley 2006).[14]

Markets and the crisis

In the OIE framework actors are positioned with evolving 'cognitive structures' in an evolving institutional context; actors and structures are mutually constituted. Economic actors are social actors operating in specific institutional environments and markets are institutionalized structures, in which power is equally important as efficiency to understand their performance. It is a fundamental misconception to present markets as neutral anonymous selection mechanisms, in which individuals independently decide, as if they were atoms. Markets are political constructs strongly regulated by informal and formal institutions. In part, these rules evolve spontaneously (especially the informal ones), but they also result from purposeful design.

However, societal interest groups heavily influence the political process of institutional design and redesign. It is characterized by struggle and conflict because a change of rules almost always implies an adjustment of the distribution of costs and benefits. Consequently markets are best perceived as evolving systems in which individual and collective action results in both intended and unintended consequences. Likewise markets are never in equilibrium, but always in a process of adaptation, transition and evolution. The existence and constitution of collective values is explicitly taken on board in the social value theory. On the one hand values underlie the formal and informal institutions of society, and through that 'filter' they determine the (economic) values as terms of exchange (see Dolfsma 2004, p. 49). On the other hand the analysis undertaken by the economist is not value-free; facts are always theory-laden and on top of that theories are value-laden. In contrast to the subjective theory of value, facts and values are not separate categories. Reality is not considered to be composed of objects to which the researcher has direct access, and which would allow for objective knowledge. On the contrary; in order to understand (complex) reality, people in daily life and researchers in scientific inquiry make use of 'ordering ideas', like concepts, categories and frameworks that allow for abstraction, and that structure reality.[15] The world of facts is complex and continuously data have to be sorted out, applying specific standards of relevance (Bush 2009). In selecting the proper standards, inevitably choices are made and then unavoidably values and value judgements are involved.[16] Facts speak as far as they are considered relevant from a specific value point of view. In the design for values, both markets and non-market institutions enable individuals to reveal their endogenous preferences and values and offer ways to decide about collective values. It is not only about 'free markets' where individuals express their subjective values, but also about rules of the game on how collective values ought to be 'revealed and implemented'. Moreover, the so-called virtue ethics is part of the social theory of values; local, contextual virtues of actors should be made explicit and are also subject to judgement: some virtues are more 'right' than others.

In the perspective of the social theory of value, markets are seen as one among the many potential instruments to realize societal values. A well-designed market can be a tool to realize specific (instrumental) values, like an efficient use of assets, but other tools can be considered more appropriate to realize other values, like a more equal distribution of income, a sustainable energy production, or more attention for the cultural heritage in the community. Moreover, designing and implementing markets to allocate goods and services is not 'value free' as the subjectivist theory of value suggests. Not only are markets, as discussed, always institutionalized, reflecting specific property and power distributions. Yet, as for instance Sandel (2012) points out, the use of markets in turn influences the norms in society and, as such, markets are not value-free and cannot be properly analysed and evaluated within an isolated economic discipline.

This also holds for non-market institutions: democratic, participatory coordination mechanisms that have an impact on the norms in society are not value-free either. In other words: which allocation mechanisms are preferable not only depends on their efficiency attributes. It should also depend on its positive or negative impact on the values and norms a society wants to endorse.

In sum: OIE works with a framework that addresses institutional issues in a dynamic, holistic and systemic way (Wilber and Harrison 1978). In doing so, actors in the theories and models are not one-dimensionally efficiency driven, but their preferences are endogenously constituted in the process of interacting and acting.[17] Correspondingly the environment is not only complex as in NIE, but structures in the environment are constituted mutually with the individuals and collectivities. In contrast to the methodological individualistic approach of the subjective theory of value, the social theory of value is characterized by so-called methodological interactionism, including both the interaction between actors and structures and the interaction among actors.

To put it differently: all values, both individual and common values, are constituted in interaction. Moreover, values both emerge and are designed. Values can be right or wrong, they are subject to (e)valuation, and they are judged and deliberated in a specific context of time and place. The social theory of value is about the social construction of values and about the social processes of judging values. To judge, values are investigated on their consequences for the well-being of the members of the society: what are the consequences of implementing specific values for realizing other more fundamental values?

Because values are contextual and dynamic, the social theory of value designs institutions that make a 'social construction' possible in such a way that individuals in the process of deliberation (a) have access to the necessary information, (b) have access to the arenas where the deliberation and decision making takes place, and (c) that they can participate and also have the capabilities to do so in a responsible way. In other words actors should be informed, knowledgeable and aware of their responsibilities.

4 Conclusion

In this chapter we have discussed that all scientific knowledge is formulated in models of the real world. In applying concepts, theories and models inevitably choices are made: in representing the real world the scientist isolates vertically and horizontally such that reality becomes ‘manageable’. These choices are not arbitrary. On the contrary: the debate among scientists is about the relevancy of specific models for on the one hand the research questions one is interested in (what causes the economic crisis?) and on the other hand about the resemblance of the assumptions in the models with the conditions in the real world.

We distinguished two schools of thought in institutional economics: one based on the methodological principles of neoclassical economics (NIE) and the other based on alternative principles (OIE).

It is shown in this chapter that NIE will explain an economic crisis as a lack of efficient institutions that are part of the ‘institutional environment’ (the informal and formal institutions are ‘not right’). The remedy is to be found in a more prominent role for subjective values (via the ‘free’ market) and a stricter environment of laws and regulations (property rights, competition law, corporate law, etc.).

Next we showed how the alternative of OIE models the real world differently and we showed how different causes of the crisis are identified and different remedies are recommended. Instead of a methodological individualistic approach in which the free market is central, OIE applies a methodological interactionistic approach with a social theory of value and a position of the ‘institutionalized’ market as one of the tools among others to realize societal objectives. A crisis is caused by a number of interacting variables which should and cannot be disentangled; the economic system is best modelled as a dynamic, holistic process instead of as a static mechanistic equilibrium. Then the market should be under strong surveillance of societal institutions that monitor developments and intervene when the ‘is’ differs from the ‘ought’. The interventions can be at the level of the norms and values of individuals, groups and society at large (informal institutions), at the level of the formal institutions (laws and regulations), at the level of institutional arrangements (organizations and contracts) and at the level of behaviour of individuals (including to forbid specific actions).

Applications of both mainstream and alternative insights can be found in actual policy measures and action undertaken by civil society. At the level of national and international governmental organization it is mostly assumed that the economic world is orderly structured and governed by universal laws and regularities similar to the natural world. The diagnosis of the crisis is one in which those laws have not been taken sufficiently into account. The remedy of new or stricter rules and regulations should be such that economic actors are again disciplined by the economic rules and market pressures so no opportunistic behaviour and abuse of power in their own interest is possible anymore. Most of the measures taken by (inter) national government are in line with this diagnosis: 'get the institutions as rules of the game right'. At the same time plenty of examples of the alternative approach can be found: often at the local decentralized level people ask themselves what are the community values and objectives to strive for? Is that security of jobs, quality of work, sustainable production and consumption, participation and social cohesion, or decision making about core investments in for instance infrastructures? Non-market governance is then mostly considered more appropriate and the models relevant to understand what is going on and how the world should be organized are not based on assumptions of an orderly structure world, but on assumptions about change, dynamics and chaos. On the edge of order and chaos new varieties emerge and innovations come about.

We concluded in this chapter that inevitably different representations of the real world exist, that different causes of economic crisis are identified and different remedies are recommended. The discussion should be about the relevancy of the different models; when to apply the one that represents the world as well ordered and that causes and remedies are located in the formal rules? When to apply to one in which the world is represented as a process, full of feedbacks and interdependencies, which is best, represented as a whole? We have discussed that the answer is not only a matter of the correct description of what is (positive), but also of what should be (normative). When we consider the different type of measures taken to remedy the crisis we learn that different models of economic reality can be relevant; it is the art of applied science to apply the right model at the right time and place.

Notes

1 Although important differences exist between a framework, theory and model (Ostrom 2005) we use in this chapter the concepts of model rather loosely as a synonym for theoretical abstraction in general.
2 This connects to the philosophy of pragmatism; for details see below and Groenewegen (2011).
3 For details see Bromley (2006) and Groenewegen (2011).
4 The following is based on Correljé *et al.* (forthcoming).
5 This section is based on Groenewegen (2011, 2013).
6 I describe the characteristics of the ideal type of positivism admitting that all kind of nuances exist under the names of post-, or neo-positivism (Friedrichs and Kratochwil 2009).
7 This is known as 'ontological realism' (Friedrichs and Kratochwil 2009).
8 Deduction and induction can be formulated in logical terms like Peirce did in his example of the beans. It can also be formulated in terms that apply to the testing in social sciences. Then deduction is of a hypothetical-deductive kind, in which a logically derived hypothesis will be tested in an empirical setting and induction refers then to the collection of empirical case material from which a classification or typology can be constructed.
9 Karl Popper, who in his 'critical rationalism' pointed out that all observed is based and coloured by 'pre-conceived theory', criticizes this point of view. Facts are

theory-laden. Popper (1959) maintained the distinction between facts and norms (so-called dualism).

10 This does not only hold for the model of pure and perfect competition, but also for the monopolistic and oligopolistic models with well-defined price or quantity reactions.

11 A distinction is made between the so-called Williamsonian and the Northian branch of NIE (Groenewegen 2011). In our interpretation we conclude that the former stays in the philosophical and methodological tradition of NCE, whereas the latter departs from it and adopted many characteristics of the original economic institutionalists (see below).

12 Original Institutional Economics (OIE) was after the emergence of NIE often called Old Institutional Economics. We prefer the terminology of Original. The label of Neo-institutionalism is also used for the post-war institutionalists like John K. Galbraith, Gunnar Myrdal and others that followed the approach of Veblen and Commons (see Gruchy 1972). In this contribution we call the pre- and post-war institutionalists both OIE (see also Rutherford 1994; Groenewegen *et al.* 1995).

13 That is what OIE economists mean when they claim OIE is problem solving and policy-oriented.

14 Interesting is the question what room is left for volition, for rational purposeful action? In this respect the distinction between habits and routines becomes important. Dewey (1927, p. 28) explains that habits also can be inquired and tested by man, i.e. man can take distance from the specific habits that cause an action and reflect on the consequences of that action. When such reflections raise doubts about the rightfulness (is the 'is' well analysed?), or desirability of the belief (do the habits contribute to the realization of the 'ought'?), then man is in the position to inquire what is wrong about the habits causing the undesirable action, and to intervene by altering the institutions (the rules of the game) to change the 'habit of thought'. In the case of routines man acts mechanically, without thought about the consequences and without valuation of the consequences of the routinized actions in the light of the societal goals. The real opposition is not between reason and habits, but between reasonable habits and unintelligently routinized habit (Costa and Caldas 2009).

15 'Structuring reality' should not be interpreted as 'creating reality'.

16 Bush (2009) makes a distinction between values (standards of judgement), valuation (the application of those standards) and value judgement (the evaluation of values in relation to (other) intrinsic values).

17 This is the core of philosophical pragmatism. In the words of Nooteboom (2013, p. 2): pragmatism 'holds that cognition, in a wide sense that includes normative judgments and goals, occurs on the basis of mental dispositions and categories that are developed in interaction with the physical and especially the social environment'. The crux of the argument is that action, practice, constitutes the actor: 'intelligence is internalized practice'. This connects well with the framework of North (2005) about institutional change.

References

Ayres, Clarence E. (1944), *The Theory of Economic Progress*. Chapel Hill: The University of North Carolina Press.

Becker, G.S. (1996), *Accounting for Tastes*. Cambridge, MA: Harvard University Press.

Bromley, Daniel W. (2006), *Sufficient Reason: Volitional Pragmatism and the Meaning of Economic Institutions*. Princeton and Oxford: Princeton University Press.

Bush, P.D. (2009), The neoinstitutionalist theory of value. *Journal of Economic Issues*, 43(2), 293–307.

Commons, John R. (1931), Institutional economics. *American Economic Review*, 21, 648–657.

Commons, John R. (1934 [1961]), *Institutional Economics. Volume 1*. Madison: University of Wisconsin Press.

Correljé, Aad and Groenewegen, John (2009), Public values in utility sectors: economic perspectives. *International Journal of Public Policy*, 4(5), 395–413.

Correljé, Aad, Groenewegen, John, Künneke, Rolf and Scholten, Daniel (forthcoming), Design for values in economics. In: J. van den Hoven, P.E. Vermaas and I. van de Poel (eds), *Handbook of Ethics, Values, and Technological Design*. Dordrecht: Springer.

Costa, Ana N. and Castro Caldas, Jose (2009), Claiming Choice for Institutional Economics. Paper presented at the EAEPE Annual Conference, Amsterdam.

Denzau, A. and North, D. (1994), Shared mental models: ideologies and institutions. *Kyklos*, 47(1), 3–31.

Dewey, John (1927), *The Public and Its Problems*. Athens, OH: Ohio University Press.

Dolfsma, W. (2004), *Institutional Economics and the Formation of Preferences: The Advent of Pop Music*. Cheltenham, UK: Edward Elgar Publishing.

Friedrichs, J. and Kratochwill, F. (2009), On acting and knowing: how pragmatism can advance international relations research and methodology. *International Organization*, 63, 701–731.

Groenewegen, J. (2011), The Bloomington School and American institutionalism. *The Good Society*, 20(1), 15–36.

Groenewegen, J. (2013), A synthesis of neoclassical and institutional economic price theory? In: W. Dolfsma and S. Kesting (eds), *Interdisciplinary Economics: Kenneth E. Boulding's Engagement in the Sciences*. London: Routledge, pp. 316–331.

Groenewegen, J. (2014), Understanding and Designing the Next Generation Infrastructures; on Mono-, Multi- and Interdisciplinrity. Valedictory Lecture, 23 May, Delft: Delft University of Technology.

Groenewegen, John and Vromen, Jack (1996), TCE and beyond: a case for theoretical pluralism. In: J. Groenewegen (ed.), *TCE and Beyond*. Dordrecht/Boston: Kluwer Academic Publishers.

Groenewegen, J., Kerstholt, F. and Nagelkerke, A. (1995), On integrating new and old institutionalism: Douglass North building bridges. *Journal of Economic Issues*, 29(2), 467–475.

Gruchy, A.G. (1972), *Contemporary Economic Thought: The Contribution of Neo Institutional Economics*. Clifton, NJ: Augustus M. Kelley.

Hodgson, Geoffrey M. (2004), Reclaiming habit for institutional economics. *Journal of Economic Psychology*, 25, 651–660.

Latsis, S.J. (1976), A research programme in economics. In: J. Latsis (ed.), *Method and Appraisal in Economics*. Cambridge: Cambridge University Press, pp. 1–41.

Mäki, U. (2011), Diagnosing the Alleged Failure of Economics as a Modeling Failure. Paper at the XII International Academic Conference on Economic and Social Development, 5–7 April, 2011, Moscow, Symposium on 'Crisis & Economics: Methodological Implications'.

Mitchell, W.C. (1927), *Business Cycles: The Problem and its Settings*, Cambridge, MA: National Bureau of Economic Research (NBER).

Nooteboom, B. (2013), A pragmatist theory of innovation. In: H. Melkas and V. Harmaakorpi (eds), *Practice-based Innovation: Insights, Applications and Policy Implications*. Heidelberg: Springer, pp. 17–27.

North, D.C. (2005), *Understanding the Process of Economic Change*. Princeton: Princeton University Press.

Ostrom, Elinor (2005), *Understanding Institutional Diversity*. Princeton and Oxford: Princeton University Press.

Popper, K. (1959), *The Discovery of Scientific Knowledge*. London: Routledge.
Rutherford, M. (1994), *The Old and New Institutionalism*. Cambridge: Cambridge University Press.
Sandel, M. (2012), *What Money Can't Buy: The Moral Limits of Markets*. London: Penguin.
Schütz, A. (1953), Common-sense and scientific interpretation of human action, *Philosophy and Phenomenological Research*, 14, 1–39.
Searle, J. (1996), *The Construction of Social Reality*. London: Penguin.
Searle, J. R. (2005), What is an institution? *Journal of Institutional Economics*, 1(1), 1–22.
Spiller, Pablo T. (2013), Transaction cost regulation. *Journal of Economic Behavior & Organization*, 89, 232–242.
Tool, Marc R. (1986), *Essays in Social Value Theory*. Armonk, NY: M.E. Sharpe.
Van Staveren, I. (2007), Beyond utilitarianism and deontology: ethics in economics. *Review of Political Economy*, 19(1), 21–35.
Veblen, Thorstein B. (1899 [1975]), *The Theory of the Leisure Class*. New York: Augustus M. Kelly.
Veblen, Thorstein B. (1904 [1975]), *The Theory of the Business Enterprise*. Clifton, NJ: Augustus M. Kelly.
Wilber, Charles K. and Harrison, Robert S. (1978), The methodological basis of institutional economics: pattern model, storytelling, and holism. *Journal of Economic Issues*, 12(1), 61–89.
Williamson, O.E. (1975), *Markets and Hierarchies: Analysis and Antitrust Implications*. New York: Free Press.
Williamson, O.E. (1979), Transaction-cost economics: the governance of contractual relations. *Journal of Law and Economics*, 22(2), 233–261.
Williamson, O.E. (1998), Transaction cost economics: how it works, where it is headed. *De Economist*, 146 (January), 23–58.

2 Causes of the 'great recession' and economic policy implications

Philip Arestis and Elias Karakitsos

1 Introduction

The global financial system has been under enormous stress since August 2007. It then spilled over to the global economy more broadly. This is actually the first such crisis since the 1929 Great Depression. The focus of this chapter is on the origins of the 'great recession', based essentially in the US, and policy implications along with whether any economic policies and institutional changes have been initiated to avoid future such crises. In doing so, we distinguish between main factors and contributory factors. The main factors contain three features: distributional effects; financial liberalization; and financial innovation. The contributory factors also contain three features: international imbalances; monetary policy; and the role of the credit rating agencies.

The discussion of the causes of the 'great recession' is followed by relevant economic policy implications, where we offer a number of general observations along with specific policy recommendations, accounting for distributional effects. We suggest that the focus of the New Consensus Macroeconomics (NCM) on price stability was shown not to work by the events that had led to the financial crisis of August 2007. We argue that fiscal and monetary policies when coordinated provide a better way forward in terms of economic policies along with financial stability. We emphasize financial stability in particular – an aspect completely ignored prior to the August 2007 financial crisis. We elaborate further on financial stability, especially in terms of what recommendations have been initiated in the US, UK and in other parts of the world, including the EU and the IMF, before we offer a summary and conclusions section.

We begin our discussion with the main causes of the 'great recession' and more specifically with the first feature of the main causes, this being distributional effects.

2 Main factors

2.1 Distributional effects

The steady but sharp rise in inequality, especially in the US, but elsewhere, too, is an important feature. The share of national output in the US taken up by profits had reached close to a post World War II high before the onset of the recession; while real wages had fallen even behind productivity. The declining wage and rising profits share were compounded by another long-term economic term: the increasing concentration of earnings at the top, especially in the financial sector (Arestis and Karakitsos, 2013, chapter 2). The share of the financial sector to GDP almost doubled in size between 1981 and 2007, and more recently accounted for 8 per cent of US GDP (Philippon, 2008). Between 1981 and 2007 the US financial sector as measured by the ratio of private credit to GDP grew from 90 per cent to 210 per cent. Also over the same period, there was a sharp, nearly six-fold, increase in the profitability of the US financial sector. Indeed, and over the same period, wages in the financial sector were higher than in other sectors, even after controlling for education (Philippon and Reshef, 2009). Financial sector relative wages, the ratio of the wage bill in the financial sector to its full-time-equivalent employment share, enjoyed a steep increase over the period mid-1980s to 2006. Still more recently, the typical US family earns less than in 1989, according to the US Census Bureau (September 2013). Household incomes have been falling for the fifth consecutive year. Median household income is now 8.3 per cent below its pre-recession peak in 2007. The share of the wealth accruing to the top 1 per cent grew by 31 per cent in the three years to 2012, while the rest rose by just 0.4 per cent (see Saez, 2013). Indeed the top 1 per cent has been close to full recovery since August 2007, while the bottom 90 per cent have hardly started recovering.

Similar but less pronounced increases in financial shares are relevant in many other countries. Germany, China and the UK are three examples but many more can be cited. In Germany, and according to the OECD (2008), income inequality over the years 2000–2005 grew faster than in any other OECD country. In China the top 1 per cent income share has gradually risen from 2.6 per cent in 1986 to 5.9 per cent in 2003. Also in China financial intermediary shares to GDP increased from 1.6 per cent in 1980 to 5.4 per cent in 2008 (Greenspan, 2010, p. 15). In the UK and over the period leading to the 'great recession' there was a significant falling share of wages and also wages fell below productivity (see Arestis and Karakitsos, 2013, chapter 2). The distributional effects discussed so far have been greatly enhanced by attempts at financial liberalization in many countries around the world. Of particular importance for our purposes was the financial liberalization framework in the US, especially the repeal of the 1933 Glass–Steagall Act in 1999. Both the redistribution and the financial liberalization policies led to a period of financial engineering in the US, which spread worldwide, and eventually caused the 'great recession'. In the words of the Chairman of the UK Financial Services Authority:

> There has thus been an increasing 'financialisation' of the economy, an increasing role for the financial sector. Financial firms as a result have accounted for an increased share of GDP, of corporate profits, and of stock market capitalisation. And there has been a sharp rise in income differential between many employees in the financial sector and average incomes across the whole of the economy.
>
> (Turner, 2010, p. 6)

2.2 Financial liberalization

The US experienced financial liberalization from around the mid-1970s. However, the apotheosis of the financial liberalization in the US took place in 1999 with the repeal of the 1933 Glass–Steagall Act. The 1933 Glass–Steagall Act was designed to avoid the experience of the 1920s/1930s in terms of the conflict of interest between the commercial and the investment arms of large financial conglomerates (whereby the investment branch took high risk tolerance). The ultimate aim of the 1933 Glass–Steagall Act was to separate the activities of commercial banks and the risk-taking 'investment or merchant' banks along with strict regulation of the financial services industry. In effect the Glass–Steagall Act of 1933 broke up the most powerful banks. The goal was to avoid a repetition of the speculative, leveraged excesses of the 1920s/1930s. The repeal of the Act in 1999 enabled investment banks to branch into new activities. And it allowed commercial banks to encroach on the investment banks' other traditional preserves. Not just commercial banks but also insurance and other companies, like the American International Group (AIG), were also involved in the encroaching. An important development that relates liberalization and distribution is the opening up of capital markets to foreign entry, namely capital account liberalization. A recent IMF study (Furceri and Lounyani, 2013) provides evidence of such link: 58 episodes of large-scale capital account reforms in 17 advanced countries provide firm evidence that such liberalization is followed by a significant and persistent increase in inequality. Furceri and Lounyani (op. cit.) refer to another contributor to increased inequality; it is the 'policy actions by governments to lower their budget deficits. Such actions are referred to as fiscal consolidation in economists' jargon and, by their critics, as "austerity" policies' (p. 26).

2.3 Financial innovation

The repeal of the Glass–Steagall Act in 1999 allowed the merging of commercial and investment banking. The merging enabled financial institutions to use risk management in their attempt to dispose of their loan portfolio. Banks set up trusts or limited liability companies with small capital base, i.e. separate legal entities, known as Structural Investment Vehicles (SIVs). The SIVs operation is financed by borrowing from the short end of the capital markets at a rate linked to the inter-bank interest rate, a short-term rate of interest; and buying the loans, essentially mortgages, of mother banks and selling them to the private sector at a rate linked to the long-term interest rate. The subprime mortgage market thereby emerged, relying heavily on the continuous rise of house prices and an upward sloping yield curve. Subprime mortgage is a financial innovation designed to enable home ownership to risky borrowers. So long as the short-term rate of interest was lower than the long-term rate, big profits materialized, which helped the housing market to produce a bubble.

Parallel banking, what is also now called shadow banking, was thereby created outside the control and the regulatory umbrella of the authorities. And to quote Greenspan (2013):

> Shadow banking is a form of financial intermediation whose funding is not supported by the traditional banking safety net – in the United States, deposit insurance and access to central bank funding. Shadow banking includes the activities of investment banks, hedge funds, money market funds, structural investment vehicles (SIVs), and other credit intermediaries acting outside the regular banking system.
>
> (p. 40)

This led to an important financial innovation. Financial institutions engineered a new activity that relied on interlinked securities, the Collateralized Debt Obligations (CDOs), mainly emerging from and closely related to the subprime mortgage market. Investors bought CDOs because they trusted the triple A-credit ratings assigned by the credit rating agencies. The sale of CDOs to international investors made the US housing bubble a global problem and provided the transmission mechanism for the contagion to the rest of the world. The size of the shadow banking is reported in Greenspan (2013), where it is stated that

> assets of shadow banking institutions globally grew from $26 trillion in 2002 to $62 trillion in 2007, and following a decline in 2008, reached $67 trillion by the end of 2011. As a share of total financial intermediary assets, shadow banking consistently accounted for 23 percent to 27 percent during that time frame.
>
> (p. 40)

The significant expansion of SIVs was accompanied by a significant move of assets and liabilities off bank balance sheets in a way that created more robust capital levels. With the August 2007 financial crisis, however, 'SIVs that carried the name and reputation of their originating banking entities were absorbed (with their risk) back into the banks' balance sheets' (Greenspan, op. cit., p. 40).

A period of rising policy interest rates (mid-2004 to mid-August 2007) emerged, after a prolonged period of abnormally low interest rates (initially 1997–1998 but more aggressively after the internet bubble of March 2000). Rising interest rates initially produced the end of the housing boom and the burst of the housing bubble in 2006. By August 2007 the yield curve was inverted, that is long-term interest rates became lower than short-term rates. And the subprime mortgage market simply collapsed. Indeed, 'And as the demand in the United States for homeownership collapsed and home prices fell, widespread defaults of mortgage-backed securities saddled banks and other highly leveraged financial institutions with heavy losses, both in the United States and Europe' (Greenspan, 2013, p. 50). The collapse of the subprime market spilled over into the real economy through the credit crunch and collapsing equity markets; and all this led to the freezing of the interbank lending market as from August 2007; a significant recession emerged, what we now label as the 'great recession'.[1]

3 Contributory factors

3.1 International imbalances

The process described so far was accentuated by the international imbalances, which were built up over a decade or more. Especially so in view of the rise of China, and the decline of investment in many parts of Asia following the 1997 crisis there, which created a great deal of savings. Those savings were channelled mainly into the US, helping to put downward pressure on US interest rates. Another factor was the capital flows from European banks, which bought a great deal of CDOs financing them in large part by borrowing from US money-market funds. All these were helped by capital account liberalization, namely the opening up of capital markets to foreign entry, and the steady decline in the number of restrictions that countries impose on cross-border financial transactions. A lot of evidence on the removal of these restrictions, over the past three decades, as reported in the IMF's *Annual Report on Exchange Arrangements and Exchange Restrictions* (see, also, Furceri and Loungani, 2013). Also, the Federal Reserve low interest rate policy pursued in the US at the same time, enabled households there to live well beyond their means; and the negative effects of greater inequality on spending power meant that ordinary families faced with a declining wage share became increasingly indebted. Low interest rates at the same time helped to push up asset prices, especially house prices, thereby enabling the financial sector to explode. The explosion of the banking sector enabled lending to households and businesses to expand substantially along with lending to other non-bank financial institutions. All these imbalances created a more buoyant market for financial institutions thereby helping in the promotion of the financial engineering innovation discussed earlier.

3.2 US monetary policy

This feature springs from the monetary policy emphasis on frequent interest rate changes as a vehicle to controlling inflation. The impact of this policy has been the creation of enormous liquidity and household debt in the major economies, which reached unsustainable magnitudes and helped to promote the 'great recession'. This was especially so after the collapse of the IT bubble (March 2000), when central banks, led by the US Fed, pursued highly accommodative monetary policies to avoid a deep recession. As a result of these developments, the transmission mechanism of Monetary Policy changed: the build-up of household debt and asset holdings made household expenditure more sensitive to short-term interest rate changes; furthermore, and mainly post August 2007, the high debt levels, combined with the difficulties in the 'real' sector, implied that lenders and equity holders stay away from the market place. Not forgetting the presence and magnitude of toxic assets (the CDOs and other relevant securitized assets, most if not all of which became worthless after August 2007), which posed real problems that needed to be sorted out.

Looking at debt statistics, we find that, between 1998 and 2002 in the US, outstanding household debt was 76.7 per cent to GDP; between 2003 and 2007 it increased to 97.6 per cent of GDP. Outstanding household debt in the UK was 72.0 per cent of GDP over the period 1998–2002 (in 1960 it amounted to less than 15 per cent of GDP); and between 2003 and 2007 it shot to 94.3 per cent of GDP. In the Euro Area outstanding household debt increased from 48.5 per cent to 56.6 per cent respectively in the same periods as above. Over the period 1997–2007 the ratio of US financial sector debt to GDP rose by 52 per cent, and the total US private debt to GDP rose by 101 per cent over the same period. US total private credit grew from around 70 per cent in 1945 to well over 200 per cent in 2008. Similar numbers apply in the case of other developed countries, notably Ireland and Spain (see BIS, 2008, for all the data referred to above).

Consequently, the dangers with the type of monetary policy pursued at the time are clear: frequent changes in interest rates can have serious effects. Low interest rates cause bubbles; high interest rates work through applying economic pressures on vulnerable social groups. It clearly follows that regulatory and prudential controls become, then, necessary.

3.3 Role of credit rating agencies

There is sufficient consensus by now that credit rating agencies contributed to the August 2007 financial crisis and to the 'great recession'. Credit rating agencies erroneously assigned AAA status to many worthless papers; the assignment did not reflect the true risks inherent in those securities. This unfortunate episode emerged in view of the credit rating agencies accounting only for the credit default risk and not market or liquidity risk. A further problem is the role of credit rating agencies in the economy. This is to forecast the probability of default on the repayment period of the issuer of a debt liability. Their job is, therefore, relevant forecasting. In which case, the accuracy of their forecasts is clearly an important issue, which should be susceptible to *ex post* accountability. On this score there is no check on their forecasts since it is left to the credit rating agencies themselves precisely what to publish.

Conflict of interest is another important feature of the credit rating agencies. Credit rating agencies are paid by the issuers, not by investors. In fact, the larger credit rating agencies receive most of their revenues from the issuers they rate. These fees were enhancing their revenues and profits substantially during the boom, thereby creating potentially a serious conflict-of-interest case. It is also the case that credit rating agencies were central to the capital needs of banks. The conflict of interest just mentioned was thereby reinforcing their contribution to the 'great recession'.

The credit rating agencies have been accused of bestowing AAA credit rating on toxic assets, which were thereby treated as completely safe. In fact, some

80 per cent of the total value of CDOs were given AAA credit rating, thereby treated as completely safe (Goodhart, 2009). The study by Ashcraft *et al.* (2010) calculates that on a value-weighted basis 80–90 per cent of CDOs received the AAA credit rating. Greenspan (2010) also comments that: 'The venerated credit rating agencies bestowed ratings that implied AAA smooth-sailing for many a highly toxic derivative product' (p. 13); and that 'despite their decades of experience, the analysts of the credit rating agencies proved no more adept at anticipating the onset of the crisis than the investment community at large' (p. 12). More recently, Greenspan (2013) adds to this when he suggests that the credit rating agencies' 'favorable ratings of many securities offered a false sense of security to a great many investors' (p. 46).

4 Economic policy implications

4.1 General observations

The analysis so far implies certain policy implications. Perhaps the most important one is that price stability, which had been achieved prior to August 2007, did not and does not guarantee stability of the economy as a whole; nor do interest rate adjustments. These are important implications in terms of the economic policies that follow from the theoretical framework of the New Consensus Macroeconomics (see, for example, Arestis, 2007). Furthermore, cyclically balanced budgets in normal times are not enough; fiscal policy should be used both in the short term and in the long term to address demand issues. Even more important, is the proposition that coordination of monetary and fiscal policies is vital, along with discretion in applying them (Arestis, 2012). It is also of paramount importance to never forget the significance of accounting for 'distributional effects' in both economic theory and policy, which have been fatally ignored recently, and not so recently, as suggested above in the relevant sub-section. The main operations of any Central Bank should be directed towards financial stability, so that prudential authorities take a system-wide perspective in regulation and supervision. The focus on the solvency of individual institutions as the case had been prior to August 2007 is simply not enough. The events leading to the 'great recession' testify to this important requirement; financial stability has not been addressed properly, and as such it requires further investigation and proper policy initiatives to account for it.

The focus of financial stability should be on proper control of the financial sector so that it becomes socially and economically useful to the economy as a whole and to the productive economy in particular. Banks should serve the needs of their customers rather than provide short-term gains for shareholders and huge profits for themselves. Proposals that aim to ensure financial stability have been put forward around the world and we comment on them in an attempt to answer the question of whether if these financial stability proposals were implemented and in place, a similar crisis of August 2007 would be avoided. We discuss in what follows in section 5 the various proposals suggested around the world in an attempt to answer this question.

4.2 Financial stability proposals

There have been several financial stability proposals around the world since the 'great recession'. We discuss them in what follows, beginning with probably the most important one; this is the US proposal, known as the Dodd–Frank Act of 2010.

4.2.1 The US Dodd–Frank Act of 2010

The US President's relevant proposal, initially known as the Volcker Rule, and now incorporated as part of the proposal, which was signed into law on 21 July 2010, and became the Dodd–Frank Act of 2010, is the one we discuss in this sub-section. The rule contains a number of important constituent elements, with the ones relevant to this contribution being as follows:[2]

- Eliminate proprietary investments (namely to prohibit banks that take insured deposits from running their own trading operations), and also ownership of hedge funds by banks;
- In the final Act this was modified so that banks would be allowed to hold proprietary investments of 3 per cent of their core capital, and also severely restricts their ability to invest in hedge funds and private equity; this is what is now known as the Volcker rule;
- Size matters: no financial firm should be allowed to become 'too big to fail';
- End of taxpayer bailouts: the legislation grants government the power to wind down failing institutions, not just banks, if they threaten the financial system;
- A new 'orderly liquidation' authority is equipped with the power to seize a failing 'systemically important' institution;
- Credit rating agencies: this is another important aspect of the Dodd–Frank Act, which is the introduction of a new Office of Credit Ratings to supervise credit rating agencies;
- 'Shadow banking' and non-bank financial services companies are also to be regulated.

The Financial Services Forum (FSF) in particular, which represents 18 US top banks, has argued that the President's proposals misdiagnose the causes of the financial crisis.[3] The proposed separation of commercial banking from investment banking is too complicated and too costly to achieve; that the proposals put jobs at risk, damage US competitiveness and might even threaten growth in the US economy. Another argument from the American Bankers Association (as reported in the *Financial Times* on 11 December 2013) insists that banks and customers would suffer from the 'enormous, highly complex and burdensome rule'. This is so since banks would not be able to provide certain services that pose no risk to the financial system. Still another argument is that the interests of the US banks would be severely harmed in a way that would give a competitive advantage to their rivals in the rest of the world. In this sense, so the argument goes, not only the activities of foreign lenders operating in the US would be affected but also the business they undertake in the rest of the world. It has also been proposed that proprietary trading should be limited to a percentage of overall assets or business; this was granted as mentioned above. Tackling the 'too big to fail' institutions should be undertaken instead through more effective supervision. The most frequently used argument against the proposals is that they are by far too complicated. We would suggest, though, that surely they cannot be more complicated than the creation of the CDOs, as described above. Indeed, compared to CDOs that were one of the main causes of the crisis, the new proposals are delightfully simple.

The Volcker rule was of course part of the Dodd–Frank Act of 2010; indeed it was, and still is, the centrepiece of the 2010 banking reform but it has been under enormous pressure and difficulties in its implementation as a result of opposition mainly from the banking industry. As a result of this enormous challenge, and four years of protracted negotiations, the Volcker rule was only ratified on 10 December 2013 by the five agencies ruling on the measures and which will administer the rule, after the US Treasury Secretary had given them an end of the year 2013 deadline to finally report.[4] The final Volcker rule gives the banks more flexibility on market-making activities, whereby they trade on securities and bonds on behalf of their customers. It maintains, however, its stringent restrictions on hedge funds and private equity funds activities of the banking sector. Banks have now until 21 July 2015 to comply with the rules as ratified.[5]

This Act may not be the Glass–Steagall Act of 1933, but it is the most sweeping and wide-ranging overhaul of the US financial regulations since the 1930s. An interesting and relevant question is whether this Act would make the US banks safer and thereby whether it would have prevented the 'great recession' or indeed another similar occurrence. Our response is on the negative in view of the non-separation of commercial and investment entities. Such separation would make banks safer, as it did during the Glass–Steagall Act of 1933 period, namely 1933–1999, for it would ban the banks from taking all risky activities altogether. It should also be noted that banking is a very complex institutional system, and as such it should be heavily regulated.[6]

4.2.2 The UK proposal

The US initiative and proposals have been followed by the Bank of England officials. A government-appointed commission on banking was set up in the summer of 2010 to provide a year-long analysis of whether banks should be split up into commercial and investment entities; and whether a version of the Dodd–Frank Act is appropriate for UK banking. The Vickers report, as it is now known, produced its preliminary thinking in September 2010, its interim Report in April

2011 and its final Report in September 2011. It recommends 'ring-fencing' banks' retail operations from their investment banking activities, whether conducted by UK or foreign-owned banks. It thereby aims to protect retail banking activities from losses incurred in investment banking operations (see, also, Vickers, 2013).

There are problems with the Vickers report. The main problem of ring-fencing is that banks may be encouraged to take greater risk with the activities inside the ring-fencing, such as mortgages, corporate and personal assets. This could very well be so since such activities would be more likely to be bailed out. No wonder the UK Parliamentary Banking Commission proposes a review of this rule so that a full separation of the whole industry is undertaken. There is actually a provision in the bill for a reserve power that would allow split of individual banks if the ring-fence is not followed properly.[7]

In the UK financial stability has taken a step further through the creation of the Financial Policy Committee (FPC) at the Bank of England, which is in charge of macroprudential policy; it was created by the Financial Services Act 2012 and came into effect on 1 April 2013. Its focus is to spot financial crises emerging in the economy well before the kind of crash that emerged in August 2007. The FPC works with but is independent of the Monetary Policy Committee (MPC), which is responsible for achieving a set inflation target (currently 2 per cent with 1 per cent tolerance range either side of the target) through manipulating the rate of interest; but with the rate of interest currently being 0.5 per cent, Quantitative Easing (QE) is the main current monetary instrument pursued in the UK. When it comes to the question of 'forward guidance' in the UK in terms of allowing the rate of interest to rise even when unemployment is above 7 per cent, financial stability is an important consideration.

A banking reform bill has now been approved by the UK Parliament and House of Lords (the latter passed the bill on 16 December 2013). The UK Parliamentary Banking Commission amended the banking reform bill, which enacts the Vickers recommendations, for it considered it to be 'inadequate legislation'. One of the main features of the bill is the introduction of provisions for a review of the 'ring-fence' proposal, what is called 'electrified ring-fence', so as to allow a possible break-up of the banking sector, if 'ring-fencing' does not work. Another feature is that the UK Parliamentary Banking Commission proposed for the Prudential Regulation Authority (PRA)[8] to prepare a report on proprietary trading soon after the ring-fence is implemented. This is to be followed by a review of the banking reform bill within three years after the passing of the bill and to consider the possibility of banning proprietary trading if it became necessary to protect financial stability. The banking commission also places increased weight on the leverage ratio (debt to assets ratio) and proposes that the FPC is given power over this ratio before 2018 when the UK government plans to introduce it (see, also, HM Treasury, 2012, 2013).[9] The passage of the banking reform bill, and according to the UK government as reported in the *Financial Times* (17 December 2013), completes 'the final legislative phase of the plan to create a banking system that supports the economy, consumers and small businesses'.

4.2.3 The EU proposal

A similar trading ring-fence proposal comes from the Committee commissioned by the European Commission and headed by the Governor of the Finnish Central Bank, Erkki Liikanen. The committee suggests ring-fencing banks' trading business, not of retail activities as in the Vickers report. In the report's view, similar to that of the Vickers report, 'the specific objectives of separation are to ... limit a banking group's incentives and ability to take excessive risks with insured deposits' and to 'prevent the coverage of losses incurred in the trading entity by the funds of the deposit bank, and hence limit the liability of taxpayer and the deposit insurance system'.[10] This report, like the Vickers one, has been criticized on two grounds: there is no predefined 'resolution regime', which can wind banks up in the case of a disaster scenario; banks, even ring-fenced ones, may still be bailed out by governments in a crisis. And such a reform could disrupt the flow of corporate funding; companies may very well turn away from bank loans to capital markets for bond funding. As reported in the *Financial Times* (11 December 2013) the Erkki Liikanen reform effort has been stalled at the stage of its passage through the European Commission in view of vocal opposition from a number of banks, especially German and French ones.

There are differences between the UK Vickers report and the EU Erkki Liikanen report. These are summarized by Vickers (2013) as follows:

> There are differences, some of which reflect the different geographic scope. Thus, for example, a common European approach to trading book risk weights makes sense, whereas a single-country approach could have detrimental consequences for geographic arbitrage. A more surprising difference concerns securities underwriting, which Liikanen would allow with deposit banking. Besides the historical observation that this is the opposite of Glass–Steagall, economic logic suggests that securities underwriting belongs with trading, as it involves writing large put options. Corporate customers could still obtain a comprehensive array of banking services, including underwriting, from a single bank, but with the risk lying outside the deposit bank entity.
>
> (p. 7)

Ring-fencing assets as suggested by the EU Erkki Liikanen report, though, would limit the liquidity of corporate bond trading, thereby making this form of financing more expensive. Interestingly enough, though, France is the only country outside the US that has reached closest to the Volcker rule. In the summer of 2013, a banking reform law was passed in France that requires banks to introduce proprietary trading via a ring-fenced subsidiary.[11] However, on the whole, radical measures to increase stability and competition in the EU financial sectors have been bypassed. What is required is a complete institutional separation of retail banking from investment banking.

4.2.4 The IMF proposal

Further proposals that intend to deal with the size of financial institutions come from the IMF. These proposals include more and higher capital requirements, as well as more liquid assets, along with the adoption of legal regimes that provide for the orderly resolution of failing institutions. Strong and effective supervision, along with political support, is an essential part of any serious and lasting reform of the financial sector. A complement to these regulatory reforms is to tax the financial sector. This would discourage excessive size as well as wholesale financing, two serious problems in the 'great recession'. The IMF bank tax proposals, for the G20 finance ministers, are relevant in this context and rely heavily on the need for a global approach. They are designed to ensure that financial institutions bear the direct costs of future failures or crises. In this way, future bailouts would be funded by the banks paying the costs of financial and economic rescue packages. These tax plans comprise of: (i) a financial stability tax, in the IMF language a 'Financial Stability Contribution' (FSC) tax, which would require banks and other financial institutions to pay a bank levy, initially at a flat rate. This would be later adjusted to reflect risk so that financial sector activities that pose a greater risk would pay a higher rate. This type of tax is designed to fund future government support, and thereby avoid 'moral hazard' problems. At a later stage, (ii) a financial activity tax (FAT) is proposed, which is a tax on the sum total of profits and remunerations paid by financial institutions. The sum would be a kind of Value-Added Tax (VAT), a tax from which financial institutions are currently exempt. So that imposing such a tax could make the tax treatment of the financial sector similar to other sectors. This would deter the financial sector from being too large on purely tax reasons. It would also contain the tendency of the financial sector for excessive risk-taking. It might be, though, that neither 'too big to fail' nor taxing the financial institutions should be considered in isolation. They are both necessary and should be treated as such.

International agreement on such proposals is paramount. Not likely, though, in view of disagreements among the G20 members; the EU, however, is determined to go it alone. Objections to this proposal have been raised by the central banks of mainly Australia, Brazil, Canada and Japan, the least affected countries by the 'great recession', who argue that taxing banks reduces in effect their capital thereby making them more, not less, vulnerable to financial crises. No doubt banks would argue, and have argued, that taxing liabilities and transactions to stave off future financial crises carry their own problems. Most important of which is that taxes would not reduce risk in the system; on the contrary, it might increase risk by implicitly building in insurance for bank's risky behaviour.

Another objection is that under such plans the financial sector would not be able to provide the products and services demanded by their customers. Such rules might create a new credit crunch if introduced without full consideration of these possibilities. Requiring banks to hold more capital could actually result in banks providing less lending than otherwise. Banks have, thus, resisted reform, on weak grounds really, but with powerful lobbying. And yet substantial and far-reaching reforms are absolutely necessary to avoid another similar crisis.[12]

4.2.4 The Basle III proposal

The 27-member countries of the International Basel Committee on Banking Supervision of the Bank for International Settlements with the Group of Central Bank Governors and Heads of Supervision at their meeting on 12 September 2010 reached an agreement on regulatory issues. Further discussion took place at the first 2011 G20 meeting in Paris. The so-called 'Basel III package' is concerned with bank capital and liquidity standards. The new ruling, phased in from January 2013 with full implementation to be achieved by January 2019, has only dealt with bank capital. It requires banks to hold equity requirements of at least 7 per cent of risk-weighted assets (RWA); or up to 9.5 per cent for banks of global systemic importance. It also includes liquidity standards with a liquidity coverage ratio, which requires banks to meet a 3 per cent leverage ratio. The timetable is a victory for the banks, which gives them longer to earn profits to offset against losses accumulated during the 'great recession' and in the process tax advantages emerge.[13]

The new capital ratios are lower than they might have been and also they are not to be fully implemented until 2019. This long phase-in period seems to have been a concession to small banks, especially in Germany. These are the banks that will struggle with the new rules presumably because of undercapitalization. Another problem is that unlike the US Dodd–Frank Act, which provided relevant regulations in the case of banks migrating to the 'shadow banking' sector and to the lightly supervised non-bank financial services companies, Basle III does not contain such provision. A further problem concerns the definition of the capital ratio, which is defined in relation to RWA, not to total assets. An implication of this is that toxic leverage is highly probable: when the RWA is a small proportion of total assets, then the exposure of the banking sector to risk would be very high indeed.

The IMF in its *2012 Global Financial Stability Report* argues that Basle III rules would exacerbate the too-big-to-fail problem. It is suggested that 'Big banking groups with advantages of scale may be better able to absorb the costs of the regulations; as a result, they may become even more prominent in certain markets, making these markets more concentrated'.[14] The IMF is particularly concerned that banks with large shares of their activity in fixed income, currencies and commodities markets will become even more dominant. The IMF also cautions that Basle III rules raise the incentive to develop new products to circumvent the framework. There is also a 'high chance' that the framework would push riskier activity into less regulated parts of the financial system.

Clearly, then, Basel III has failed to correct the mechanism through which the main cause of the 'great recession' emerged. Under such circumstances it should not be surprising for another similar crisis to take place. All in all, and given the key role of Basel III in the global regulatory system, it would appear that financial stability remains unresolved and elusive.

4.2.5 Role of credit rating agencies

In any type of reform, the role of credit rating agencies should be seriously revised. Abolishing them in view of their unacceptable performance in over-rating might be one way forward. Changing the way of their remuneration is another: looking carefully into the conflict of interest that arises from their fees paid by the issuers, rather than by the investors, thereby introducing a strong incentive to boost ratings, is long overdue. Credit ratings should be more transparent: publishing their methodologies and including more details on their work, so that investors can easily check, is very important.

The Dodd–Frank Act of 2010 has provided a way forward in an attempt to tackle this issue, as stated above. The President of the European Commission has suggested the placing of credit rating agencies under the direct supervision of a 'European Securities markets' authority. The Chancellor of Germany and the President of France proposed 'a clampdown on credit rate agencies'. The Bank of England and to a lesser extent the ECB, signal a clear break away from credit rating agencies. In this way the judgements of the credit rating agencies have been called into question since the eruption of the financial crisis in August 2007. But still no positive action has been taken.

5 Summary and conclusions

We have highlighted the origins of the August 2007 financial crisis and the subsequent 'great recession'; and in doing so we have distinguished between main causes and contributing factors. The main factors we have suggested are a combination of distributional effects and financial liberalization in the US, but also elsewhere, both of which enabled the creation of the shadow banking in the US, thereby initiating the emergence of the financial innovation of CDOs and other similar toxic assets. We have also proposed three contributory factors: international imbalances, monetary policy and the role and performance of the credit rating agencies.

We have also discussed the policy implications of the 'great recession' to suggest that more intervention on the policy front is desperately needed. We also need to have a properly regulated and functioning banking system to allow economic activity to expand. In this respect financial stability is paramount. We have discussed a number of suggestions on this front but, unfortunately, progress on financial reform is extremely slow; and there is worrying poverty of action. In fact, nearly four years since the US Dodd–Frank Act of July 2010, and other proposals as discussed above, and still banking reforms remain a work in progress across the world. Indeed, and as Vickers (2013) concludes: 'The financial crisis began more than five years ago. The prolonged macroeconomic and fiscal costs of financial crises are manifest to all. Yet the progress of banking reform has been mixed, and much unfinished business remains' (p. 8).

Notes

1 It is interesting to note that according to the Economist (30 November 2013, p. 28), the crisis that started in August 2007 in the US

> did more harm to Britain than to America. Britain had the first bank failure, and it had the biggest one. In just 18 months between 2008 and 2009 GDP dropped by 7.2% more than it had in the 1930s. As unemployment rose, benefits kicked in and the budget deficit swelled: by 2010 Britain had the largest of any G20 nation.

2 A summary of the very lengthy Dodd–Frank Act of July 2010 is available at: www.banking.senate.gov/public/_files/070110_Dodd_Frank_Wall_Street_Reform_comprehensive_summary_Final.pdf.

3 Examples of this critique are available, for example, at: www.sifma.org/issues/item.aspx?id=25260.

4 The five agencies mentioned in the text are: the Federal Reserve, the Federal Deposit Insurance Corporation, the Office of the Controller of the Currency, the Securities and Exchange Commission (SEC) and the Commodities Futures Trading Commission. The US Treasury also played a role.

5 The relevant details of the revised version of the Volker rule, stretching to 800 pages, are available at: http://online.wsj.com/public/resources/documents/1210volcker preamble.pdf.

6 Despite its ratification on 10 December 2013, it is expected that industry groups, such as the Chamber of Commerce, but not individual banks, might engage in litigation to block the measures of the Volcker rule.

7 See the Independent Commission on Banking (2011) for the details of the Vickers Report. See, also, Vickers (2013).

8 The Prudential Regulation Authority (PRA) was created by the 2012 Financial Services Act and was given, on 1 April 2013, the responsibility for the prudential regulation and supervision of banks, building societies, credit unions, insurers and major investment firms. It sets standards and supervises financial institutions at the level of the individual firm, thereby being in charge of microprudential policy; and it is part of the Bank of England.

9 As reported in the *Financial Times* (9 December 2013), the HSBC bank, which operates in 80 countries around the world, is thought to be seriously considering reallocation in Hong Kong to avoid the UK ring-fencing.

10 The Erkki Liikanen report under the title 'High Level Expert Group on Reforming the Structure of the EU Banking Sector' is available at: http://ec.europa.eu/internal_market/bank/docs/high-level_expert_group/report_en.pdf. See, also, Liikanen (2012) and Vickers (2013).

11 Germany has pursued a similar route to that of France but there is a long way for this initiative to be ready for potentially becoming a relevant law.

12 The IMF proposals under the title 'A Fair and Substantial Contribution by the Financial Sector' is available at: http://news.bbc.co.uk/1/shared/bsp/hi/pdfs/2010_04_20_imf_g20_interim_report.pdf.

13 Admati and Hellwig (2013) have suggested that a very much higher capital requirements than Basel III is necessary.

14 The IMF *2012 Global Financial Stability Report* is available at: www.imf.org/External/Pubs/FT/GFSR/2012/02/pdf/text.pdf.

References

Admati, A. and Hellwig, M. (2013), *The Bankers' New Clothes*, Princeton, NJ: Princeton University Press.

Arestis, P. (2007), *Is There a New Consensus in Macroeconomics?*, Houndmills, Basingstoke: Palgrave Macmillan.

Arestis, P. (2012), Fiscal policy: A strong macroeconomic role. *Review of Keynesian Economics*, Inaugural Issue, 1(1), 93–108.

Arestis, P. and Karakitsos, E. (2013), *Financial Stability in the Aftermath of the Great Recession*, Basingstoke: Palgrave Macmillan.

Ashcraft, A., Goldsmith-Pinkham, P. and Vickery, J. (2010), MBS Ratings and the Mortgage Credit Boom, *Federal Reserve Bank of New York Staff Report 449*, New York: Federal Reserve Bank of New York.

Bank of International Settlements (BIS) (2008), *Annual Report*, June, Basel, Switzerland: Bank for International Settlements.

Furceri, D. and Loungani, P. (2013), Who Led the Gini Out? *Finance & Development*, December, 50(4), 26–27.

Goodhart, C.A.E. (2009), *The Regulatory Response to the Financial Crisis*, Cheltenham: Edward Elgar Publishing Limited.

Greenspan, A. (2010), The Crisis. Available at: www.brookings.edu/~/media/Files/Programs/ES/BPEA/2010_spring_bpea_papers/spring2010_greenspan.pdf.

Greenspan, A. (2013), *The Map and the Territory: Risk, Human Nature, and the Future of Forecasting*, London: Penguin Books for Allen Lane.

HM Treasury (2012), *Sound Banking: Delivering Reform*, London, October.

HM Treasury (2013), *Banking Reform: A New Structure for Stability and Growth*, London, February.

Independent Commission on Banking (2011), *Final Report: Recommendations*, London.

Liikanen, E. (2012), *Final Report of the High-level Expert Group on Reforming the Structure of the EU Banking Sector*, Brussels.

OECD (2008), *Growing Unequal? Income Distribution and Poverty in OECD Countries*, October. Paris: Organisation of Economic Co-operation and Development.

Philippon, T. (2008), The Evolution of the U.S. Financial Industry from 1860 to 2007, *Working Paper*, November, New York University.

Philippon, T. and Reshef, A. (2009), Wages and Human Capital in the U.S. Financial Industry: 1909–2006, *NBER Working Paper No. 14644*, Washington, DC: National Bureau of Economics Research.

Saez, E. (2013), Income Inequality: Evidence and Policy, *Mimeo*, University of California, Berkeley.

Turner, A. (2010), What Do Banks Do? What Should They Do and What Public Policies Are Needed to Ensure Best Results for the Real Economy?, Speech given at the CASS Business School, London, 17 March. Available at: www.fsa.gov.uk/pubs/speeches/at_17mar10.pdf.

Vickers, J. (2013), Banking Reform in Britain and Europe. Paper presented at the *Rethinking Macro Policy II: First Steps and Early Lessons* Conference, hosted by the International Monetary Fund, Washington, DC, 16–17 April.

3 Financialization, financial systems and sustainable development

Malcolm Sawyer

Introduction

An ecologically sustainable growth path has many prerequisites: amongst those would be the construction of a financial system which is itself sustainable and which is consistent with the funding of investment which supports a sustainable growth path. The financial system has often been viewed as something of a driver for economic growth, and as such lower and sustainable growth requires some taming of the financial system. The first part of the chapter discusses the relationships between financialization, growth of the financial sector and growth of economic activity. It is particularly concerned with whether indeed the financial system fosters growth, and whether more recently the relationship between financial growth and economic growth has changed. The second is based on the argument that there is not a general shortage of finance for investment particularly in a slower growth era, and that much more attention should be paid to ensuring that the direction of finance is towards environmentally friendly and 'green' investment. It cannot be expected that a financial system will ensure such a direction of finance, and that measures will be needed in terms of regulation and restructuring the financial system to aid the re-direction of finance.

Financial sector, financialization and economic growth

The central concern in debates over the relationship between financial development and economic growth has been over what types of developments in the financial sector (e.g. growth of equity markets) would favour economic growth, and what effects of regulation and liberalization would have on economic performance and notably growth. The presumption in those debates has been that faster growth and more output were desirable ends, and little regard was given to the composition of growth.[1]

It has generally been argued that there is a positive relationship between financial development and economic growth: this has been discussed theoretically and empirically. Within that literature there has been dispute over the directions of causation between financial development and economic growth.[2] What is termed financial development has been viewed in terms of the size and structure of the financial sector: the size has meant bank deposits to GDP and the ratio of stock market capitalization to GDP, and structure has referred to the relative roles of the banking system and the stock market. Although the term financial development is used in this literature, it is more the size of the financial sector which is measured in the empirical work.

In what may be termed the era of financialization (broadly since circa 1980 in the industrialized world), the financial sector has grown substantially, and measures such as size of banking system and stock market have increased. Whilst this growth has involved some rise in measures of size such as that of the stock market, it has also involved growth of derivatives and securitization and trading in those derivatives, and in the scale of financial institutions through expansion of their assets and liabilities, developments which have fed into increased instability of the financial system. Causal observation suggests that in industrialized economies the growth of the financial sector has outpaced the growth of the real economy, and the increased scale of the financial sector has not been associated with faster economic growth. More formally, in some recent papers the positive relationship between financial development and economic development has been found wanting. For example, 'Up to a point, banks and markets both foster economic growth. Beyond that limit, expanded bank lending or market-based financing no longer adds to real growth' (Gambacorta *et al*., 2014, p. 21).[3] Law and Singh (2014) report, based on a sample consisting of 87 developed and developing countries, that their

> empirical results indicate that there is a threshold effect in the finance-growth relationship. In particular, we find that the level of financial development is beneficial to growth only up to a certain threshold; beyond the threshold level further development of finance tends to adversely affect growth. These findings reveal that more finance is not necessarily good for economic growth and highlight that an 'optimal' level of financial development is more crucial in facilitating growth.
>
> (p. 33)

Others, e.g. Epstein and Crotty (2013) have argued that the financial sector has become too large; and that the ways in which the financial sector has expanded in recent times (through securitization for example) have aided instability and have engaged in activities which are resource-using but which do not contribute to the financing and funding of investment.[4] There have been arguments advanced to the effect that financialization (of the recent era) has been associated with a lower rate of investment (and associated with that a somewhat slower rate of growth in the industrialized world in the neoliberal era, though without assigning causality).[5]

One may be tempted to argue that further growth of the banking and financial sector should be encouraged in order to reduce investment and the growth of the real economy! But we resist that temptation by recognizing that not only could the resources deployed in the banking and financial sector be put to socially beneficial use, it is also necessary to ensure that the growth which does occur is not environmentally damaging and is ecologically sustainable.

The most widely cited definition of the term 'financialization' is probably that given by Epstein (2005) in his introduction to his edited book *Financialization and the World Economy*: 'here we will cast the net widely and define financialization quite broadly: for us, financialization means the increasing role of financial motives, financial markets, financial actors and financial institutions in the operation of the domestic and international economies' (p. 3). Although many have focused on the period since circa 1980 as an era of financialization, at least some of the processes identified by Epstein have been an ongoing feature of capitalism, if not before, though taking different forms and at different speeds (and it may be possible to think of periods of de-financialization with the 1930s as one such period). The debates referred to above would also suggest that financialization is long-standing as financial development is generally measured in ways related to the size of the financial sector (or at least the banking sector). In the period since 1980, financialization has generally gone alongside neo-liberalism and a rise in inequality (and we do not delve here into the relationship between them). In the project on Financialisation, Economy, Society and Sustainable Development (FESSUD), and following Fine (2011), eight features of financialization have been identified.[6] These are:

> First, it refers to the large-scale expansion and proliferation of financial markets over the past thirty years...
>
> Second, the process has been closely interwoven with de-regulation of the financial system itself and the economy more generally...
>
> Third, financialisation, understood as both the expansion and the proliferation of financial instruments and services, has been associated with the birth of a whole range of financial institutions and markets...
>
> Fourth, at a systemic level, financialisation has been located in terms of the dominance of finance over industry...
>
> Fifth, financialisation is strongly associated with market mechanisms, complemented or even reinforced by policies that have underpinned rising inequality of incomes and of inequality more generally...
>
> Sixth, though, consumption has often been sustained by the extension of credit, not least through the use of capital gains in housing as collateral...
>
> Seventh, it is not merely the expansion and proliferation of financial instruments and markets that are striking but also the penetration of such financing into a widening range of both economic and social reproduction – housing, pensions, health, and so on...
>
> Finally, financialisation is associated with a particular culture which is to be interpreted broadly.

Financialization and the growth of the financial sector have gone alongside somewhat slower growth in the industrialized countries and rising inequality. Financialization has also been associated with rises in the occurrence of financial crises. The history of capitalist economies is littered with financial crises of which the 2007–2009 financial crises were amongst the more global and extensive; but it should not be overlooked that there were other major crises (notably the East Asian 1997). Laeven and Valencia (2012) (from their Figure 4) record 346 financial crises in the period 1970–2011, of which 99 were banking crises, 18 sovereign debt crises and 153 currency crises, 11 banking and debt, 28 banking and currency, 29 debt and currency, and eight combined all three elements. After a lull in the early 2000s, a total of 25 banking crises are recorded for 2007–2011. Their paper also gives estimates of the large-scale costs of financial crises. Financial crises have often been associated with recessions, and these recessions have often, but not always, associated with a fall in economic output (particularly when compared with what would have happened if previous growth rate had continued) which is not fully recovered, even though growth itself at around the previous rate is resumed. But

> the impact of the 2008–2009 global financial crisis (GFC) on emissions has been short-lived owing to strong emissions growth in emerging economies, a return to emissions growth in developed economies, and an increase in the fossil-fuel intensity of the world economy.
>
> (Peters *et al.*, 2012, p. 1)

One might even be inclined to argue that financialization is good for the environment in that it may tend to slow down growth, and the recessions coming from the financial crises lower future levels of output and may tend to diminish carbon emissions. In contrast we base our arguments on the need for slower growth in the future, and that the growth which does arise has to be of the 'right type'. It has to be growth which is 'green', environmentally friendly and low carbon, and does not leave a massive ecological footprint. The direction of investment (and research and development) becomes particularly important. It is much more a matter of the 'quality' of investment than the 'quantity'. The downward pressures under financialization on investment may not, of course, have been restraints on the 'right sort' of investment: indeed the short-termist aspects of financialization could well steer investment towards short-term gains rather than investment which has a long term pay-off, and away from investment, particularly research and development, which has uncertain pay-off.

A sustainable financial system for environmental sustainability

Development which is sustainable from ecological and environmental perspectives has many perquisites. It will require that the 'ecological footprint'[7] from economic activities (and human activity more generally) does not continue to outstrip the capacity of the eco system to absorb; it will require that the nature of energy use and carbon emissions does not lead to excessive CO_2 and climate change which cannot be coped with. Formulas such as the Kaya identity relating the level of human impact on climate in the form of emissions of the greenhouse gas carbon dioxide to population, GDP per capita, energy use per unit of GDP, carbon emissions per unit of energy consumed and a more general PAT where human impact is the multiple of population (P), affluence (A) and technology (T) are simple representations which point to a host of ways by which the environmental impact could be reduced. For the approach of this chapter, the role of technology is particularly significant: in the Kaya identity through influencing energy use relative to GDP and carbon emissions relative to energy consumed, and in the PAT formula with the direct mention of technology.

The rate of economic growth (as measured by GDP or similar)[8] will probably need to be somewhat lower in the future (as compared with the pace in industrialized countries over the past seven decades). With a near constant capital-output ratio this would imply a lower requirement (relative to GDP) for investment. The shifts in technologies could have some effects on the average capital-output ratio – for example, a shift towards services would likely involve a lower capital-output ratio, whereas shifts from non-renewable energy resources to renewable could involve higher capital requirements.[9] In Fontana and Sawyer (2015) we have argued that the consequences of lower investment intensity would involve higher consumption (public and private) propensity, the need for a larger budget deficit (to in effect offset the gap between private savings and investment) to ensure that full employment becomes a reality (though involving shorter working time).

In an earlier paper (Fontana and Sawyer, 2012) we set out three types of growth rate: the demand-led rate of growth which is itself driven by investment demand linked with the expected rate of growth; the supply-side rate of growth based on labour force and labour productivity growth; and the rate of growth compatible with the 'ecological footprint'. The latter depends on the nature and form which economic growth (or lack thereof) takes including the carbon content of that growth and its energy use, the speed of destruction of nature and the latter's ability to replenish itself. Ensuring a compatibility between the growth of the effective labour force and the growth of economic activity is not central here, though we have to say that full employment (with employment including unpaid as well as paid) is an important component of sustainability, and that appropriate macroeconomic policies are required to ensure that a lower growth rate (and likely lower investment requirements) does not lead to high unemployment. Other policies on working time would also be required.

Bringing the demand-led rate of growth into compatibility with the sustainable 'ecological footprint' will require a lower rate of investment (based on a view that future growth of output will have to be lower) and the direction of loans and funds into 'green', environmentally friendly and low carbon investments. Market forces and the pursuit of profit are not conducive to the drive for a lower rate of growth (and as we argue in Fontana and Sawyer, 2015 a lower rate of growth may well lead to a lower rate of profit).

The working assumption here is that future economic growth of economic activity, particularly in the industrialized world, will need to be lower in the future than in the past decades (notably the period since WWII) for reasons of environmental sustainability. The extent to which growth will need to be lower in the future is fiercely disputed from those thinking a few tenths of a percentage point per annum through to zero or de-growth. Some (including IPCC) have viewed output being lower than otherwise in a few decades time, but that translated into lower growth of one or two tenths of a per cent. Others (e.g. Piketty, 2014) view slower growth, perhaps of the order of 1–1½ per cent per annum for industrialized economies, though this may come more through limits on the speed of technical change. Anger and Barker (2015) suggest a growth rate for the world over the period to 2050 of the order of 2.5 per cent per annum. Others such as those in the Centre for the Advancement of the Steady State Economy, Dietz and O'Neill (2013), Victor (2008) would place the sustainable rate of economic growth at zero (or less). Chancel *et al.* (2013) postulate a growth rate of between 0 and 1 per cent per annum.

The macroeconomic adjustments to a lower rate of growth undertaken to preserve high levels of employment would include using monetary and fiscal policy to bridge the gap between (lower) investment and savings – that is using a budget deficit to in effect absorb the difference between savings and investment, and indeed to enable the savings to be realized.

One of our starting points is that the quantity of investment (as conventionally measured) required in industrialized countries in the coming decades is unlikely to be greater (relative to the overall size of the economy). It is rather the quality and composition of investment which becomes of crucial concern. This is reflected in statements such as 'There is a significant green investment gap. The current level of green investment is running at less than half of the level needed to deliver the decarbonisation implicit in national and international targets. A significant scale-up is needed' (House of Commons Environmental Audit Committee, 2014). It is also a basic tenet within post-Keynesian economics that investment generates savings, and that the issue of there being sufficient savings do not arise but rather the issue is the provision of finance (in the form of bank loans) which enables the investment to take place.

It is argued here that, in general, there is not a shortage of savings for investment of the 'right type'. Current patterns of savings and investment in many countries, and the associated budget deficits, suggest a tendency for savings to exceed investment. However, a constraint on investment comes from *initial finance*; that is the provision by banks of loans which enable investment (and more generally production) to occur. Whilst banks typically offer loans to creditworthy customers on the terms which the bank sets, nevertheless the banks have it within their power not to provide loans. Further, banks have the power as to whom those loans are provided; in effect who the banks regarded as creditworthy. It has long been argued that in practice banks adopt credit rationing which discriminates against certain groups; whether on grounds of ethnicity, gender, of size of firm, or on nature of activity. When initial finance has been provided, investment activity stimulates income and saving, and sufficient savings will be generated to *ex post* provide funding for the investment. Investment requires finance and liquidity; and thereby sufficient savings are generated. The savings thereby generated within a period match the investment which has occurred in that period in terms of quantity from macroeconomic considerations.[10] But, usually through the financial markets and institutions, the savings have to flow to the individual investment projects (and the firms who have undertaken them). Hence the focus should be on the direction of finance and funds rather than concern over sufficient savings. But the allocation of finance and funds is in the hands of the financial institutions and markets, and there is no assurance that that allocation is in accordance with sustainability. It would involve that the financing of investment, initial and final in the terminology of the circuit approach, is channelled towards socially desirable and environmentally friendly investment, and not towards financial asset accumulation speculation. It also indicates that the thrust of the operations of the banking and financial system should be on the financing and funding of real investment, and not financial investments, rather than be engaged in securitization, derivatives, etc.

It may be rather fanciful to seek to structure a financial system which is sustainable in the sense that it expands smoothly in a manner compatible with the growth of economic activity and avoids major booms and busts, financial crises and the after effects of those. The construction of a banking and financial system in a capitalist economy which does not involve instabilities, credit and asset price booms and busts and periodic financial crisis is difficult if not impossible. It is an inherent feature of banking and financial systems to involve such instabilities. Minsky, for example, argued that 'the readily observed empirical aspect is that from time to time capitalist economies exhibit inflations and debt deflations which seem to have the potential to spin out of control' (Minsky, 1994, p. 153) in his introduction to a piece of the 'financial instability hypothesis'. Minsky states (1986, p. 327) that 'turbulence – especially financial instability – is normal in capitalist economy; the tranquil era between 1946 and 1966 was an anomaly'. The recent focus on the financial crises of 2007/2009 and its global dimensions has tended to overlook the frequency of financial crisis.

A banking and financial system is required which is itself robust and not subject to crises which lead to recessions and unemployment. It also requires that the banking and financial system does not develop in ways which generate instabilities in other parts of the economy. The interactions of the banking and financial system with the property market are sources of asset price bubbles and subsequent bursting. The development of securitization and derivatives based on commodities serves to generate instabilities in other parts of the economy: notably recent examples have been food and energy markets in 2007/2008.[11]

Whilst a financial system structured and regulated to be less prone to financial crises is a worthy aim, and some of the proposals put forward here may well contribute towards that aim, our main purpose is the relationship between the financial sector and environmental sustainability.

Credit rationing is a pervasive feature of the behaviour of banks and other financial institutions in the sense that banks have to assess the risks of non-payment and default of loans, and the interest rate charged and the other conditions of any loan will reflect that risk assessment. There will be credit rationing in the sense that potential borrowers are not able to borrow all they wish at the loan rate, and indeed the loan rate charged by banks increases with the scale of borrowing as the perception of default increases. The credit allocation processes depend on risk assessments which in an uncertain world can only be perceptions of frequency of default, etc., rather than based on well-established probability distributions. There have been many large literatures on how banks and other financial institutions approach lending to different social, ethnic groups and gender, and in effect discriminate against some and practice financial exclusion. The structure of the financial system and the legal framework must be such as to ensure that credit rationing practices do not operate against 'green investment', and more generally environmentally friendly investment. The creation of specialist 'green' banks, requirements for a proportion of loans to be allocated to specified types of environmentally friendly investments and the underwriting of certain types of loans by public insurance can be mechanisms by which some of the obstacles on environmentally friendly investments could be addressed.

The distinction is often drawn between a bank-based financial system and a market-based one,[12] and much has been written on the effectiveness of the two systems. In practice, each financial system contains major elements of both (and indeed it is difficult to conceive of a financial system without an extensive banking system through which loans are granted, money created and a payments technology provided). The bank-based vs market-based dichotomy can be viewed through the lens of 'voice vs exit' (Hirschman, 1970), which is further discussed below. Here we note that the 'exit' option operates in the market in that an economic agent can express their disapproval through exit – selling or not buying the good concerned (in the stock market case, shares in a company). In face-to-face economic relationships though 'voice' can be expressed. '[T]he fundamental distinction between financial systems can be seen to be not whether they are bank- or capital market-based, but rather whether they are dominated by exit or voice mechanisms' (Pollin, 1995, p. 29). The voice-exit distinction can be summarized (though much more is involved) when Hirschman (1970) argues that consumers can signal their dissatisfaction to a firm either through the exit option (stop buying the firm's product) or through the voice option (express dissatisfaction to the firm). Similarly workers can signal dissatisfaction by leaving the firm or by voicing their complaints. A bank-based system lends itself more to the operation of voice rather than exit effects, whereas market-based operate through the latter. In a bank-based system, it is rather less difficult to guide the nature of lending than it would be under a market-based system.

At a general level, the essential requirement is for a banking and financial system which serves the rest of the economy rather than the rest of the economy serving the interests of the financial sector. Apart from the provision of a well-functioning payments technology, the key requirements which should be made for a financial system are that:

i it expands in a way which is consistent with the environmentally sustainable rate of growth;
ii it channels loans and savings into the social desirable types of investment.

We now sketch four components of a strategy towards the financial sector which could aid environmental sustainability.

Financial transactions taxes

The first component envisages a role for financial transactions taxes as a means of reducing the financial sector's trading activities in existing financial assets, which we would argue are not related with what should be the key functions of the financial sector of the financing and funding of investment.[13] The trading of existing financial assets, the growth of 'fictitious capital' and the rise of assets and liabilities (relative to GDP) contribute little to that key role. The resources which engaged in such trading would be released for more productive activities, and there can be beneficial effects on the volatility and fragility of such markets.

The essential rationale for a financial transactions tax remains and is indeed reinforced by financialization and the specific direction which financialization has taken in the past three decades with the growth of securitization and derivatives. The advocacy of a financial transactions tax is not to preclude other taxes on the financial sector such as financial activity taxes. The advantages of a financial transaction tax would not only dampen down the resources deployed in the buying and selling of existing financial assets which are of little social benefit, but also serve as a source of tax revenues which can be deployed for the funding of public green investment.

Green development banks

A second component is the establishment and/or greater role for state-sponsored development banks. Such development banks often raise substantial funds in the capital market as well as more direct funding by government. The advantages of a development bank model include the clear setting of objectives for the way in which funds are to be allocated, which sectors and which activities are to be favoured. It can enable funds to be provided on more favourable terms than would be forthcoming from private financial institutions through implicit government subsidy of its operations (e.g. the mark-up of the interest rate charged over the costs of funds in the capital market is kept low). The range of investments funded by a development bank could also focus on the type of investments which are shunned by the financial markets. These would include investments which have a long-term rather than short-term pay-off, and those subject to high degrees of uncertainty: a notable example here would be research and development activities. There are, of course, examples of banks operating along such lines including the German KfW, the UK Green Investment Bank and the European Investment Bank.

Insofar as a state-sponsored development bank was drawing on government funds it would run into the objection that it adds to budget deficit and to the public debt. Our response to that would be that borrowing for investment also adds to the assets of the public sector (whether through infrastructure investment or through onward lending to the private sector), and that the concern should be that the funds are well used, adding to the desired direction of investment, and aiding the achievement of full employment. There is no 'tipping point' for the national debt to GDP ratio which threatens growth. But also note that as with the European Investment Bank any lending by governments can be leveraged through direct borrowing by the development bank, and that such borrowing (as is the case with the European Investment Bank) does not appear on the balance sheets of any national or EU organization.

A state development bank has the potential for the prioritizing of funds for socially desirable investments. This is not to underestimate the obstacles of assessing the social desirability of investment projects, nor the threats of 'mission creep' whereby those financial institutions which initially have wider objectives than profit maximization become focused on profits.

Guided lending

There has been a long history, particularly in the context of industrial development, of requirements being placed on banks on the sectors of the economy to which loans are made, for example, the prioritizing of investment in sectors which are regarded as strategic for industrialization, and limiting loans to households. Banks and other financial institutions make loans and provide funds according to their assessments of profitability for themselves which is based on their assessments of the profitability of the proposed investments and the risks associated with such investments and of default. An important element of the promotion of greener investments is to seek to ensure that funds flow in the direction which is compatible with that objective. The proposal here is some degree of guided lending for banks – that is requirements that a specified proportion of their lending is to what is identified as green and environmentally friendly investment. This could draw on the US experience of the Community Reinvestment Act (CRA), introduced in 1977 and revised in 1995, whereby banks and other financial institutions are legally required to direct a portion of funds to lending to the local community.

> The Community Reinvestment Act is intended to encourage depository institutions to help meet the credit needs of the communities in which they operate, including low- and moderate-income neighborhoods, consistent with safe and sound operations. The CRA requires that each depository institution's record in helping meet the credit needs of its entire community be evaluated by the appropriate Federal financial supervisory agency periodically. Members of the public may submit comments on a bank's performance. Comments will be taken into consideration during the next CRA

> examination. A bank's CRA performance record is taken into account in considering an institution's application for deposit facilities.
>
> (www.federalreserve.gov/communitydev/cra_about.htm; accessed March 2014)

Another avenue could be the use of bank disclosure on the lending decisions made by banks. For example, Dayson *et al.* (2013, p. 7) explore the use of a Banking Disclosure Act as

> it is believed that disclosure could support research into the determinants of underinvestment and lending, which in turn would aid by enhancing our understanding of financial exclusion and underinvestment. In particular, it would help identify groups and areas less likely to access financial services.

This should not be taken to underestimate the practical difficulties involved here, of which the most obvious one would be the specification of the forms of investment which would qualify and which would not. It is though possible to point to banks and many organizations which adopt ethical and environmental factors into their decisions on lending and financial investments. An ethical bank such as Triodos (triodos.co.uk), financial institutions seeking Shiria compliant investments, etc. have to draw up codes of conduct for their investment behaviour. The 'guided investment' approach would be along similar lines, though recognizing that mistakes will be made, and the monitoring of such an approach should not be understated.

The underlying philosophy is that banks are making credit allocation decisions all the time, and the decisions which come out are not necessarily socially desirable. The purpose here would be to seek to ensure that sufficient credit is channelled in the directions consistent with the overall sustainable strategy.

Concluding comments

An environmentally sustainable growth path requires, inter alia, that the financing and funding of investments are undertaken which will aid the re-structuring of economic activity in a more environmentally friendly direction. The financial sector is involved in many activities which detract from its function of the financing and funding of investment. Further, the financial sector cannot be relied on to channel funds into 'green' investments. In this chapter we have offered some outline suggestions on ways to restructure the financial sector and to redirect funds in appropriate ways.

Notes

1 I am referring here to what may be termed the mainstream literature as reviewed in, for example, Levine (2005). There have been alternative literatures which are concerned with industrialization and the role of development banks in the processes of industrialization.

2 For recent view of this literature and elaboration of points made in this paragraph see Sawyer (2014a).
3 For some further discussion on this point see Sawyer (2014a).
4 See Sawyer (2012) for further discussion on this point.
5 See Hein (2012) for work in that direction.
6 See Sawyer (2014b) for further discussion.
7 The Global Footprint Network views the ecological footprint as 'a measure of how much area of biologically productive land and water an individual, population or activity requires to produce all the resources it consumes and to absorb the waste it generates, using prevailing technology and resource management practices.' The ecological deficit/reserve is then the difference between the biocapacity and ecological footprint of a region or country. 'An ecological deficit occurs when the Footprint of a population exceeds the biocapacity of the area available to that population. Conversely, an ecological reserve exists when the biocapacity of a region exceeds its population's Footprint' (www.footprintnetwork.org/en/index.php/GFN/page/glossary/).
8 GDP here is viewed as a measure of output which uses up inputs, and imposes an ecological footprint; it is not to be regarded as a good measure of economic welfare, and it has well-known deficiencies as a measure of material prosperity.
9 The capital-output ratio for non-renewable energy, of course, omits from the calculation the use of the non-renewable resource.
10 This is cast in terms of a closed private economy: some recasting of the argument would be needed for an open economy to include government deficit and net exports in the discussion.
11 On this see Verchelli (2014).
12 See Sawyer (2014c) for discussion and critique of this dichotomy.
13 For an overall assessment of financial transactions taxes see, for example, Arestis and Sawyer (2013).

References

Anger, A. and Barker, T. (2015), 'The effects of the financial system and financial crises on global growth and the environment', in P. Arestis and M. Sawyer (eds), *Finance and the Macroeconomics of Environmental Policies*, Basingstoke: Palgrave Macmillan.

Arestis, P. and Sawyer, M. (2013), 'The potential of financial transactions taxes', in P. Arestis and M. Sawyer (eds), *Economic Policies, Governance and the New Economics*, Basingstoke: Palgrave Macmillan.

Chancel, L., Demailly, D., Waisman, H. and Guivarch, C. (2013), 'A post-growth society for the 21st century: does prosperity have to wait for the return of economic growth? (CIRED). Studies No. 08/2013. Available at www.iddri.org.

Dayson, K., Vik, P., Rand, D. and Smith, G. (2013), *A UK Banking Disclosure Act: From Theory to Practice*, Dorking, UK: Friends Provident Foundation.

Dietz, R. and O'Neill, D. (2013), *Enough is Enough: Building a Sustainable Economy in a World of Finite Resources*, San Francisco: Berrett-Koehler Publishers.

Epstein, G. (2005), 'Introduction: financialization and the world economy', in G.A. Epstein (ed.), *Financialization and the World Economy*, Cheltenham: Edward Elgar.

Epstein, G. and Crotty, J. (2013), 'How big is too big? On the social efficiency of the financial sector in the United States', PERI, Working Paper series, No. 313.

Fine, B. (2011), 'Financialisation on the rebound?', mimeo.

Fontana, G. and Sawyer, M. (2012), 'Towards post Keynesian ecological macroeconomics', mimeo.

Fontana, G. and Sawyer, M. (2015), 'The macroeconomics and financial system requirements for a sustainable future', in P. Arestis and M. Sawyer (eds), *Finance and the Macroeconomics of Environmental Policies*, Basingstoke: Palgrave Macmillan.

Gambacorta, L., Yang, J. and Tsatsaronis, K. (2014), 'Financial structure and growth', *BIS Quarterly Review*, March, 21–33.

Hein, E. (2012), *The Macroeconomics of Finance-Dominated Capitalism – and its Crisis*, Cheltenham: Edward Elgar.

Hirschman, A.O. (1970), *Exit, Voice and Loyalty: Responses to Decline in Firms, Organizations and States*, Cambridge, MA: Harvard University Press.

House of Commons Environmental Audit Committee (2014), *Green Finance: Twelfth Report of Session 2013–14*, HC 191, London: The Stationery Office.

Laeven, L and Valencia, F. (2012), 'Systemic banking crises database: an update', *IMF Working Papers*, WP/12/163.

Law, S.H. and Singh, N. (2014), 'Does too much finance harm economic growth?', *Journal of Banking & Finance*, 41, 36–44.

Levine, R. (2005), 'Finance and growth: theory and evidence', in P. Aghion and S.N. Durlauf (eds), *Handbook of Economic Growth*, Amsterdam and London: Elsevier.

Minsky, H.P. (1986), *Stabilizing an Unstable Economy*, New Haven, CT: Yale University Press.

Minsky, H.P. (1994), 'Financial instability hypothesis', in P. Arestis and M. Sawyer (eds), *The Elgar Companion to Radical Political Economy*, Cheltenham: Edward Elgar.

Peters, G.P., Marland, G., Le Quéré, C., Boden, T., Canadell, J.G. and Raupach, M.R. (2012), 'Rapid growth in CO_2 emissions after the 2008–2009 global financial crisis', *Nature Climate Change*, 2, 1–4.

Piketty, T. (2014), *Capital in the Twenty-first Century*, Cambridge, MA: The Belknap Press of Harvard University Press.

Pollin, R. (1995), 'Financial structures and egalitarian economic policy', *International Papers in Political Economy*, 2(3), 1–36.

Sawyer, M. (2012), 'Re-structuring the financial sector to reduce its burden on the economy', in P. Arestis, R. Sobreira and Jose Luis Oreiro (eds), *The Recent Financial Crisis, Financial Regulation and Global Impact: Volume 1: The Financial Crisis: Origins and Implications*, Basingstoke: Palgrave Macmillan, pp. 114–136.

Sawyer, M. (2014a), 'Financial development, financialisation and economic growth', *FESSUD Working Paper*, No. 21. Available at fessud.eu.

Sawyer, M. (2014b), 'What is financialization?', *International Journal of Political Economy*, 42(4), 5–18.

Sawyer, M. (2014c), 'Bank-based vs. market-based financial systems: a critique of the dichotomy', *FESSUD Working Paper*, No. 19. Available at fessud.eu.

Verchelli A. (2014), 'The neoliberal trajectory, the great recession and sustainable development', in P. Arestis and M. Sawyer (eds), *Finance and the Macroeconomics of Environmental Policies*, Basingstoke: Palgrave Macmillan.

Victor, P.A. (2008), *Managing Without Growth*, Aldershot: Edward Elgar.

4 Financial capitalism trapped in an 'impossible' profit rate

The infeasibility of a 'usual' profit rate, considering fictitious capital, and its redistributive, ecological and political implications[1]

Wolfram Elsner

Introduction

In the present chapter, we will try to put forward, and illustrate with some rough calculations, the thesis that, when using the simple logic and dynamics of Marx' profit rate (PR) and particularly considering a *corrected PR including fictitious capital* – i.e. nominal, fluid, money-like, interest-begging capital that, however, is no longer designed to go the 'productive' way – it will turn out that a historically *usual PR* on the exploding amounts of that fictitious money-capital (which by far has become the largest share of all capital) has become *infeasible* after four decades of 'neoliberal' transformation and redistribution from the bottom to the top ranks.

It will be argued that '*neoliberalism*' itself (neither 'neo', new nor liberal for working people, as we know), when it was pushed into a practical counterrevolution in the 1970s, was a reaction to a shrinking PR under the late Keynesian welfare-state constellation, which in turn had pushed, through its very growth success, oligopolization and over-accumulation – and a decline of the PR. 'Neoliberalism', however, by its very means and mechanisms – *redistribution, financialization,* pecuniary *speculation, rent-seeking* and real *asset and income stripping* for interest income – even has continued, if not accelerated and aggravated, the *long-run fall of the (corrected) PR*, despite of its massive redistribution into the profit mass.

An average corrected PR (across a bubble cycle) not only has turned out to be untenably low but also tends to continuously decrease, rather than increase, as many PR-theorists have shown for the conventional PR, and at least for the first gold-rush phase of 'neoliberalism'. The corrected PR has decreased to such low levels that none of the most powerful corporate financial entities would want to accept it, considering their claims of a 'usual' PR of 20 per cent or 25 per cent or more, as 'culturally adopted' under the financialization regime – and they could not anyway given their ongoing rivalry and race for PRs.

This 'impossibility theorem' will have some most severe implications for capitalists' expectations, moods and behaviours, and the prospects of the current speculation capitalism, such as a comprehensive, reinforced and *accelerated redistribution* race. The latter includes, and eventually *exceeds*, the redistributable amounts of the *profits of the minor capitals*, of the *tangible industrial surplus value* and of *conventional capital*, of the money-capital of the *private wealthy*, of the *wage sum*, of the *public budgets* and of the whole *national GDPs*. Therefore, the fight for profit has to proceed not only to a comprehensive income and capital-asset stripping but to the plundering of all other assets of the earth of some lasting and potential future value, i.e. *resources and land-grabbing*.

The *comprehensive redistribution race* triggered that way, which includes all kinds of *taxpayers' money* and the *resources of humankind*, also turned out to be *incompatible with democracy* – even with the reduced variants of a representative, parliamentary, oligopolistic inter-party system, as we used to know it – and eventually with any *reasonable human development* at large.

1 The Marxian PR: a tool to explore typical socio-politico-economic constellations

Specific values of the PR do not automatically trigger specific expectations, moods or actions of capitalists and therefore do not entail specific competitive and macroeconomic consequences. Particular values are highly *contingent* and need to be considered *in context* rather. If properly embedded in specific *socio-politico-economic micro- and macro-constellations*, the PR formula may indicate typical expectations, sentiments and resulting behaviours – all driven and mediated by different degrees of rivalry and collaboration among the individual capitals – and their related macro effects. It thus may help analysing and illustrating the systemic crisis of financial capitalism, reinforced redistribution races and increasing social costs imposed on the real-economic, ecological, social, political and moral subsystems. The PR, however, is an *average macro-economic* phenomenon in the first instance, which only provides indications for reactions of individual capitals and resulting inter-corporate rivalry and redistribution races.

The PR, as an indication of average capitalists' experiences, expectations, sentiments and actions, under certain stylized constellations, is used here in the following form:

$$\pi = \frac{s}{c+v} = \frac{\frac{s}{v}}{\frac{c}{v}+1},$$

where s is the capitalists' surplus value over the sum of applied (conventionally tangible) constant capital c and variable capital v in the industrial value production process, with s/v the labour exploitation rate (or rate of surplus value) and c/v the composition of total capital. If considered at the macro-level, the values may be considered realized in monetary values, while for an individual capitalist a produced surplus value, of course, might not be realizable, under certain conditions, in terms of sales revenues.

A strictly formal logic and true formal dynamics of the PR in typical constellations would, of course, need to be elaborated in much more detail than is considered sufficient for our purpose, if to be used in formal modelling, exact quantification and eventually application to empirical research (for more detail on that logic, see, e.g. Heinrich 2012).[2] The PR, however, shall be illustrated and applied here as a heuristic and illustrative tool only, to demonstrate how far we can get with it to characterize the current crisis and comprehend diverse processes resulting, including seemingly very disparate phenomena.

2 Some insights into profitability development and the current crisis in the recent PR literature

A look at some instances of the recent literature on *fictitious capital*, the *PR* and the antecedents, causes and consequences of the *crisis*, provides some insights into the contexts and developments of profitability.[3]

(1) *Claude Serfati* (2009, 2012), for instance, has argued that the dominance of *fictitious capital* stems from the increasing use of *intangible assets* in the process of profit generation of the largest multinational corporations under the 'neoliberal' regime – profit that no longer has had sufficient incentive to be invested in real-economic value-production but has strived to go the 'short way', *M–M′*, through stripping tangible assets and conventional surplus value and the income streams derived from that. Among others, financialization and liquid (and, in fact, objectively 'superfluous' and excess) *money-capital* thus have led to an increasing (and also more volatile) divergence between *book accounting values* and *stock-market values*.[4] Increasing waves of mergers and acquisitions have taken place at the borderlines between real value production and financial speculation. The power dimension of the conglomerate 'big corporate economy' and 'big speculation industry' then established what traditionally was called a *rentier economy*, a dominant economy of rent-seeking, asset speculation and asset and income stripping through crediting and debt service, where traditional industrial profit and other traditional incomes on the one hand and speculation rents on the other have both blurring boundaries against each other and competition for resources. Rent-generation in fact *dismantles the real economy*.

Serfati (2009) considers the value distribution of *s* between *v* on the one hand and investment in conventional (tangible) *c* and *speculative purposes* (generating more fictitious capital) on the other at the core of an accelerated crisis of the PR. Notably, the *crisis of profitability* emerged in spite of *highest levels of labour exploitation* and the growth of the *profit mass and share*. The share of wages in value-added drastically declined in leading OECD countries from somewhat below 70 per cent in the mid-1970s to somewhat above 55 per cent at the onset of the crisis in 2007, and productive investment in tangible capital continuously declined. The public rescue packages 2008ff., in turn, also had distinct distributional effects reinforcing that trend.

Serfati estimates a *fictitious-capital stock* of more than US$680 trillion (Tn) just in over-the-counter (OTC) *derivatives* and a (similarly over-speculated) *equity stock* of more than US$100 Tn (each 2008).

(2) *Michael Hudson* (2010, 2012) and co-author(s) (e.g. Hudson and Bezemer 2012) also have elaborated on financialization, *fictitious capital*, financial capitalism as an unproductive, neo-feudal *rent-(seeking) system*, the financial burden of comprehensive asset and income stripping and *debt services*, the crisis of profitability and the resulting crises. At the core is 'the hope of the financial class: to capitalize the entire surplus into debt service' (Hudson 2010: 2).

Hudson clearly states that the amount of *fictitious capital cannot be 'real'-ized over time*, although it strangles the whole real economy, destroying the host economy's ability to pay, and needs to *transform* its pretences into *real values* before a crash. The implications sweep into the whole socio-political economy and natural environment, with corporate *raiding*, *fraud*, freeing rent from taxation and subsequent taxpayer (specifically labourer-taxpayers) bailouts.

Hudson has provided an account of the origins and mechanisms of fictitious capital as considered in the light of the crisis 2008ff. While mechanisms of fictitious-capital dominance cause the conventional PR to fall, the PR that considers increasing fictitious capital exhibits what he calls '*a pseudo-falling of the rate of profit*' (2010: 4; emphasis added) – what we call here a *fall of the corrected PR*.

Also Hudson considers the *interactions of finance with the real economy, particularly real estate and monopolies*. The speculative sector organizes a permanent raiding on the real economy and, in particular, *on labour incomes, savings and pension rights*.[5]

Hudson also analyses the short-cut *M–M′* way of stripping economy, society and environment. He explains, through ubiquitous excess capital, (i) simultaneous *inflated debt*, *debt interest-rate deflation* and *asset inflation*, (ii) the *Ponzi* scheme of a growing credit-debt system and (iii) simultaneous *asset inflation* and *real-economy (wages and commodities) deflation*. The *state* and its *(ex-)public enterprises* contribute to all this after having been turned into tollbooth agencies to extract rent, recycling it into bank bailouts. On top of that, *debt financing* is privileged over equity financing through the *tax deductibility* of interest payments.

The *bubble mechanism* is used to postpone the inevitable crash as long as possible, and particular action is to be taken before the bubble bursts. While he mentions hit and run strategies like *manager salaries*, *bonuses* and *dividend* explosion, he seems to overlook the ultimate ways to *transform fictitious capital into more value-maintaining forms*, such as the speculation on the *natural assets* of the earth.

But Hudson and Bezemer (2012) realize another mechanism that impacts the natural environment, namely that *assets typically get run down* in the process of their repeated financialization: '...high indebtedness leads to increased natural resource exploitation as well as more unsustainable patterns of resource use ... absentee landlords ... pay their mortgages by not repairing their property but letting it deteriorate' (p. 10).

(3) *Maniatis* (2012), in a recent conventional PR analysis, shows how the tendency of the falling PR explains the end of the 'golden age' of post-WWII and the

subsequent profitability crisis of the 1970s. While 'neoliberalism' has triggered a dramatic *increase of the exploitation rate* (s/v), and technological change (the IT-revolution) even has dampened for some time the accumulation of conventional constant capital, a fall in the capital-output ratio, profitability (the conventional PR) overall 'has not recovered sufficiently' in the end under the 'neoliberal' regime, 'due to the survival of *lagging capitals* and the increasing use of *unproductive labor*' (2012: 6; emphasis added). The 'neoliberal' feeding of capital through redistribution and privatization apparently not only caused real-economic slack and low profitability, financialization and excess fictitious money-capital, but also allowed *less productive capitals* to survive and capital to deploy ever more *unproductive overhead labour (particularly pecuniary 'services')*. Despite claims of the contrary, the 'neoliberal' regime caused *low productivity growth* even along with falling real wages (which normally would have fuelled productivity growth, but could not do so due to the circuit effect of weak demand and real-economic slack). But since all that could be monetized was reaped for capital income, the surplus mass, surplus share of GDP and rate of surplus s/v continued to grow.

A usual approach of Marxists (see also, e.g. Shaikh and Tonak 1994) has been to split the PR (π) into the following components:

$$\pi = \frac{\Pi}{K} = \left(\frac{\Pi}{Y}\right)\left(\frac{Y}{Z}\right)\left(\frac{Z}{K}\right)$$

with Π the mass of profits (s), K the total capital stock ($K=c+v$), Π/K the PR, Y the net output (national income, thus Π/Y the profit share), Z the maximum capacity output (Y/Z the capacity utilization rate) and Z/K the (technical) output-capital ratio (technical capital productivity).

In this frame, the *crisis of profitability* has been explained by the following stylized constellation, even under conditions of growth (↑, ↓, ~: increases, decreases, remains unchanged); see Appendix 1 for algebraic conditions:

$$\pi\downarrow = \left(\frac{\Pi\uparrow\uparrow}{K\uparrow\uparrow\uparrow}\right)\downarrow = \left(\frac{\Pi\uparrow\uparrow}{Y\uparrow\uparrow}\right)\uparrow\left(\frac{Y\uparrow}{Z\uparrow}\right)\sim\left(\frac{Z\uparrow}{K\uparrow\uparrow\uparrow}\right)\downarrow\downarrow$$

where mainly the falling (technical) output-capital ratio (*falling capital productivity through the growth of capital*) makes up for the falling PR, while the *profit share may even increase* through redistribution, privatization and all ways of reaping values for surplus (even if capital utilization remains constant).

This constellation by all means, be it a conventional or corrected PR calculation, applies to the *second ('decadent') and immediate pre-crisis period of 'neoliberalism'*, i.e. the years from the end of the 1990s up to 2007. But this will particularly be the case when we *correct* this constellation by including an exploding amount of fictitious capital.

The *conventional PR* of the corporate sector, as given by Maniatis for the US, on average was around 14 per cent for the 'golden age' (1948–1968), around 9 per cent for the Keynesian crisis period (1969–1982), falling over the period, and around 9 per cent again over the 'neoliberal' period (1982/1983ff., slightly increasing over the period until 2007). During the 'neoliberal' period, the result was increasingly due to the *profits of the financial sector* while the *traditional industrial sectors* faced a clearly *declining PR*.

The 'insufficient increase' even of the conventional PR under the 'neoliberal' regime was due to the fact that 'neoliberalism' increasingly caused *capital to become 'obese'* and *prevented the classical capitalist cyclical self-cleaning* through crisis and devaluation; in other words, 'due to the survival of lagging capitals, as the presence and size of the state did not allow for a massive devaluation of capital, and the continuous increase in unproductive labor necessary for the reproduction of the system' (Maniatis 2012: 26). The *burst of the bubble* with its necessary deleveraging will then reveal 'the weak fundamentals of the real economy' and, thus, the perspective of a 'deep and prolonged crisis' (ibid.).

(4) *Basu and Vasudevan* (2012) also provide a recent empirical investigation of the conventional PR from WWII to now and its significance for the current crisis. Reviewing the state of the art of contemporary Marxist profitability analyses, they also come to distinguish between the *gold-rush phase* of 'neoliberalism' with its *profit(ability) boom* that had ended the 1970s profitability crisis for nearly two decades, and the repercussions of that very boom in the *decadent phase*. In that second phase, *excessive* (tangible and fictitious) capital has become '*obese*' and '*idle*' and increased in spite of real-economic slack and real-investment failure, just through continuing *redistribution, wage (share) reduction*, an *increased exploitation rate* and through the *self-multiplication of fictitious capital in the growing bubble*. Also according to this analysis, both decreasing productivity of capital and an increasing share of unproductive overhead labour eventually caused the crisis and made the PR eventually decline.

In all, there are *different ways to conceptualize, model, quantify and measure the PR*. One may start from the measure of *profit* as all income flows other than compensation for employees, v; one may then successively remove depreciation, indirect taxes, interest payments and direct taxes. Similarly, *capital* might be broadly measured as fixed assets + raw materials + unfinished and finished commodities + money + depreciation funds + financial assets.[6] It might be measured as the stock of fixed assets net of depreciation and financial liabilities, both either at historical or replacement costs. In that way, Basu and Vasudevan operationalize and quantify several broader and narrower measures of the PR, using, for instance, net value added (less employee compensation, then net of production and import taxes, i.e. a 'net operating surplus') for profit, before or after depreciation and before or after direct taxes.

They show, for instance, that the PR, using *net operating surplus*, as compared before and after capital taxes, reveals considerable *capital subsidies through tax reliefs* from the 1970s on. Using *gross* total fixed assets and gross profits *after tax*, the PR increases to the levels of the mid-1960s, i.e. between 11 per cent and 16 per cent, from the 1990s to 2007. The *non-financial* corporate business sector generally is somewhat below that level and does not recover that clearly in the 1990s and 2000s, so that there is an *increasing burden of the real economy* that mirrors *profit redistribution* between the two subsectors.

The decomposition analysis (see equation above) also confirms that under the 'neoliberal' regime the *profit share has grown continually* (from the early 1980s onwards), while the *capital productivity has drastically shrunken*, particularly in the *decadent phase* of 'neoliberalism' (in the 2000s). Considering the decline of the *output-capital ratio* and the growth of *capital intensity* (c/v) in the 2000s, when labour productivity and the exploitation rate grew, and contrasting it to the relatively little capital accumulation in the last pre-crisis period (the 2000s), this in fact indicates how far the 'decadent-neoliberal' period has deteriorated the real economy in favour of fictitious capital (Basu and Vasudevan 2012: 23ff.).

According to the conventional calculations of the PR, the crisis was not an obvious crisis of profitability. But this is not the last word on profitability in a wider sense. We need to consider the fundamental shifts between conventional and fictitious constant capital. We will estimate a *corrected PR* incorporating fictitious capital, suggesting that former historical levels of the PR have increasingly become infeasible, and that this has caused a *continuous and increasing crisis of profitability, even in the gold-rush phase* of 'neoliberalism'.

(5) Notably, *Alan Freeman* (2013) published an article with the same idea of *correcting the usual Marxist PR calculations*, which use conventional constant capital and result in high and increasing PRs for most of the time of 'neoliberalism' (at least the gold-rush phase 1982–1999). Freeman's results, in contrast, indicate *considerably lower PRs* – a third for the UK and somewhat above half for the US (each for 2006), *continuously declining*. He does, however, not discuss the further implications on the reinforced redistribution race, the bubble as a redistribution mechanism and the race for 'real' values, i.e. resource and land-grabbing, which will be addressed in the present chapter.

3 The 'neoliberal' transformation of capitalism: in all, redistribution to the top ranks

The elements of the 'neoliberal' paradigm, a secular policy and state-bureaucratic project, and of the new theoretical models and ideologies of 'markets', 'competition', 'the state' and 'money', have been critically analysed for long and are well-comprehended theoretically and historically today (see, e.g. Palley 2012). We just roughly sketch (without particular references) some core elements of that decades-long planned political-economic project (e.g. Schoenbaum 2012) and its implications for the components of the PR.

(1) *'De-regulation' of the markets*, according to the new paradigm of the ideal 'market', a thought-experimental chimaera of an 'optimal' and self-stabilizing mechanism, stridently misconceiving and *misrepresenting real-world markets*. This fundamental misconception triggered the largest acceleration of the *self-degeneration (endogenous erosion) of the markets*, further accelerating concentration and centralization, power-ization and structures of narrow oligopolies in virtually all relevant industries.

(2) '*Globalization*', allegedly the promotion of 'international competition', in fact the mutual opening of home markets for the most over-accumulated foreign

rivals to provide them new action space (sales, investment and labour control). Above mutual intrusion, this was meant to create an *exclusive layer of capital action*, capturing their *control over labour* worldwide, and *lowering variable-capital value* on a global scale. The project was designed to exclude the rest of society and societal organizations, including the states themselves, from any similarly effective organization or action at the global level, thus deliberately preventing future re-embedding of capital interests into society and states.

(3) *Privatization*: The PR was further fed through underpriced sales of public wealth and utilities as established over the past centuries and decades, usually with state-guaranteed, protected and profitable production and sales fields, further strengthening protected narrow oligopolies. The 'neoliberal' governments shovelled *large amounts of underpriced* Δc into the largest capitals' value productions and PRs, which then could be used to generate and extract high amounts of safe Δs in usually already well-cultivated fields (with each millions of dependent households).

(4) *Labour market (de-)regulation*, and promotion of labour- and capital-saving technological change: The value of variable capital was further reduced this way. This went particularly far in the case of Germany, where 'neoliberal' social democrats and greens created a large state-bureaucratic, coercive and authoritarian sub-labour-market with enforced close-to-zero wages.

(5) The political paradigm change towards *political-economic austerity*: The restrictive austerity-oriented ('anti-inflation' and 'balanced-budget') *fiscal and monetary policies* were made centre-stage, and, in particular, tight monetary policy established as the most powerful policy area and tool-set ever, notably strictly beyond and above the political and democratic area. Thus, the factual main policy tools were set *aside from 'politics'* and *above democracy* – assigned to the new isolated mega-power of the *Central Banks* (CB) in order to guarantee, stabilize and feed private banks' balances.

(6) Finally, an endless number of measures in the fields of *taxes*, budget *expenses*, education, *social insurance* (health, unemployment, pensions,...), media, etc. were elaborated – by the 'neoliberal (think) tanks', both within and across the tops of the big capitals and the(ir) governments – to further redistribute income, wealth, public property, power and prestige from bottom to top, utilizing the century myths of 'effective markets', 'private entrepreneurship', 'global competition', 'innovation', public 'budget consolidation' and the 'inferiority' of any collective rationality, publicity and commonality. Margaret Thatcher had internalized the message most dully, crudely and brutally: 'There is no such thing as society.'

4 Consequences I: self-degeneration of the markets, real-economic slack, financialization and the explosion of 'fictitious' capital

Uncertainty, over-complexity, volatility, turbulence and crises

De-regulated and dis-embedded markets today display an intensified over-complexity, radical uncertainty, volatility and turbulence. In this way, they push exploitative and redistributive behaviour for short-run speculative profit rather than productive behaviour for average industrial profit, tend to decrease real investment, tend to trigger often insufficient effective interior consumptive demand and slacking GDP growth. Obviously, more and deeper financial crises have occurred this way, such as the stock market crisis 1987, the Japanese crisis 1986ff., the Asian crisis 1997–1999, the Russian crisis 1998, the Dotcom-speculation crisis 1999/2000, the Argentinian crisis 1999–2002 and the global crisis 2007ff.

Accelerated self-erosion of markets

Unleashed markets have *degenerated into an unprecedented power system*: The 40 largest financial conglomerates do control, in a multi-layered system, the 43,000 largest international corporations, according to a recent study at ETH Zurich, the largest international corporate-network study ever (see *The Network of Global Corporate Control*, Vitali *et al.* 2011). It is a closed shop of mutual control, uncontrollable itself from outside. Involved are only several hundred top-rank individuals, who largely know each other, plus some hundred mega-rich private individuals as their shareholders and creditors. 'Markets'? Any conspiracy theory of the left turns out to be a harmless bedtime story compared to 'neoliberal' reality.

Real-economic slack and (self-)drainage of industrial capital for financial speculation

Real-economic slack has been made structural through an economically counter-productive extreme *redistribution* of wealth, income and power, with relative *under-consumption* and subsequent structural *under-investment*. And the less the real economy provided opportunities for real investment, the more even conventional *manufacturing corporations moved into financial speculation*. An accelerated *drainage of the real economy* took place. Rather than getting a PR of, say, 5–10 per cent (after taxes and net of depreciation; see above, *Section 2*) through real value-production efforts, as was the case in 'good old producing' capitalism, they increasingly were after a PR of 20 per cent, 25 per cent or more, as was promised to be yielded forever by the speculation industry – and realized (for themselves) for most of the time through blowing up bubbles.

As an *example* from the World exports vice-champion, the German foreign trade surplus 2000–2009 was about €1 Tn, whereof €700 billion were immediately returned into US financial speculation. That is why the German banks have turned out, and – even after years of crisis, some adaptation, and much 'outsourcing' of junk bonds to the CBs and other bad banks – still are, the most over-speculated ones among the leading OECD countries.

In face of the *negligence of the real economy* and shrinking opportunities of real investment, while the corporations had been made rich through 'neoliberal' redistribution, the increasing financial surplus of the big corporations in the conventional industries went to the speculation centres, and the manufacturing corporations became financial speculators, seeking to redistribute existing wealth and income, rather than producing real values.

For Germany, a *real-investment gap* has cumulated to around €1 Tn since 1999 and real-investment slack causes a gap of 0.6 percentage-points of GDP growth p.a. (DIW 2013).

Most uneven distribution ever

In all, the top 0.1 per cent rich have been made richer; the top 0.01 per cent super-rich were made mega-rich, and the top 0.001 per cent mega-rich have become giga-rich. UN and World Bank's *World Development Reports* have shown that the most uneven distributions have been created in the 'neoliberal' era, and in every respect so (personal, functional, social, inter-regional, international,…), compared to any distribution since the year 1800, from when data could be reconstructed.

The example of the *German wage ratio* may provide a rough idea of the size of nominal money redistributed: The ratio shrank by 10 percentage-points of GDP in 25 years. It has been calculated recently that only between 2001 and 2012, around €1 Tn has been redistributed through the shrinking wage share (see Memorandum 2013, 6).

'Financialization': a debtor-creditor system, Ponzi style

Financialization and the dominance of financial 'investment' necessarily generated a cumulative and exponential growth of the credit-debt volumes, a growing bubble independent of the basic fundamentals, which eventually had to shift into a *Ponzi* system, with 'Structural Investment Vehicles' (SIVs), 'Collateralized Debt Obligations' (CDOs), etc., a system of speculations and wagers that yielded *higher PRs* than any productive economic activity ever could. It generated undreamt of high PRs in the largest entities of the speculation industry through the sales of structured, derivative nominal claims – systematically and increasingly, and in the end unavoidably, including *'subprime' and other 'toxic' content*. Over all, this could not work without system(at)ic *fraud*. But, as is well-known, as soon as the growth rates in such pyramid sales systems decrease, the crisis becomes inevitable.

Household and corporate indebtization

While hundreds of millions of usual households had been forced into a system of increasing indebtedness through the 'neoliberal' *pressure on wages*, and at the same time lured into speculative borrowing by promises of endless *asset (i.e. housing) price inflation*, conventional industrial corporations started borrowing in order to speculate and satisfy the increasing income and wealth demands of their shareholders, creditors and top personnel. This supported the drainage of the real economy in favour of the enrichment of institutional creditors and the personal enrichment of individual creditors and owners: Manager salaries, interest rates, bonuses, dividends exploded and money surplus were redirected into financial speculation, corresponding with real disinvestment (see, e.g. Hudson and Bezemer 2012).

Debt inflation and interest-rate deflation, asset inflation and wage and commodity deflation

When an asset-inflationary bubble implodes, the interest rates still need to be paid. The debtor then will be in even greater need for new credits. A global, dominantly redistributive *creditor-debtor economy* thus emerged from what once was a largely value-producing economy.

Therefore, while interest rates deflate (because of the inflating supply of nominal credit) and further support the deflation of the real economy (wages and commodities), asset prices inflate through financial speculation. *Inflation* of the speculative areas and *deflation* of commodity prices illustrate a *split economy*, dominated by the *rentier* sector (Hudson 2010; Hudson and Bezemer 2012).

Money-capital multiplication, the short-cut way

In sum, the unleashing of the money sector was designed to trigger, through a number of complex interconnected channels, a historically unmet redistribution from bottom to top, in any respect (small vs large capitals; personal distribution; distribution among social groups and classes; poorer vs richer regions and countries; etc.) and in this way an *explosion of fictitious money*: Making money shifted from conventional industrial surplus production,

$$M{-}C{-}M'$$

(money–produced commodity value–more money), to speculative multiplication,

$$M{-}M'$$

(money–more money), where increasing parts of M and M', the *fictitious capital*, may be considered part of a *corrected total capital stock,* $c_{corr.}$, and the fictitious part of $\Delta M = M - M'$ now part of a corrected s_{corr}.

The stylized constellation of 'neoliberalism'

In all, we have considerable indication of the fact that the income redistributed in around 30 years fed the expansion of fictitious capital, which, of course, also seeks a profit yield and a maximum PR. Such large-scale redistribution did, in fact, *increase the profit mass and profit shares*. This happened in the classical way, i.e. by relatively *shrinking* v (i.e. v's share in total capital). A stylization, with $s = s_{corr.}$ and $c = c_{corr.}$:

$$\pi = \left[\frac{\left(\frac{s \uparrow\uparrow}{v \downarrow\downarrow} \right) \uparrow\uparrow\uparrow\uparrow}{\left(\frac{c \uparrow\uparrow\uparrow}{v \downarrow\downarrow} \right) \uparrow\uparrow\uparrow\uparrow\uparrow + 1} \right] \downarrow,$$

with $\Delta v < 0 < \Delta s < \Delta c$ as necessary conditions for numerical values.

It caused the PR to fall.

5 Consequences II: the impossibility of a historically 'usual' average global PR, reinforced redistribution, the bubble as the redistribution vehicle and the transformation of fictitious capital into real values

The 'impossible' PR

The explosion of fictitious capital is indicated by the ca. US\$200 Tn 'market value' of fluid *personal wealth stocks* seeking interest yield, as currently estimated on average by different banks and insurance companies, the ca. US\$700 Tn 'market value' of *derivative papers* (CDOs) (according to the BIS statistics), which now are revived again by J.P. Morgan Chase and Morgan Stanley (WSJ 2013) and ca. US\$60 Tn 'market value' of CDS. What of this can be added into a global amount of the private fictitious capital stock, however, still is largely unexplored. The latter also includes the speculative parts of traded *equity capital*, which is *over-priced* in face of the exploding amounts of interest-seeking fictitious capital, and in line with the general *asset inflation*.[7] Furthermore, what is the *institutionally held* money-capital wealth stock of banks, investment banks and funds, hedge funds, pension funds, insurance companies and private equity companies? And what is the amount of fictitious capital held by more conventional manufacturing corporations? On top of that, it has been estimated that up to 60 per cent of the total stock might be *'invisible' in official statistics*, i.e. secret *offshore money-capital* flowing to tax heavens (see, e.g. Tax Justice Network 2012). So what would be the *true size of the global fictitious capital*? This still remains an unanswered and even largely unexplored question so far.

From indications that we have, we probably are not completely wrong assuming around *1 Quadrillion (Qn) US\$ (10^{15}) of global fictitious capital stock*, while the global GDP currently is *c.*US\$75 Tn. If we, for the sake of simplicity, assume this to be the surplus (gross, before tax) in a corrected average global PR, the *yield on that capital stock* (with $c_{corr.}$ now considered to be largely *fictitious capital*),[8] then would be 7.5 per cent gross and before tax – which would be a historical low for a PR before depreciation and tax (compare with numbers given above in *Section 2*), particularly somewhat between one-half and one-third

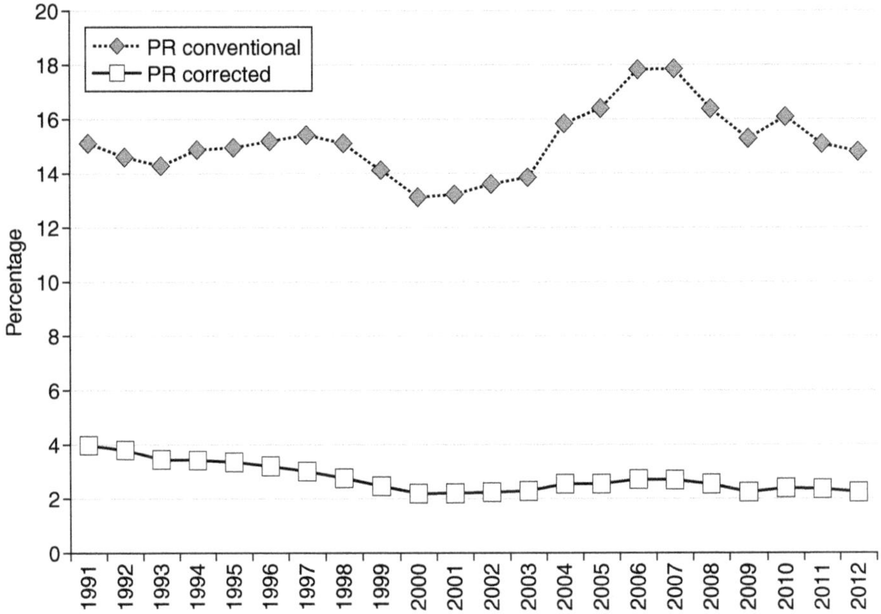

Figure 4.1 PR for Germany, conventional and corrected (source: own calculation from data of the German Statistical Office (DeStatis)).

of what has historically appeared most of the time. (Note that around US$45 Tn of global wage income (v) would not add a particularly significant amount to the 1 Qn and thus not drop the rate significantly.) Thus, a *general impossibility of a 'usual', historically known, average PR* becomes comprehensible. Such average (corrected) PR obviously cannot work in the long run for the big capitals.

For a calculation of a PR for Germany in conventional and corrected ways, see Figure 4.1 above. For the data and their description, see Appendix 2.

Enforced redistribution required for a 'standard PR'

This implies two things:

- that the crisis 2008ff. in fact was a *crisis of profitability*, and
- that such a low average PR becomes a critical factor for *exacerbating rivalry and redistribution among the capitals*, on top of the redistribution between labour and capital, between capital and the state budget, and between capital and the global real resources of humankind. The *standard PR requirement* of the largest financial entities has been 25 per cent and more even in crisis years (all before depreciation and tax): Consider the *redistribution required* (and mostly realized so far), compared to the average possible yield rate of somewhat above 7 per cent.

Benchmark PR requirements, of course, are never guaranteed, individually or collectively, in the course of a crisis, and with exploding bank balances and simultaneously deteriorating real-economic conditions, those PR standards will no longer be realized in general nor individually – but rather displaced by '*bank crises*' as we experience in the Eurozone currently. But even fiercer the redistribution races will be – as the capital stocks largely still are there.

Ubiquitous redistribution races

Against the background of a *longer-run and continuing crisis of 'corrected' profitability*, the excess fictitious capital is not only the cause, but also provides the 'solution' for *private household needs to maintain a consumption level* that are insufficiently met by household wage incomes under conditions of wage deflation. Further, the overshoot of fictitious capital will continue to be loaned by *speculating manufacturing corporations* to further increase their PR through financial 'investment', particularly when their PR from real-economic activity remains insufficient. Finally, also, the *public budgets* have been pushed into larger *structural deficits* by their bank flooding during the crisis. The credit needs of private and public budgets thus meet an increasing need of overshoot fictitious capital to yield an interest-rate based profit, i.e. to be loaned as credit. Under these conditions, the *loan-debt-economy* will be further built up. *Asset prices* will be further inflated this way, and should asset prices collapse the debt service nevertheless will have to be paid – with obvious further redistribution effects.

The bubble as a system(at)ic redistribution mechanism

In order to inflate that kind of business and redistribute more (fictitious) yield into one's own PR at the expense of others' PRs, derivatives and derivatives of derivatives (SIV, CDS) need to be expanded, becoming more and more *opaque* and risky. An explicit argument of J.P. Morgan Chase and Morgan Stanley for launching CDOs again recently with high-risk tranches was that there is so much private profit-seeking capital 'out there' that this just must be done again (WSJ 2013). In fact, *blowing up a bubble* and trying to 'manage' that bubble until its burst has become a *main redistribution vehicle*.

Transforming fictitious capital into real values before the bubble bursts: draining the real economy and the resources of the earth

However, while the bubble still is inflated, fictitious capital needs to be transformed into something of real value that is capable of *surviving the coming implosion of the bubble* with relatively little loss of value, or that may relatively quickly grow in value again thereafter and maintain its value across the bubble cycle. Thus, they must *pull out of fictitious capital* as much as possible and transform it into real values. Among the measures to do so figure those flows out of the fictitious capital that go into

- the *exploding luxury consumption*;
- a further transfer of *public wealth* into the private PR (Greece's public wealth, for instance, has just been sold to the German corporations); and
- as the *wage sum* is largely squeezed, *privatization* is largely exhausted, *public budgets* are largely ruined, and also conventional *industrial capital stock* and the whole *GDP* do not provide sufficient extractable money-capital *s* for a PR required – the *appropriation of all potential value stocks of the earth.* Capitalism in that way returns in many respects to its bloody land-grabbing roots.[9] Transforming fictitious money-capital into real values implies that the money circuit again will be transformed, adding commodifyable (particularly natural) assets as *C*, from $M-M'$ to $M-M'-C$.

Such further redistribution of income flows just within the quantitative frame of the GDPs, let alone just of the public budgets, does *not provide sufficient s* for a sufficiently high PR – considering the *sheer quantities* of fictitious capital.

Also, luxury consumption commodities and further privatization of public utility stocks are not sufficient *c* (including *c* for future *s* generation) that could survive the burst of the bubble with sufficient value maintenance, also considering the sheer quantitative relations with the fictitious capital the value of which is to be maintained when the bubble bursts. An increasing general *land- and resource-grabbing* and a *speculation on anything that will have some real value in the future* (as it will be *needed by humankind* for future living and survival) is therefore what we can observe today – a *drainage of the earth.*

6 'Neoliberal' state intervention: bailing out the 'too-big-to-fail', subsequent enforced austerity policy, and double and triple 'dips' – required redistribution vs democracy

After the inevitable outbreak of the open crisis, the 'neoliberal' governments/states will intervene in largely predetermined ways. The 'neoliberal' state intervention under given conditions will aggravate the real-economic and social downturn:

- bailing out the 'too-big-to-fails' or 'systemic': bank guarantees and bank balance flooding with the money of current and future taxpayers generations;
- subsequently reinforced austerity policies for 'budget consolidation', worsened redistribution, thus the classical state generated double (and perhaps triple) dips (with the new public rhetoric now reversing cause and effect, making politics the causer of the crisis);
- followed by again reinforced austerity policies.

A more realistic macro-circuit relation among 'neoliberal' governments, the financial speculation sector and the corporate real-estate and manufacturing sectors than provided in usual macro-circuit models, with an important role for the government bailout of the speculation sector, will therefore have to include the financing of politicians in public office through the speculation industry (see Hudson and Bezemer 2012: 8).

The taxpayer's full burden of bailing out the banks

And the full burden for the taxpayer has rarely been made transparent. For example, in Germany, on top of the ca. €550 billion *extra debt officially displayed in the public budget* (€786 billion government liability incl. bank guarantees, both for 2011), the full risk uploaded on current and future taxpayers, in fact, adds up from

- public purchases of bank shares;
- public crediting and guarantees for private banks;
- tax breaks and deferrals for speculation industry entities (e.g. private equities do not pay taxes at all in Germany);
- the German share of the risks taken over from the private banks by the ECB (toxic papers, negative real interest);
- the German share of IMF credit lines for EU countries under German export pressure;
- the German shares of the Eurozone 'rescue parachutes' EFSF and ESM;
- and as a German specific feature, German CB's 'Target2' credits to other CBs, partly financing German exports to Eurozone countries under pressure.

With these, the whole additional German taxpayer's burden 2008ff. has piled up to ca. €2 Tn, approaching the amount of the German GDP p.a.

Prohibiting structural change, innovation and re-redistribution

Bailing out virtually any individual bank (at least in Germany this was the case) has also implied the weird effect of prohibiting any structural change in, or major *adaptation pressure* on, the speculation sector. But also, public protective intervention has largely *prohibited a structural re-redistribution* (beyond the devaluations of the stocks of the over-speculated banks and super-rich individuals and the general profit consequences of the enduring crisis), saving the super- and mega-rich, the shareholders and creditors of the banks, *absolving them (so far) from any contribution to really solve the crisis* and to bear its costs through a *massive reduction of fictitious capital.*

With all that the current and future taxpayers' burdens explode, and with the *CBs' fresh money for over-speculated junk papers*, a *secular inflation* becomes a real option – despite the real economy's current deflation tendency. In a more critical future phase, if the money from today's QE waves should infiltrate the real economy, the CBs will not dare to pull that money out again to trigger a major crisis. In fact, a *future expropriation* of wage earners, savers and retirees through a secular inflation today is considered again, among the ranks of the 'elites', an appropriate way out of the debt burdens of governments – as it has been 'successfully' exercised repeatedly in the history of the twentieth century. The money explosion through the speculation sector, the CBs and the governments will not be easily revocable by the CBs at any time, nor can be confined to the asset sector in the longer run.

Public speculation against a superiority of private 'financial mass destruction weapons'

With the *Eurozone* policies to set up the EFSF and ESM, in particular, but also with any ordinary QE, a *speculative race of the states* (the taxpayer) *against the speculation industry* began in order to regain the 'confidence of the markets' – a *battle that is already lost* for the taxpayer from its very beginning, if we consider again the *sheer relative amounts* of the 'financial mass destruction weapons' (W. Buffett) of the *private fictitious capital vs the public budget* allocated on both sides of the 'taxpayer vs the speculation industry' gamble. The 'hostage-taken' taxpayer has no chance in this gamble in the longer run.

Two QE waves of the ECB in 2011 and 2012, plus its continuing current further QE policy have already piled up to €1.6 Tn. But nevertheless, the deteriorating real economy, in its *government-induced austerity and double/triple dip mode*, has unavoidably added, on top of the financial and state budget crises, the *bank crises* that necessarily were to come in spite of public bank flooding. Thus, earlier bank credits given to the real economy tend to increasingly fail.

Required redistribution incompatible with democracy

Obviously, such amounts of redistribution through public budgets, through other channels within the GDPs, and through the social and natural resources of the earth have become increasingly *incompatible with democratic decision procedures*. There have rarely been majorities in the general populations for those bailouts in polls. Classical *parliamentary procedures* have been increasingly annulled by the governments since the crisis 2008ff. Parliaments have neither been properly informed nor have alternatives been presented. The 'neoliberal' political credo '*TINA – there is no alternative*' (Thatcher) is unswayed in the political process. The 'neoliberal' parties of all (earlier) colours have even come to form factual super-large coalitions. In the Euro countries under pressure, the big parties had to formally sign declarations to continue the policies dictated by the EU, regardless of who delegates the government personnel. Only a few members of the parliaments still complain about their being cut off from information. So even the surrogate-democratic parliamentary systems, with their duopolistic/oligopolistic (and now mostly collective-monopolistic) inter-party gambles, have become 'unserviceable' to those redistribution processes, of making squeezable virtually all the wealth of the public budgets, the national economies and the global natural environment for the PRs of the fictitious capital.

Eurozone and EU pioneering post-democracy

In the Eurozone and the EMU, which have their own specific birth defects on top of the general (fictitious) over-accumulation crisis, there is a particular tendency towards *technocratic and authoritarian governance*: The EU '*Economic and Financial Governance*' – to be run by the President of the EU Commission, the ECB president, the heads of IMF and ESM, the Councils of Economic, Finance, and Prime Ministers, and the top bankers – may easily become the *post-democratic prototype* and even a pre-dictatorial governance structure against national sovereignty and democracies of the weaker countries that have come under pressure of the German export tank (see, e.g. Macartney 2013). Presidential systems, such as that of the US, have always been more akin to decision structures beyond classical parliamentary systems anyway. And again, the CBs have become the actual *main protagonists of any proactive policy* anyway – entities that have deliberately been put beyond democracy by the 'neoliberal' counterrevolution 40 years ago.

7 Conclusion: no way out other than…

Saving the banks (notwithstanding the organization of their further concentration with public support), and saving their mega-rich shareholders and creditors from any contribution to pay for the crisis and its social costs made the *fictitious capital grow even during the crisis*. *Classical capitalist crises* and the required *meltdown of (fictitious) capital* have been prohibited so far, and, thus, *no 'solution' for the PR* and for degenerated capitalism is conceivable. The average PR 'with fictitious capital' still remains historically low and tends to further decrease. Capital has become fully '*obese*', '*sclerotic*' and no 'cleaning' appears feasible.

In addition, consider the *values still at risk in the bank balances*, which even further increase through the real-economic downturn. In early 2009, the EU Commission found in a confidential document that then 44 per cent (around €18 Tn) of the nominal assets of the EU banks were toxic, *non-marketable*.[10] This portion might have declined by now through their transfer into the taxpayers' pockets (the ECB), but may also have increased through the continuing real-economic crisis and bank crisis. This all will have to be bailed out, and their standard PRs maintained, to restore the 'confidence of the markets'.

The *amounts to be claimed for redistribution* in order to maintain the standard PRs for the big financial players seem to *exceed the redistribution capacities* of the national wage sums and the public budgets (and wealth stocks), i.e. the GDP shares that realistically can be further redistributed. They might sooner or later even *exceed the potentials of the CBs*, which may also become subject to certain 'moral' limits. Since public budgets' and GDPs' limits already seem to be approached, and CBs' limits may be approached in some foreseeable future, the *weird run for potential future real values in the earth's natural stocks*, in order to generate more M' (and s), becomes comprehensible. To further redistribute risks and values of the sizes implied here and saving the speculation industry by playing its gamble and betting 'against' it with taxpayers' money will further generate high *social costs*.

Without designing a *new secular re-redistribution project*, freeing the PR and the real-economy from *'obese' excess fictitious capital*, and freeing economy and society from the bottleneck of the PR in general, making the economy somehow workable again for society, there will be no way out. 'Neoliberal' redistribution has been a *40-year-long political-economic project*. There is no way out other than to *reverse that very process* in the same dimension and strictness in order to restore a somehow functioning productive real economy. On this way, a *solid and "boring" credit sector for the real economy* with very moderate PRs, if at all, needs to be created, *independent of the speculation sector*. As far as the speculation sector still may be allowed to exist, it needs to be *strictly reduced to gambling for own account* of the super- and mega-rich and their special institutes, with the slightest public bailout strictly prohibited.

A corrected PR exploration appears to be a fruitful device to contextualize and explain antecedents and consequences of the crisis that often are not considered in proper context. It seems worthwhile to continue exploration along these lines.

Appendix 1: some general logical conditions of the PR to increase or fall

$$\pi' = \pi + \Delta\pi = \frac{s'}{c' + v'} = \frac{s + \Delta s}{c + \Delta c + v + \Delta v}$$

and

$$\Delta\pi = \frac{s + \Delta s}{c + \Delta c + v + \Delta v} - \frac{s}{c + v} = \frac{(c+v)(s+\Delta s) - s(c+v+\Delta c+\Delta v)}{(c+v)(c+v+\Delta c+\Delta v)}$$

$$= \frac{\frac{\Delta s}{\Delta c + \Delta v}(c+v) - s}{\frac{(c+v)(c+v+\Delta c+\Delta v)}{\Delta c + \Delta v}}$$

In order to explain the intended resulting value (i.e., the algebraic sign) of $\Delta\pi$, we may consider the different combinations of the terms of the numerator and denominator.

The sign of change of the *PR*, $\Delta\pi > 0$ or $\Delta\pi < 0$, is determined by the values of

$$\frac{\Delta s}{\Delta c + \Delta v}(c+v) - s \text{ and } \frac{(c+v)(c+v+\Delta c+\Delta v)}{\Delta c + \Delta v}.$$

Four general conditions can be derived from this:

(1) If $\Delta c + \Delta v > 0$ and $\frac{\Delta s}{\Delta c+\Delta v} > \pi$, then $\frac{(c+v)(c+v+\Delta c+\Delta v)}{\Delta c+\Delta v} > 0$ and $\frac{\Delta s}{\Delta c+\Delta v}(c+v)-s > 0$, then $\Delta\pi > 0$.

(2) If $\Delta c + \Delta v > 0$ and $\frac{\Delta s}{\Delta c+\Delta v} < \pi$, then $\frac{(c+v)(c+v+\Delta c+\Delta v)}{\Delta c+\Delta v} > 0$ and $\frac{\Delta s}{\Delta c+\Delta v}(c+v)-s < 0$, then $\Delta\pi < 0$

(3) If $\Delta c + \Delta v < 0$ and $(c + v + \Delta c + \Delta v) > 0$, and $\frac{\Delta s}{\Delta c+\Delta v} < \pi$, then $\frac{(c+v)(c+v+\Delta c+\Delta v)}{\Delta c+\Delta v} < 0$, and $\frac{\Delta s}{\Delta c+\Delta v}(c+v)-s < 0$, then $\Delta\pi > 0$.

(4) If $\Delta c + \Delta v < 0$ and $(c + v + \Delta c + \Delta v) > 0$, and $\frac{\Delta s}{\Delta c+\Delta v} > \pi$, then $\frac{(c+v)(c+v+\Delta c+\Delta v)}{\Delta c+\Delta v} < 0$, and $\frac{\Delta s}{\Delta c+\Delta v}(c+v)-s > 0$, then $\Delta\pi < 0$.

Appendix 2: data from national accounts for PR calculation and results (traditional and corrected), Germany, 1991–2012

Year	*Property Income*	*Compensation of Employees*	*Gross Output*	*Constant Capital*	*Financial Assets*	*PRtrad*	*PRcorr*
	(a)	*(b)*	*(c)*	*(d) = (c)-(a)-(b)*	*(e)*	*(a)/ [(b)+(d)]*	*(a)/ [(b)+(d)+(e)]*
1991	356	861.2	2710.12	1492.92	6587.325	15.12%	3.98%
1992	365.2	933.22	2864.39	1565.97	7092.75	14.61%	3.81%
1993	362.16	954.67	2896.55	1579.72	7948.55	14.29%	3.45%
1994	391.94	978.56	3025.56	1655.06	8801.575	14.88%	3.43%
1995	411.14	1012.76	3159.29	1735.39	9496.675	14.96%	3.36%
1996	423.68	1020.98	3211.06	1766.4	10429.75	15.20%	3.21%
1997	441.56	1024.11	3304.44	1838.77	11793.725	15.42%	3.01%
1998	447.26	1044.91	3406.64	1914.47	13251.725	15.11%	2.76%
1999	436.35	1071.26	3526.85	2019.24	14603.15	14.12%	2.47%
2000	429.73	1111.2	3704.79	2163.86	16310.825	13.12%	2.19%
2001	445.14	1131.93	3810.95	2233.88	16845.775	13.23%	2.20%
2002	452.51	1138.84	3778.71	2187.36	16847.75	13.60%	2.24%
2003	466.86	1141.61	3837.85	2229.38	17069.175	13.85%	2.28%
2004	541.42	1145.39	3959.18	2272.37	17825.15	15.84%	2.55%
2005	576.05	1137.64	4088.72	2375.03	19074.9	16.40%	2.55%
2006	652.64	1156.08	4314.54	2505.82	20402.925	17.82%	2.71%
2007	690.22	1187.11	4557.59	2680.26	21747.71667	17.85%	2.69%
2008	660.97	1229.74	4695.15	2804.44	21965.35	16.38%	2.54%
2009	578.84	1233.41	4364.84	2552.59	21993.925	15.29%	2.25%
2010	648.33	1270.98	4677.63	2758.32	23060.70833	16.09%	2.39%
2011	656.65	1327.97	5006.76	3022.14	23467.075	15.10%	2.36%
2012	657.42	1377.64	5098.07	3063.01	24952.025	14.80%	2.24%

Notes

1 Paper given at the international EU-COST-Action Conference 'Democracy and Financial Capital', University of Kassel, Germany, October 2012. The author is grateful to the discussants at that conference, particularly to Christoph Scherrer, University of Kassel, Beat Weber, Austrian Central Bank, Vienna and Daniel Muegge, University of Amsterdam. Also thanks to Claude Serfati, who has commented on an earlier version. The paper was also given and discussed at the EAEPE summer school, Rome, 1–5 July, 2013. Thanks to the participants and discussants. An earlier version was published in the *real-world economics review* in December 2012 (see Elsner 2012), and I have gratefully received a number of useful comments from Edward Fullbrook, an anonymous reviewer of the *rwer*, and several readers. Furthermore, I am grateful for helpful comments to my assistants and PhD students: Dr Shuanping Dai, Yasar Damar, Dr Torsten Heinrich; Dr Henning Schwardt, and Yanlong Zhang. Shuanping Dai provided the algebraic exercise on some general conditions for profit-rate changes as given in Appendix 1. Yasar Damar provided the empirical comparative calculations for Germany and the empirical data.

2 We will generally use just an intuitive illustration of the changes of the PR, with arrows up and down, the different numbers of which indicate the *relative ordinal sizes of change* of its constituents. A more exact (cardinal) algebraic display might start with *partial derivatives* of the PR after its constituents, $\partial\pi/\partial s$, $\partial\pi/\partial v$ and $\partial\pi/\partial s$, if we would consider only a change of one variable at a time. Otherwise, whether we could define functional relations among the three constituents, such as, e.g. $s \rightarrow c$ or $v \rightarrow s$ (how complex or crude ever, linear or non-linear, recursive or not), or assume changes among them largely independent (albeit simultaneous), we might consider a *total derivative* in order to relate the changes of the PR to the changes of its constituents more exactly, or even employ more sophisticated methods. If we just would want to mirror the simple intuitive illustrations used here by discrete changes of its constituents, Δs, Δv, and Δc (as will be done in the following), we will have to consider that these conditions would not hold for all numerical values, but would hold only if, particularly, the differences between Δs and Δc are large enough. In Appendix 1, we have provided some general conditions for the PR to increase or decrease, depending on the relative values of Δs, Δv and Δc, and s, v and c.

3 Note the long tradition of economic theorizing on *financialization* from the early twentieth century on. For the early days, Veblen's *Theory of the Business Enterprise* (Veblen 1904) or Lenin's imperialism theory (Lenin 1917) might be considered. Both considered financialization a late form of capitalism only and could not foresee yet its degeneration into a deadly drainage of both the productive economy and the resources of the earth. For recent publications on the *new role of fictitious capital*, beyond those cited in the following, see, e.g. McNally 2009; Norfield 2012; Palley 2013.

4 On the recent bubble in the stock market, see, e.g. Keen 2013.

5 For attempts to extend macro-models through a newly conceptualized financial sector, in order to make the interactions between the financial and the real sectors and the causes of the financial crises visible, see, e.g. Peetz and Genreith 2011.

6 The *stock-flow issue* would of course need to be discussed more in-depth. While Marx himself used idealized *annual flows* even for *constant capital c*, assuming that constant (and variable) capital's lifetimes were exactly one year, contemporary empirical measurement, even when referring to 'stocks' of (constant) capital, often is also based exclusively on regular *national accounts*, i.e. annual flows. Time series for tangible capital stocks proper do exist, though, and would need to be combined with an assumption of an *average lifetime* of a unit of constant-capital stock in order to estimate the true constant-capital *stock* value c that exists in a certain year and requires an *annual PR* (when *vintage capital* has not been fully amortized through earlier years' PRs yet). But independent of whether constant capital stock is a strictly *annual or a multi-annual conception*, the PR is an annual conception. And independent of whether capital stock is an

annual or a multi-annual conception, the *capital stock may accumulate. Fictitious capital* can *accumulate particularly fast* through its *credit-derivatives chains*. On the general, and now topical, issue of stock-flow-consistent macro modelling, see Goodley and Lavoie (2007).

7 Again, see Keen (2013).

8 It is of course debatable whether one can apply the PR, considered for value production, to fictitious capital, which is designed 'just' to re-distribute surplus and labour income from value production through permanent and increasing debt service into its own interest income. However, again, since fictitious capital has come to increase itself largely independent of real value production and to be dominating over conventional constant capital, it also has become a *competitor for profit*. In that, the two capital forms seem to be comparable: They both are begging for a PR, and competing for real values and the real resources of the world.

9 See, e.g. Harvey (2003: 137ff.); id. (2010: 244ff.).

10 Note that this news only made it into the *Daily Telegraph* for one day (11 February, 2009), and thereafter was withdrawn and tabooed.

References

Basu, Deepankar, and Vasudevan, Ramaa, 2012, 'Technology, distribution and the rate of profit in the US economy: understanding the current crisis', *Cambridge Journal of Economics*, 37(1), 57–89.

DIW 2013, *Fehlende Investitionen kosten Deutschland jedes Jahr 0,6 Prozentpunkte potentielles Wirtschaftswachstum*, Berlin: DIW, June 2013.

Elsner, Wolfram, 2012, 'Financial capitalism – at odds with democracy. Or: caught in the trap of an "impossible" profit rate', *real-world economics review*, 62, 132–159.

Freeman, Alan, 2013, 'The profit rate in the presence of financial markets: a necessary correction', *Journal of Australian Political Economy*, 70, 167–192.

Godley, Wynne, and Lavoie, Marc, 2007, *Fiscal Policy in a Stock-Flow Consistent (SFC) Model*, The Levy Economics Institute, Working Paper No. 494, Annandale-on-Hudson, NY.

Harvey, David, 2003, *The New Imperialism*, Oxford, UK; New York, US: Oxford University Press.

Harvey, David, 2010, *The Enigma of Capital and the Crises of Capitalism*, Oxford, UK; New York, US: Oxford University Press.

Heinrich, Michael, 2012, *An Introduction to the Three Volumes of Karl Marx's Capital*, New York: Monthly Review Press.

Hudson, Michael, 2010, 'From Marx to Goldman Sachs: the fictions of fictitious capital', downloaded on 16 January, 2013 from: http://michael-hudson.com/2010/07/from-marx-to-goldman-sachs-the-fictions-of-fictitious-capital1/.

Hudson, Michael, 2012, *The Bubble and Beyond: Fictitious Capital, Debt Deflation and the Global Crisis*, Dresden, Germany: ISLET Publ.

Hudson, Michael, and Bezemer, Dirk, 2012, 'Incorporating the *rentier* sectors into a financial model', *World Economic Review*, 1(1), 1–12.

Keen, Steve, 2013, 'A bubble so big we can't even see it', *real-world economics review*, 64, 3–10.

Lenin, Vladimir I., 1917, *Imperialism, the Highest Stage of Capitalism: A Popular Outline*, in: id., *Selected Works*, Moscow: Progress Publishers, 1963, Vol. 1, 667–766.

Macartney, Huw, 2013, *The Debt Crisis and European Democratic Legitimacy*, London; Basingstoke: Palgrave Macmillan.

Maniatis, Thanasis, 2012, 'Marxist theories of crisis and the current economic crisis', *Forum for Social Economics*, 41(1), 6–29.

McNally, David, 2009, 'From financial crisis to world-slump: accumulation, financialisation, and the global slowdown', *Historical Materialism*, 17, 35–83.

Memorandum 2013, Arbeitsgruppe Alternative Wirtschaftspolitik, *Umverteilen – Alternativen der Wirtschaftspolitik*, Bremen, www2.alternative-wirtschaftspolitik.de/uploads/memorandum2013_grafiken_.pdf (accessed 3 November 2014).

Norfield, Tony, 2012, 'Derivatives and capitalist markets: the speculative heart of capital', *Historical Materialism*, 20(1), 103–132.

Palley, Thomas I., 2012, *The Economic Crisis: Notes From the Underground*, Washington DC: (Self-published).

Palley, Thomas I., 2013, *The Economics of Finance Capital Domination*, London; Basingstoke: Palgrave Macmillan.

Peetz, Dietmar, and Genreith, Heribert, 2011, 'The financial sector and the real economy', *real-world economics review*, 57, 41–47.

Schoenbaum, Thomas J., 2012, *The Age of Austerity: The Global Financial Crisis and the Return to Economic Growth*, Cheltenham, UK; Northampton, MA, USA: Edward Elgar.

Serfati, Claude, 2009, *The Current Financial Meltdown: A Crisis of Finance Capital-Driven Globalization*, Draft prepared for the International Conference 'Whither Financialised Capitalism?', SOAS, University of London, November 2009; downloaded on 16 January, 2013 from: www.researchonmoneyandfinance.org/media/conference-07-09/Serfati.pdf.

Serfati, Claude, 2012, 'Die finanz- und rentengetriebene Logik der multinationalen Unternehmen', *PROKLA*, 42(4), 531–556.

Shaikh, Anwar, and Tonak, Ertugrul A., 1994, *Measuring the Wealth of Nations: The Political Economy of National Accounts*, Cambridge, UK: Cambridge University Press.

Tax Justice Network 2012, 'Magnitudes: dirty money, lost taxes and off offshore', downloaded on 7 November, 2012 from: www.taxjustice.net/cms/front_content.php?idcat=103.

Veblen, Thorstein B., 1904, *The Theory of Business Enterprise*, New Brunswick, NJ: Transaction Publ., 5th pr. 2005.

Vitali, Stefania, Glattfelder, James B. and Battiston, Stefano, 2011, 'The Network of Global Corporate Control', Study at the TU Zurich, *PLoS ONE*, 6(10), downloaded on 16 January, 2013, from: www.plosone.org/article/info%3Adoi%2F10.1371%2Fjournal.pone.0025995.

WSJ 2013, Die gefährlichste Wette der Wall Street kehrt zurück, *The Wall Street Journal Deutschland*, 5 June, 2013.

5 The battle of ideas in the Eurozone crisis management

German ordoliberalism versus post-Keynesianism

Brigitte Young

Introduction

Many observers of the Eurozone crisis blame much of the hardship experienced by indebted countries on Germany's insistence on austerity policies (Blyth 2013). That Germany has a particular political-economic tradition of an ordoliberal form of monetarism is not a new insight. It was Razeen Sally in 1996 who introduced Anglo-Saxon scholars to the German variant of neoliberalism which forms the theoretical basis of the Social Market Economy. Sally concludes that

> German neoliberalism presents a distinctive variety of political economy with eminently classical concerns, incorporating sociological and legal dimensions, even though some of its constructivist elements and willingness to accept discretionary government intervention run against the grain of the classical tradition.
>
> (Sally 1996: 250)

At the turn of the century, the political scientist and German scholar Christopher Allen (2005) argued that 'ordoliberalism' has trumped Keynesianism in the Federal Republic of Germany, but that the pressures of globalization, Europeanization and the considerable costs of Germany unification may see greater movement toward neoliberalism (of the Anglo-Saxon type of laissez-faire) and away from its half-century of ordoliberalism (Allen 2005: 220). Surely, there is some evidence that the united Germany has turned to a more Anglo-Saxon neoliberalism starting with 'Agenda 2010' of the coalition government of Chancellor Schröder (Bruff and Ebenau 2012).

However, with the Eurozone crisis ordoliberalism has again started to dominate the discussion both in terms of the diagnosis of the crisis and solution to the economic problems. Yet there is a divergence between preferences of the southern European countries for more activist Keynesian demand-led growth, and the ordoliberal commitment of the north for balanced budgets, and a general framework for orderly market competition policies with an export-led growth model. As Peter Hall (2012) remarked the dividing line is between those who argued the crisis could be resolved by fiscal austerity and others who maintained that only demand-driven measures in southern as well as northern Europe would be necessary. Four years into the Eurozone crisis, the verdict is still out on who is right. Germany's Finance Minister, Wolfgang Schäuble, has spoken of the increasing (albeit minuscule) improvement of economic growth in indebted peripheral countries, while Keynesians point to the slow recuperation due to the austerity policies.

The chapter intends to focus on the divergence of economic ideas, and argues that while German ordoliberal ideas are to a large extent present in the German Bundesbank, the German Federal Ministry of Finance, the Federal Ministry of Economics, and some of the economic associations such as the Federal Association of the German Industry (BDI) and the Federal Association of the German Employers (BDA), there are other voices even within the German Council of Economic Experts (Sachverständigenrat) and some economic think tanks which endorse a more Keynesian demand-led growth strategy to resolve the Eurozone crisis. Nevertheless, the chapter argues that ordoliberal ideas have a veto power over other alternative economic thinking. This has strongly influenced the discourse present in German economic strategies in both the diagnosis of the crisis and its solution. As a result, there is little hope that the ordoliberal values and ideas still dominant in the Bundesbank and the Federal Ministry of Finance will shift to a more Keynesian type of demand-led growth model.

The chapter is structured as follows. The first section introduces the theoretical tools of veto players and change agents. In contrast to Tsebelis (2002) who focuses on political actors or institutions as veto players, the approach taken here is to focus on ideas as agenda setters, and agents using these ideas against alternatives as veto players. At the centre of the analysis are the ordoliberal ideas of the *Freiburg School.* This approach is more appropriate to explain why Germany's rule-based legal approach is to be found in many of the measures taken at the EU level to resolve the crisis. This includes the enactment of fiscal discipline through a 'fiscal compact' which stipulates a constitutionally mandated 'debt brake' to limit the fiscal debt of all EU countries, its defence of the independence of the Central European Bank, its strict adherence to price stability, and its support for recapitalizing banks through the ESM on condition that the ESM would control banks which gain access to bail-out funds. These measures reflect the ideas of *Ordnungspolitik* (Dullien and Guérot 2012; Berghahn and Young 2013; Young 2014). After introducing the ideas of the Freiburger ordoliberals as agenda setters and as veto players against the more interventionist Keynesian ideas, the next section analyses the vitriolic dispute among German economists. The altercation broke out when Hans-Werner Sinn, the well-known ordoliberal director of the Munich-based ifo-Institute co-signed a letter in the *Frankfurter Allgemeine Zeitung* (FAZ) entitled 'Dear Fellow Citizens' on 5 July (signed by about 200 German economists) warning the German public against the 'banking union' (29 June 2012). This was seen as a ploy to introduce the mutualization of Eurozone debt. German Keynesians and international economists accused Hans-Werner Sinn and his co-author of fanning fear without providing substantive arguments, and deploring the damage done to the reputation of the German economic profession (Handelsblatt 2012a; *The Economist* 2012).

While this clash of ideas can be shrugged off as a testosterone-fuelled ego-trip among male academics, nevertheless it does demonstrate the agenda-setting power of the ordoliberal ideas. Ordoliberals hold the trump of veto power against those who try to change the status quo and move the EU forward to a more political union. Ordoliberals' unwavering belief in sound fiscal policy and price stability stands in stark contrast to those who view these rigid measures as self-defeating and counter-productive in resolving the Eurozone debt crisis. The problem for Keynesian economists is that the austerity ideas play on familiar territory, since the rhetoric is firmly anchored in the German tradition of frugality which means 'living within your means'. In the final section, the impact of the ordoliberal discourse on the German public, which has turned against any further bail-outs of indebted countries, is discussed. In fact, the irony is that while Angela Merkel started to defend the Eurozone with her repeated slogan 'if the Euro fails, so fails the European Union' starting around the end of 2011, she is faced with German negative public opinions against the Euro, hostile back-benchers in her own party, and now even a new political party, *Alternative für Deutschland* (*AfD*) which is strongly anti-Euro. It seems that Angela Merkel may have lost the agenda-setting power in Germany for a more supranational Europe with an institutional structure that is needed not only to stabilize the Eurozone crisis, but to finally overcome the asymmetries in the Eurozone.

The ideas of German ordoliberalism as agenda setter and veto player

Drawing on neo-institutional approaches, Tsebelis (2002) argued that if we know the preferences of the veto players, the position of the status quo and the identity of the agenda setter, we are likely to be able to predict the outcome of the policy-making process. To arrive at policy changes the most important actors defined constitutionally have to come to an agreement to change the status quo. Veto players are those actors that are players in the policy process and are able to obstruct changes that are being proposed to alter the existing positions. Agenda setters, on the other hand, are political players who introduce policy changes and need to win the support of other veto players in order to shift the policy terrain. Tsebelis' rational choice approach focuses on actors and institutions as important gatekeepers.

Much has been written about the missing crisis management and resolution mechanisms at the European level. While the Euro area decision-making process in finance has gained wide academic scrutiny since the financial/euro crisis, much less work has been done on the veto points in the financial decision-making process in Germany. Dissecting the German position is all the more important, since not only is it the largest and most successful economy in the EU, it is also Angela Merkel who has dominated the Eurozone crisis resolution agenda with many agreements clearly showing a German hand-writing. Moreover, Angela

Merkel has relied much less on the European community method and has privileged the intergovernmental method such as in the case of creating the European Financial Stability Facility/European Stability Mechanism and the Treaty on Stability, Coordination and Governance in the Economic and Monetary Union (Fiscal Compact) in which the head of governments and state leaders are the key players. It is for these reasons that I will focus on the German domestic arena and explain why the economic ideas of ordoliberalism are an agenda setter and at the same time a veto player in facilitating a coordinated Euro crisis resolution.

If we look at the German domestic institutions, the major veto players in finance include the German Bundesbank and its mandate to guarantee price stability at virtually any macroeconomic cost, the Federal Ministry of Finance as well as the Federal Ministry of Economics, the German Chancellor, Angela Merkel, and her economic advisors coming mostly from the German Bundesbank, the private Deutsche Bank and until recently its influential chief executive officer, Josef Ackerman, the Constitutional Court in Karlsruhe which has been a key veto player on issues of European integration, the German system of coalition governments with (until the election defeat in 2013) a strong market-oriented Free Democratic Party (FDP), the opposition parties of the SPD and the Greens, as well as the print media (such as the *Bild Zeitung* addressing a more populist line and the more business-oriented *Frankfurter Allgemeine Zeitung*) and the many television talk shows trying to convey a simple message to the general public that hard-working Germans are paying for the lazy Southern Europeans.

This highly fragmented picture of German veto players in finance is nevertheless supported by a broad consensus of ordoliberal economic ideas, which are shared to a great extent across the political leadership and parties, the mainstream economic profession, the media and the general public. In this debate on the best solution to the EU crisis, this rule-based conception of political economy is not only shared by the mainstream economic profession, it is also shared by the larger public. Some members of the opposition parties of the Social Democratic Party and the Greens may sound more pro-European, but they equally endorse the austerity politics and the constitutionally mandated debt-brake (see Dullien and Guérot 2012).

To better understand the details of the dispute between ordoliberal and Keynesian economists, I will provide a short overview of the main tenets of the ideas of ordoliberalism of the Freiburg School, and also point out why ordoliberalism is such a powerful agenda setter and veto player in the Eurozone.

The legacy of ordoliberal ideas

Ordoliberalism has its antecedents in the 1930s, and was influential after World War II in the development of the Social Market Economy of Ludwig Erhard. Its most influential leaders are Walter Eucken, Franz Böhm, Wilhelm Röpke, Alfred Müller-Armack and Alexander Rüstow (Sally 1996; Berghahn and Young 2012; Bonefeld 2012; Biebricher 2014; Young 2014). In the present Euro crisis resolution scenario, the influence of ordoliberalism is most evident in the German position on price stability and its defence of the independence of the Central Bank. The German Bundesbank was created and reflects the rule-based approach of an *economic order*, within which economic processes take place (Sally 1996: 235). After World War II, the Freiburgers argued for the primacy of currency policy. For Walter Eucken, monetary policy was the constituting principle of the *Ordnungspolitik:* 'All efforts to institute a competitive market economy will fail as long as price stability is not guaranteed' (cited in Issing 2000: 1). However, the goal of a sound monetary system was not just to guarantee price stability. Equally important are the automatic rules for sanctions against transgressions of price stability. The purpose is to rule out any discretionary space for central bankers to intervene in monetary policy (Young 2013).

It is this supposed violation of the mandate of the Central European Bank that led to the resignation first of Axel Weber, German Chief Economist at the European Central Bank, and then some months later of Jürgen Stark. Both central bankers, schooled in ordoliberalism, disagreed with other members of the Central Bank's Executive Committee to discard the 'no-bail out clause' of the Maastricht Agreement and the Treaty of Stability and Growth Treaty in order to bail out Greece, and then later Ireland, Portugal, and also Spain and Italy. Nobody was particularly surprised when Jens Weidmann, the current president of the German Bundesbank, voted as the only member of the 23-member Board against the unlimited 'outright monetary transactions' (OMT) programme which the ECB Governing Council agreed on 9 June 2012 to start buying sovereign bonds in the secondary markets. The stipulations are that countries have to apply first to the European Stability Mechanism and accept strict fiscal conditionality.

The majority of German ordoliberal economists see the culprit for the present Eurozone crisis in the profligacy of some countries whose governments did not abide by the rules agreed under the Maastricht Treaty and the Stability and Growth Pact. Thus if strong rules with automatic sanctions are in force for all EU countries, governments are no longer able to resort to discretionary powers to violate the rules of *volonté générale.* While ordoliberalism rejects the neoclassical separation between the state and the market, they see the state as setting the constitutional framework, an *ordo*, within which market forces can operate freely. According to Walter Eucken, 'the economic constitution must be understood as a general political decision as to how the economic life of the nation is to be structured' (cited in Sally 1996: 234).

It is in this context of the ordoliberal doctrine as both agenda setter and veto player that the dispute between German economists has to be understood. The ECB transactions were seen by many economists as violating the ECB's mandate and endangering its mandate of price stability. The Maastricht Treaty includes a no bail-out clause, which German economists insist on upholding even if it means going to the Constitutional Court in Karlsruhe. The rejection of Angela Merkel and her advisors for a more politicized ECB including the shift to common mutualization of debt in the form of Euro bonds and/or providing a common Euro fund reflect the adherence to a system of rule-based *ordo* of fiscal and monetary prudence. In the absence of a constitutional framework to ensure adherence to strict fiscal rules, Angela Merkel's statement after a long night's crisis meeting in Brussels in June 2012 that she will not agree to Euro bonds 'as long as she lives' makes sense in the context of Germany's unwavering belief in sound fiscal policy and price stability symbolizing both order and stability (Young 2013). The opposite is true of lax monetary policy, budget deficits, leading to inflation and thus endangering political stability as happened during the Weimar period of the early 1920s (Issing 2000).

The dispute between German ordoliberal and Keynesian economists

The public letter drafted by the economic statistician Walter Krämer gained the necessary publicity and notoriety when the renowned Hans-Werner Sinn, director of the ifo-Institut Munich was brought on board. The letter published in the business pages of the *Frankfurter Allgemeine Zeitung* (Sinn and Krämer 2012), eventually signed by about 200 German economists, attacked the entire crisis resolution strategy of Angela Merkel as 'wrong' and warned, based on ordoliberal orthodoxy, that the proposed banking union is opening the flood gates to socialize banking debts in the Eurozone which violates the mandate of the Maastricht Treaty. Tax payers, pensioners and small depositors were warned about huge losses which would accrue as a result of the inflationary spending orgy of southern countries. As if these dire warnings were not enough, they continued to berate politicians for their unavoidable inability to safeguard the mandated conditionality as long as the indebted countries are in the majority in the Eurozone. Their parting shot was that neither the Euro nor the European idea will benefit from further rescue measures' the beneficiaries would be Wall Street, the City of London and a string of indebted domestic and foreign banks.

It did not take long before German Keynesian economists countered with public rebuttals to save the economic profession from complete ridicule. Namely, many foreign star economists were indignant and ridiculed the open letter as 'rich in heated rhetoric but poor in factual details', as Barry Eichengreen stated, and in the same article (FTD (2012a), Charles Wyplosz, the Swiss finance expert, went even further and said that the text was nothing less than a disgrace from a political point of view, and demonstrates that the economists do not even understand what a banking crisis is all about. Frank Heinemann, a Berliner economist, and Martin Hellwig, Max Planck Institute Bonn, initiated with others a rebuttal declaring the banking union as essential since its proclaimed aim is to 'break the vicious circle between banks and sovereigns', but only 'when an effective single supervisory mechanism is established'.[1] In the meantime, this second call also gathered more than a hundred supporters, ironically nine of which signed both the Krämer/Sinn call rejecting the Banking Union and the one supporting the political rescue measure.

A second rebuke, entitled 'Keine Schreckgespenster!' followed in the *Handelsblatt* (2012a) drafted by Keynesians including Peter Bofinger, a member of the German Council of Economic Experts, Gustav Horn, Director of the Institute of Macroeconomics, and others[2] criticizing the Krämer/Sinn text for fanning fear without providing substantive arguments. Not only did they deplore the damage Krämer/Sinn inflicted on the political process, they deplored the damage done to the reputation of the German economic profession. In a public rebuttal, Gustav Horn attacked the nine economists who had signed both initiatives and called on them to at least distance themselves from the rabble-rousing language of the Krämer/Sinn initiative. Other Keynesian economists, such as Rudolf Hickel, Bremen, who supports the banking union as an opportunity to improve Eurozone regulation, belittled the intervention as little more than *Stammtisch slogans* espoused by 'irate economists (Wutökonomen) with a tunnel vision' who yearn back to the time of the D-Mark (Hickel 2012).

But this is not the end of the story. The German Council of Economic Advisors (also known as the Five Wise Men) intervened in the dispute with a Special Advisory Opinion strongly supporting the EU summit decision to create a banking union, and suggesting further steps not precluding mutualization of Eurozone risks, a step Angela Merkel strictly rejects. Concretely, the Economic Advisors laid out details for a temporary euro area redemption fund, in which national debts above 60 per cent are deposited, and guaranteed collectively by the Eurozone countries, retiring the debt over a period of 25 years (Sachverständigenrat 2012). Last but not least, the German pro-euro camp received support from the Institute for New Economic Thinking (INET), a New York think tank, funded in part by George Soros. The INET Council on the Euro Zone Crisis (ICEC) comprising 17 economists, including two of Germany's wise men, Peter Bofinger and Lars Feld, issued a *Master Plan* warning Europe 'is sleep-walking into a catastrophe'. As alternative to the present austerity course, they endorse both a banking union endowed with a banking licence and a temporary redemption fund, arguing that the European Stability Mechanism is too small to help larger countries such as Spain and Italy (Süddeutsche.de 2012; *The Economist* 2012).

Not surprisingly the German government immediately rebuffed the Krämer/Sinn initiative claiming that they failed to cite the Euro decision accurately, since the Euro Area Summit Statement on 29 June 2012 does not contain any reference to mutualizing Eurozone debts (FAZ 2012). Equally sharp was the rebuke from Norbert Lammert, president of the German Bundestag, who in fact stated that of all the possible ways to provide input in resolving the Euro crisis the least helpful was that of economists (FTD 2012b). But Hans-Werner Sinn did not stop simply with the Krämer/Sinn initiative. Addressing a hearing before the Federal Constitutional Court in Karlsruhe to decide the fate of the European Stability Mechanism (ESM) in early July, he referred to the euro bailout as a 'bottomless pit', as a 'machinery of asset destruction', which failed to provide a solution.

The impact of the austerity discourse on the German domestic arena

The German public has been inundated with a discursive framing of national cultural characteristics to explain the debtor ('sinner') as 'lazy Greeks' and

Germans as victims, since 'we pay for the rest of Europe'. In this debate for Europe in Germany, the leadership 'has lost the forest for the trees' (Guérot 2012). Thus Sinn's strident ordoliberal orthodoxy is overwhelmingly supported in the television talk shows and by the public at large. Bombarding the public with a continuing dose of disciplinary discourse against bail-outs, and instrumentalizing the high inflation trauma of Weimar Germany has caused a groundswell of anti-Euro sentiments:

> 52% of Germans don't like the idea of a United States of Europe and are against changing the Basic Law in order to save Europe, 74% of German disapprove of the idea of a common European state and only 33% agree with Schäuble's idea of a directly elected EU president, and 73% are against the introduction of Eurobonds.
>
> (Guérot 2012: 1)

This is all the more tragic since German negative public opinion over the future of the Eurozone has been further fuelled by the numerous complaints filed with the Constitutional Court challenging the European Stability Mechanism. No less than 37,000 citizens have signed on to challenge the ESM at the Constitutional Court in Karlsruhe 'on the grounds it exposes German taxpayers to funding the ESM without proper democratic control over how those funds are used' (Spiegel 2012). While the Constitutional Court did not strike down the Outright Monetary Transaction (OMT) policy of the ECB in February 2014, it nevertheless ruled that the final decision of buying bonds issued by Eurozone countries has to be taken by the European Court of Justice (Voßkuhle 2014). The decision of that body of law is still pending.

It is ironic that this strong gale force from the legal system is happening at the very moment when European leaders and head of states agree to 'more Europe' (since June 2012), and the 'ECB is ready to do whatever it takes to preserve the euro' and has done so with Draghi's announcement first, that 'the Euro is irreversible' and second, to start an unlimited 'outright monetary transaction' (OMT) programme to buy bonds on the secondary market on the condition that they apply to the ESM first. As already pointed out, Jens Weidmann, the president of the German Bundesbank, was the lone wolf among the 23 board members to vote against the OMT. His principled dissention follows in the footsteps of his mentor, Axel Weber, and also Jürgen Stark, both of whom had resigned from the ECB in 2012. Despite Draghi's repeated admonition during the press conference that bond buying on the open market was a 'standard instrument of policy', the German Bundesbank interprets buying government bonds as overstepping the boundary between monetary and fiscal policy. Not without a certain hint of *Schadenfreude* did the *Financial Times* report the day after the vote on Weidmann's isolation as the lone holdout to 'outright monetary transaction' (*Financial Times* 2012).[3] However, this isolation was confined to the foreign press. In Germany, Weidmann's No-vote was celebrated as defending the ordoliberal tradition of the Bundesbank.

Most surprising was the Chancellor distancing herself from the Bundesbank's veto after a meeting with the Spanish prime minister, Mariano Rajoy, in Madrid, emphasizing her respect for the independence of the Bundesbank, but reiterating that in the end it was up to politicians to stabilize the Eurozone (Frankfurter Rundschau 2012). Despite the Chancellor's endorsing more non-ordoliberal policies of the ECB, the German media has strongly rallied against the ECB's ruling. The popular *Bild-Zeitung* ran a headline with 'a blank cheque for the debtor states', with the question 'whether he [Draghi] ruins the Euro?' (*Bild-Zeitung* 2012: 2). More serious papers were no more supportive. The more left-leaning *Frankfurter Rundschau* ran a headline, 'bond buying without limits' (Frankfurter Rundschau 2012), and the conservative *Die Welt* painted a doomsday scenario by declaring that the 'financial markets rejoice at the death of the Bundesbank'. The Italian media, on the other hand, saw it as a blow against the German arrogance. The critical foreign commentary came overwhelmingly from the political right. Thus Berlusconi's economic advisor, Renato Brunetta, demanded a Truth Committee to highlight all the political and economic mistakes Germany has pushed through against other countries and against democratic principles.

But the backlash was not just fought in the (German) media. More serious is the headwind in Merkel's own party and from some of the members of her coalition partners, which has considerably narrowed her political space for more European integration. Merkel was no longer able to muster a chancellor majority for the vote in the German Parliament to approve the Fiscal Pact and the European Stability Mechanism and had to rely on the opposition for its approval. Not only have some members of the CDU joined the Bavarian Free Voter Party (Freie Wähler Partei) to create the 'Election Alternative 2013' as a protest against creating the ESM in 2012, but more problematic politically is the newest Party 'Alternative für Deutschland' (AfD) which was created in February 2013 mostly from CDU and FDP disgruntled economists and lawyers whose goal is to disband the Eurozone. Their populist slogan 'Schluss mit diesem Euro!' (Get Rid of this Euro!) reflects the German public misgivings about the Eurozone crisis management. These new political parties believe that the legal boundary between monetary and fiscal policy has been exceeded. In other words, according to their argument, the European Central Bank is solely responsible for monetary policy, while fiscal policy is the area of national responsibility. While the German anti-Euro AfD was not as successful as its counterparts in the United Kingdom with the United Kingdom Independence Party (Ukip) and the French Front National of Marine Le Pen in the European parliamentary elections in May 2014, nevertheless the AfD won seven parliamentary seats.

Although the front pages of newspapers have given way to geopolitical reports of the conflicts in the Ukraine and the crisis in the Middle East, the Eurozone turmoil measured by the large public debts (with Greece leading with around 180 per cent of GDP, followed by Italy with around 135 per cent of GDP) is clearly not resolved. Angela Merkel faces now a huge dilemma. While she sided since the outbreak of the debt crisis with the ordoliberal austerity orthodoxy and rejected Keynesian demands to use the ECB's 'firepower' to safeguard the monetary transmission to the real economy, she has welcomed the ECB bond-buying as a useful short-term measure. This is trying to square the circle, since Germans trust Angela Merkel (at least, until now) as the defender of monetary stability characterized in the caricature of *the Swabian housewife.* A more cynical reading of not publicly coming to the rescue of Jens Weidmann is that since Merkel can no longer count on the Chancellor's majority in pushing through any further rescue measures in the German Bundestag, she now is willing to accept the ECB's sovereign bond-buying scheme in order to gain time. The near mutiny among many CDU rebels as well as the Bavarian sister party (CSU) has translated into the formation of a new anti-Euro party. While the AfD does not provide a challenge to the existing political parties, nevertheless its populist austerity discourse provides further fuel for national solutions and prevents a much needed domestic discourse on further European integration.

Conclusion: from a legalistic to a democratic Eurozone

Given the polarization in Germany between those that are nostalgically looking backward to the time of the DM when German ordoliberals guarded the stability of the money in the Bundesbank and others trying to shift the debate away from this introspective understanding of the Euro crisis blaming either the debtor countries or feeling victimized 'as the paymaster of Europe', Chancellor Merkel will find it difficult to gather support for a political union, and possibly even for a constitutional Convention, to deepen European integration with a banking union, fiscal union, political union and an economic union. Essentially, there are only two possible strategies left to resolve the crisis: either to return to national currencies in the entire EU area and be subject to the volatility of highly speculative currency markets, or laying the groundwork for deepening the Eurozone with a political union, banking union, economic union and a fiscal union with the goal to regain the political space at the transnational level lost to global market forces (Habermas et al. 2012). It has dawned on many political and economic leaders that a break-up of the Eurozone would be a costly calamity. And the biggest loser will be Germany, if the Eurozone fails (Cameron 2012). This may be one reason why Angela Merkel has taken the strong lead for *more Europe.* At the same time, it has also become apparent that the institutional design of the EMU is deeply flawed, and needs the 'E' as in economics in addition to the monetary in EMU as Jean-Claude Trichet pointed out in his acceptance speech of the *Karlspreis* in Aachen 2011.

The only possible way forward is to design an institutional framework which allows executive decisions to be made which are democratically accountable to Europe's citizens. This means also that the European Parliament has to be empowered to control executive decisions. Making the European Parliament more representative is all the more important since the German Constitutional Court cited in 2009 that Berlin cannot surrender fiscal power to Europe in the absence of democratic representation in Brussels. The same lack of accountability is also evident in the European Council consisting of heads of states and leaders of government. These political leaders report back to their national citizens, but 'the Council as a whole is accountable to no one' (Véron 2012: 4). While the European Commission is, on paper at least, accountable to the European Parliament, however in the early phase of the debt crisis, the Commission has largely been ignored by the head of states and the leaders of government (Young and Semmler 2011). The same lack of democratic accountability is also to be found in the two intergovernmental institutions, the Eurogroup made up of national finance ministers, and the Economic and Financial Affairs Council (ECOFIN) composed of the Economic and Financial Ministers of the 28 member states. However, nothing harmed the trust of citizens as much as the disregard for the French and Dutch No-vote on the European Constitution in 2004, which was then repacked in the Lisbon Treaty in 2007. A similar fate befell the Irish voters who first rejected the Lisbon Treaty in 2008, and were subsequently asked to change their vote in 2009. '[T]he democratic shortfall has been widely cited as a factor in the rise of populist anti-European parties in recent elections in several member states' (Véron 2012: 4).

The question the Eurozone is facing after four years of Euro crisis management is whether Germany will impose its legalistic rule-based system upon the rest of the member states of Europe or 'move from the legalistic mindset that prevails at present to a democratic system' (Grjebine 2012).

Notes

1 Euro Area Summit Statement, Brussels, 29 June 2012.
2 Others include Michael Hüther, Dalia Marin, Bert Rürop, Friedrich Schneider and Thomas Straubhaar (see Handelsblatt.2012b: 8).
3 In the meantime, it has been confirmed that Jens Weidmann has considered resigning several times from the ECB but was persuaded to stay by Angela Merkel and Wolfgang Schäuble (Welt-Online 2012).

References

Allen, Christopher S. 2005: 'Ordo-Liberalism' Trumps Keynesianism: Economic Policy in the Federal Republic of Germany and the EU, in: B. Moss (ed.), *Monetary Union in Crisis: The European Union as a Neo-Liberal Construction.* London: Palgrave, pp. 199–221.

Berghahn, Volker and Brigitte Young 2013: Reflections on Werner Bonefeld's 'Freedom and the Strong State: On German Ordoliberalism' and the Continuing Importance of the Ideas of Ordoliberalism to Understand Germany's (Contested) Role in Resolving the Euro Zone Crisis, *New Political Economy* 18(5): 768–778.

Biebricher, Thomas 2014. The Return of Ordoliberalism in Europe – Notes on a Research Agenda, in: i-lex. Scienze Giurdiche, Scienze Cognitive e Intelligenza artifiale. Rivista quadrimestrale Online. 21 May. www.i-lex.it.

Bild-Zeitung 2012: A Blank Cheque for the Debtor States. 9 September: 2.

Blyth, Mark 2013: *Austerity. The History of a Dangerous Idea.* Oxford: Oxford University Press.

Bonefeld, Werner 2012: Freedom and the Strong State: On German Ordoliberalism, *New Political Economy* 2: 1–24.

Bruff, Ian and Matthias Ebenau 2012: Verabschiedet euch vom 'Modell Deutschland'! in: Cicero Online. 5 April. www.cicero.de/weltbuehne/britische-kritik-am-eu-krisenkurs-verabschiedet-euch-vom-modell-deutschland/48871.

Cameron, David 2012: Why the Eurozone Will Survive. Written presentation for the American Political Science Conference, September (personal communication).

Dullien, Sebastian and Ulrike Guérot 2012: *The Long Shadow of Ordoliberalism: Germany's Approach to the Euro Crisis*. Policy Brief. February. London: European Council on Foreign Relations.

Euro Area Summit Statement 2012: 29 June. Brussels.

Financial Times 2012: Weidmann Isolated as ECB Plan Approved. 7 September: 2.

Financial Times Deutschland 2012a: Eichengreen gegen Sinn: Deutscher Aufruf empört Starökonomen. 9 July.

Financial Times Deutschland 2012b: Ökonomieschelte. 9 July: 14.

Frankfurter Allgemeine Zeitung 2012: Merkel wehrt sich gegen Ökonomen-Kritik. 'Es geht überhaupt nicht um zusätzliche Haftung'. 5 July. www.faz.net/aktuell/wirtschaft/merkel-wehrt-sich-gegen-oekonomen-Kritik-es-geht-überhaupt-nicht-um-zusätzliche-Haftung-1.

Frankfurter Rundschau 2012: Anleihekäufe ohne Grenzen. 7 September: 1.

Grjebine, André 2012: The Radical Reform That Should Be on the Agenda in Brussels. *Financial Times*, 18 October: 9.

Guérot, Ulrike 2012: He Who Comes Too Late Is Punished by Life, European Council on Foreign Relations. 11 July. http://ecfr.eu/blog/entry/he_who_comes_too_late_is_punished_by_life.

Habermas, Jürgen, Sigmar Gabriel, Peter Bofinger and Julian Nida-Rümelin 2012: Einspruch gegen die Fassadendemokratie, in: *Frankfurter Allgemeine Zeitung*, 4 August: 33.

Hall, Peter 2012: The Economics and Politics of the Euro Crisis, *German Politics* 21(4): 355–371.

Handelsblatt, 2012a: Keine Schreckgespenster! Peter Bofinger, Gustav Horn, Michael Hüther, Dalia Marin, Bert Rürup, Friedrich Schneider und Thomas Straubhaar. 6 July: 8.

Handelsblatt 2012b: Gipfelbeschlüsse 'gehen in die richtige Richtung'. Zweiter Gegen-Aufruf von deutschen Ökonomen zur Bankenunion. Handelsblog, 6 July. http://blog.handelsblatt.com/handelsblog/2012/07/06/gipfelbeschlüsse-gehen-in-die-richtige-Richtung/.

Hickel, Rudolf 2012: Gastkommentar: Der Tunnelblick der 'Wutökonomen', *Handelsblatt*, 16 July.

Issing, Otmar 2000: *Walter Eucken: Vom Primat der Währungsunion*, Vortrag: Freiburg Walter Eucken Institut, 17 March. www.ecb.int.

Sachverständigenrat zur Begutachtung der gesamtwirtschaftlichen Entwicklung 2012: Nach dem EU-Gipfel, Special Expert Opinion, 5 July. www.sachverstaendigenrat-wirtschaft.de/fileadmin/dateiablage/download/publikationen/sg2012.pdf.

Sally, Razeen 1996: Ordoliberalism and the Social Market: Classical Political Economy from Germany, *New Political Economy* 1(2): 233–257.

Sinn, Hans-Werner und Walter Krämer 2012: Protestaufruf. Der offene Brief der Ökonomen im Wortlaut. *Frankfurter Allgemeine Zeitung*. Wirtschaft. 5 July.

Spiegel, Peter 2012: Burden of Fixing Euro Falls to Leaders. *Financial Times*, 8/9 September: 2.

Süddeutsche.de 2012: 'Schlafwandelnd in die Katastrophe'. 5 July. htttp://article.wn.com/view/2012/07/25/Schuldenkrise_Schlafwandelnd_in_die_Katastrophe/.

The Economist 2012: German Economists in a Momentous Tiff: Germany's Economists Bicker Publicly About the Euro Crisis. 4 August. www.economist.com/node(/21559964/ (accessed 8 August 2012).

Tsebelis, George 2002: *Veto Players: How Political Institutions Work*. New York: Russell Sage Foundation/Princeton University Press.

Véron, Nicolas 2012: Challenges of Europe's Union. Prepared Statement before the US Senate Committee on Foreign Relations: Subcommittee on European Affairs. Hearing on The Future of the Eurozone: Outlook and Lessons (1 August).

Voßkuhle, Andreas 2014: Europa als Rechtsgemeinschaft – Gefährdungen und Herausforderungen, Presentation at the Berlin-Brandenburg Akademie der Wissenschaften, 6 March.

Young, Brigitte 2013: Neoliberalismus – Laissez-Faire – Ordoliberalismus, in: Joscha Wullweber, Maria Behrends and Antonia Graf (eds), *Theorien der Internationalen Politischen Ökonomie*. Wiesbaden: VSA.

Young, Brigitte 2014: German Ordoliberalism as Agenda Setter for the Euro Crisis: Myth Trumps Reality, *Journal of Comparative European Policy* 22(3): 276–287.

Young, Brigitte and Willi Semmler 2011: The European Sovereign Debt Crisis: Is Germany to Blame? *German Politics and Society* 29(1): 1–24.

Welt-Online 2012: Merkel Herself Asked Weidmann to Continue. 1 September. www.welt.de/108918802.

6 From economic decline to the current crisis

A comparison between Italy, France and Germany[1]

Pasquale Tridico

1 The political background of the economic decline

At the beginning of the 1990s the Italian economy incurred a very important structural and institutional change. Such a change was pushed by several factors which include both politics and economics. Italy experienced an important recession of GDP in 1992, which occurred during the same period of troubles and scandals well known as 'Tangentopoli', the corruption scandals which dominated most Italian political parties running the country since the post-Second World War. The *recession* came immediately after a period of marked financial turbulence (Miniaci and Weber, 1999) and in September of 1992, the Italian lira, strongly devaluated, was forced out of the European Exchange Rate Mechanism (ERM). A few months after, two important events occurred: most Italian politicians involved in the corruption scandals were condemned in the famous courts of 'Mani pulite' (clean hand) and, from an economic point of view, Italy signed the Maastricht Treaty which would have resulted in the country joining the Eurozone at the beginning of 2002. These are two important institutional changes which called for economic changes and new regulations and policies. We will focus on the economic aspects of this change, which can be characterized by the following five stylized facts or empirical evidences.

1. First, after the recession of 1992, Italy began a strong de-regulation process, with less involvement of the State in the economy. Corruption scandals, recalled above, convinced many people that State owned and controlled companies would favour corruption. Following this assumption, a minimum-state involvement in the economy was required and a process of liberalization and privatization started. Both processes however were carried out in a very unstable way which lacked efficiency, in particular the process of liberalization. As a result, the partial liberalization of the market coupled with the privatization process resulted in the creation of private monopolies (CNEL, 2007).
2. Inflation was considered a major problem. Moreover, the main contributor to inflation was considered to be the strong power of trade unions and the mechanism of wage collective bargaining. Hence, in July 1993, with a Tripartite

agreement (Government–Business Organizations–Trade Unions), the Government limited the use of this mechanism and introduced a decentralized mechanism for wage bargaining which had a clear objective of wage moderation. At the same time, firms accepted, as an exchange, to increase investment in innovation in order to compensate for the possible increase of profit due to wage moderation. This 'pact of exchange' was never actually respected, and investments in innovation did not fully take place (Tronti, 2005) This had negative consequences on the productivity dynamics, as we will see.

3 The withdrawal of the State from the economy meant the starting of a strong privatization process. Many State owned (or controlled) companies were sold and assets were divided. This process caused a further squeeze of the Italian economy and in particular the reduction of the industrial sector, where large State owned companies were very active. The withdrawal of the State from the economy was not in fact substituted by private investments and by new private firms. The empty space left in the manufacturing sector has simply never recovered and this meant a further reduction of the Italian industrial share in Europe and globally. Large and important firms disappeared as testified by a key book in this field written by Gallino (2003).

4 The convergence towards the Maastricht criteria meant in particular the reduction of public expenditure in order to cut deficit and public debt. This had an immediate consequence of reducing what we can call the indirect wage. Public expenditure in social dimensions and welfare declined, such as education, health, subsidies, etc. which had a negative effect on the purchasing power of workers and the middle class in particular. In the end, one can say that the Tripartite agreement and the Maastricht criteria had conflicting interests and objectives. From one side the Tripartite agreement would require increasing the welfare state expenditure in order to let trade unions and workers accept the wage moderation: this was stated in the Agreement as part of an exchange between the three parts involved. On the other side, however, the Maastricht criteria required a reduction in public expenditure (Fitoussi, 2005).

5 The Tripartite agreement was the starting point of a much deeper reform of the labour market which took place between the end of the 1990s and the beginning of the 2000s with the introduction of labour flexibility, the massive creation of atypical forms of work, the surge of temporary work and the privatization of the job allocation service in the labour market (Tronti and Ceccato, 2005). This point will be explored more deeply in the following section.

To sum up, I will argue that there are a number of factors which make the Italian economy weaker. These factors represent both direct and indirect consequences of policies implemented mainly in the 1990s and the beginning of the 2000s, listed in the five points above. These policies, which tried mainly to introduce a very market-oriented economic model, following the so called Washington Consensus approach (Williamson, 1990; Rodrik, 2004), ended up producing negative consequences on economic performances and social problems such as (Levrero and Stirati, 2005; Rodrik, 2008): high income inequality, job precariousness, declining wage share over GDP, low wage and low consumption levels and a strong profit soar; along with low education and training on the job places, low competitiveness and low labour productivity, low innovation and low R&D. All of these consequences, coupled with the historical problems of the Italian economy, are the real causes of the Italian decline and the persistency of the current crisis, such as low labour force participation, labour segmentation, regional dualism, bad transition from schools to job markets, biased politics, inefficient institutions and bad governance.

Hence, I claim, on the basis of the deteriorating income distribution, and more in general on the basis of the Italian economic decline, that there is a negative institutional change introduced mainly by law. In fact, the factors listed above are consequences of the bad policies, institutions and changes introduced in the last two decades. These factors weaken the aggregate demand, with negative results on the GDP dynamics, and enlarge the 'productivity spread' between Italy and most of other EU countries. Therefore the way out from the decline and towards a recovery after the crisis is to invert the economic policies and the economic model which is on the basis of those factors listed above and which has been pursued over the last 15–20 years. The real cause of the current crisis does not appear to be the sovereign debt issue, therefore the austerity measures implemented in Italy and in the rest of Europe in the last 2–3 years will not guarantee the recovery from the crisis.

2 The recent evolution of the Italian labour market

In the last 15 years, as we mentioned above, the Italian labour market has undergone a profound change from the legislative point of view and also from a structural and social perspective. The origin of this change can be traced back to what has happened in Italy since 1993, i.e. since the country, after the economic recession of 1992 and the signature of the Treaty of Maastricht made a decision to enter the Economic and Monetary Union (EMU). This meant first of all to respect the Maastricht criteria, first and foremost, the reduction in the inflation rate, which in Italy was particularly problematic. The Agreement of July 1993 mainly wanted by then Premier of the Government, Carlo Azeglio Ciampi, had explicitly aimed at the reduction of the inflationary spiral through wage moderation and other interventions such as income policies, the growth of innovative investments and the increase of productivity. However, as many economists have shown, most of the expected results of this agreement were largely unreached. On the contrary the policy of wage moderation and thus the disinflation has been successful (Cazes *et al.*, 1999; Rossi and Sestito 2000; Lilla, 2005).

Upon completion of this process of change more labour flexibility was introduced into the Italian labour market through the so called 'Pacchetto Treu' (Law no. 196 in 1997) and the Law no. 30 of 2003 (known as the 'Legge Biagi') that introduced radical innovations in contractual labour forms and in the labour market in general. These reforms were born under the European Employment Strategy in 1997 which led to the more complex Lisbon Strategy in March 2000 which established at the EU level, the guidelines and objectives for the reform of the labour market in order to make Europe 'the most competitive and dynamic economy in the world based on knowledge'. This strategy was then repeated and replaced by the 'Europe 2020 Strategy'. However, in Europe, the trend is to reach a social balance through a model that is commonly called 'flexicurity' which is able to ensure and combine security elements with the labour flexibility that firms require.

In Italy, there is a well-known gap between the dimension of flexibility, now widely introduced, and the dimension of social security, as the current system of unemployment benefits is complex, fragmented and disorganized and not able to cover and protect all the unemployed. Such a situation was not actually solved by the recent reform and the introduction by the Labour Minister Prof. Fornero of a new social tool called 'Aspi' (a new unemployment benefit) with the Law no. 92 of June 2012. Indeed, the latter has not expanded the audience of those entitled to unemployment benefits, who remain linked to the condition that one must have held a job placement for the previous two years before the year of unemployment. Moreover, this unemployment benefit has a limited length (eight months compared to four years in Denmark or two years on average in the EU-15) and does not cover all independent workers (the so called CO.CO.CO. or CO.CO.PRO.) who have terminated a job for a certain project, collaborators, atypical and unstable workers, who indeed constitute a big portion of new jobs, especially among young people. Finally, the Italian system of unemployment benefits is not connected, in general, to active policies, such as programmes of integration into the labour market, job search and training programmes that would facilitate the entry into the market of the unemployed. In essence, it seems we can say that in Italy, the implementation of a 'flexicurity model' should lead to improve unemployment benefits, and to increase the security elements, such as the social protection and employability. To worsen the situation, the current financial and economic crisis has led to a considerable increase in the unemployment rates and to a greater demand for income protection.

To sum up, the Italian employment security system is, therefore, still obsolete and inadequate compared to the changes that occurred in the last decade in the contractual forms and in the structural composition. It would therefore be necessary to fully adjust the social safety nets and protections in order to avoid the problem that flexible labour relations can result in precarious jobs and become a source of social exclusion and lack of income, with negative effects on consumption and aggregate demand. Moreover, in a period of economic recession like the present one, extensive social benefits and automatic unemployment subsidies are necessary in order to avoid a recessionary spiral, a weakening of the purchasing power of workers, and a further fall in consumption and in the aggregate demand. On the contrary, the recent austerity policies reduce aggregate demand further, directly and indirectly weakening the purchasing power of workers, when the indirect wages (i.e. the public expenditure on services, health, education, etc.) is cut and when wages in the public sector are reduced.

3 The model: from labour flexibility to economic decline

The labour market reforms recalled above were coupled, in the 1990s, with an uncompleted and unfair liberalization and privatization process, which favoured both the increase of rents and the worsening of income distribution. In fact privatization was introduced without a full liberalization of the goods market. Therefore, in the sectors where former public assets operated (such as: telecommunication, energy, infrastructures, public utilities, railways, etc.) mark-up and rents increased and private monopoly firms were created. Those reforms were caused on one side by a strong pressure on wages and labour (as we will see in this section), and on the other side by a lower productivity performance (as we will see in the next section).

In regards to the first aspect, the labour market reforms, we may say that the July Agreement of 1993 in the end contributed to the stagnation of wages at national level. After that, and under the pressure of the two main laws introduced in the labour market mentioned above, labour flexibility, in particular 'in entrance' increased consistently, temporary work, unstable jobs and all the atypical forms of job surged (Rossi and Sestito, 2000; Lilla, 2005; Torrini, 2005; Tronti, 2005). The process was recently completed under the law of June 2012 which introduced some forms of labour flexibility 'in exit'. However, the flexibilization in the labour market was not coupled with a higher level of public expenditure for social dimension, employability and for general labour policies (as is often the case in countries which introduced a so called flexicurity model, like Denmark or Sweden). In fact quite the opposite; indirect wages also decreased. Income inequality increased and the purchasing power of workers decreased. The wage share over the GDP fell drastically with a consequent negative impact on the level of consumption which declined drastically as well as the aggregate demand.

An examination of the relevant data for the Italian economy in comparison with its main EU and Eurozone partners such as France and Germany (and sometimes in comparison with OECD and EU member states) confirms the strong correlation between all the relevant variables discussed above. It seems clear that there is a deeper decline in the Italian aggregate demand (AD) caused by a deeper shrinking in the consumption (C) which in turn is caused by the deeper reduction of wage share (WS), the more marked decline of indirect wage (IW), i.e. the public expenditure (G) in particular in social dimensions (SD), the higher increase of inequality (Ineq) and the pressure on labour employment (L) and wage (W) caused by a stronger labour flexibility (LF) and by its correlated creation of unstable jobs (IJ). The decline in the aggregate demand is the main cause for the lower dynamics of GDP and for its deeper decline. In brief and in symbols, the mechanism goes in the following direction:

$$\uparrow LF \rightarrow \uparrow IJ \rightarrow \downarrow W \rightarrow \uparrow Ineq \rightarrow \downarrow WS\ (+\downarrow IW) \rightarrow \downarrow C \rightarrow \downarrow AD \rightarrow \downarrow GDP \qquad (1)$$

All the data reported below confirm this mechanism, starting with labour flexibility, which is measured as protection for regular and temporary employment, as components of the Employment Protection Legislation index (EPL) from the

OECD. This indicator shows the level of protection offered by national legislation to workers. In other words, how regulated the employer's freedom to fire and hire workers is. Traditionally, European economies maintain higher levels of EPL in comparison with Anglo-Saxon economies and in comparison to the USA in particular (Nickell, 2008).

In the Italian case this indicator under the pressure of the flexibilization of the labour market fell drastically as we can see in Figure 6.1 and Figure 6.2 below.

Although labour flexibility is increasing everywhere, in Europe the policy agenda is moving toward a so called 'flexicurity' which would promote some

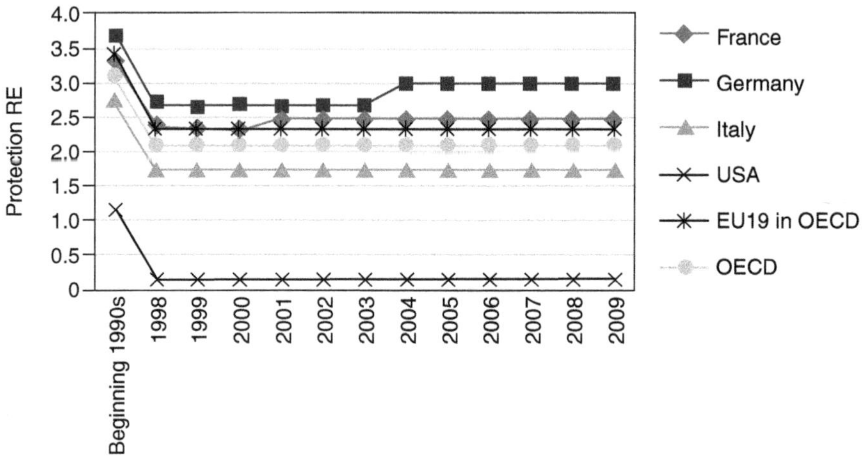

Figure 6.1 Labour flexibility of regular employees (source: own elaboration on OECD (2012)).

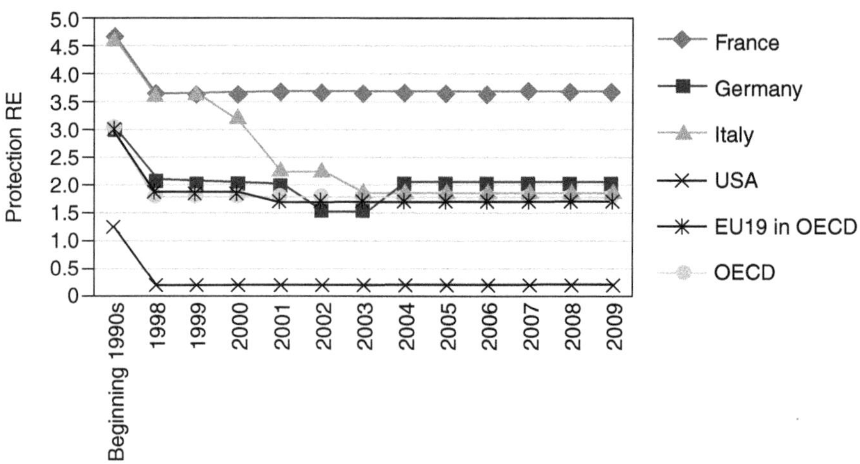

Figure 6.2 Labour flexibility of temporary employees (source: own elaboration on OECD (2012)).

type of job security while accounting for the need for flexibility on the part of firms (Kok Report, 2004; Boyer, 2009; Tridico, 2009). The Italian levels are below the Germany and France ones, and as well as below most of the OECD and UE countries, as the averages values for both show.

Flexibility goes hand in hand with temporary work which increased consistently in Italy in the last 15 years as Figure 6.3 below shows, above the values of the main EU partners and above the OECD average, in particular after 2003, when the Law no. 30 mentioned above was introduced in the Italian labour market.

In this context, real wages were pressed, because labour flexibility operated mainly in the direction to reduce costs, at least in the case of Italy. Average annual wages today in Italy are at the same level as the ones at the end of the 1990s (Figure 6.4), as the Bank of Italy several times reported (Draghi, 2007; Banca d'Italia, 2012). Even in Germany, despite the so called 'internal devaluation' which allowed for a wage moderation in the 2000s as a consequence of an agreement between Trade Unions, Industrial Organizations and Government, and despite a higher initial level, the wage increased more than in Italy (3.5 per cent against 1.4 per cent), and in France even more (12.2 per cent), while in the rest of the OECD old member states (i.e. Australia, Austria, Belgium, Canada, Denmark, Finland, Greece, Ireland, USA, UK), the increase was around 9 per cent, since 2000.

As a consequence of such a pressure on labour, the wage share declined, and of course this decline was more marked in Italy, where labour flexibility and wage stagnation were more incisive, in comparison with Germany and France and many other EU countries (see also Levrero and Stirati, 2005).

The issue of the declining wage share in advanced economies was already raised by several heterodox contributors such as Barba and Pivetti (2009), Fitoussi and Stiglitz (2009), Fitoussi and Saraceno (2010), Brancaccio and Fontana (2011) and Stockhammer (2013), who identify structural problems in the economic systems of advanced economies. These structural problems are the deep causes of the recession and of the global disorder. They refer to the income distribution bias

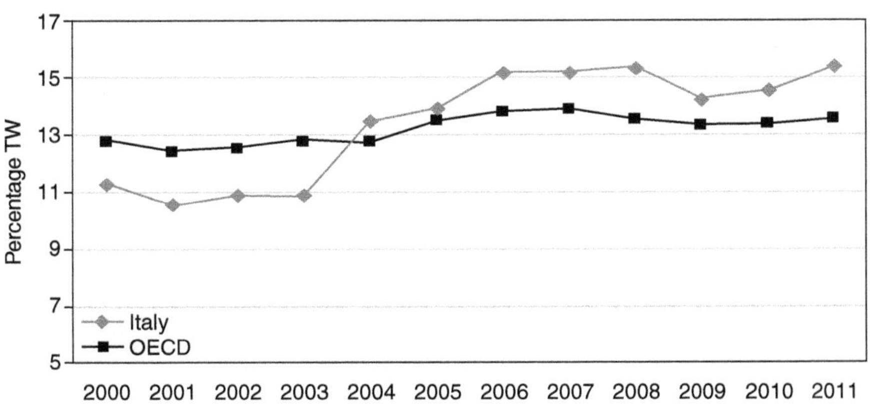

Figure 6.3 Labour flexibility – temporary work (source: own elaboration on OECD (2012)).

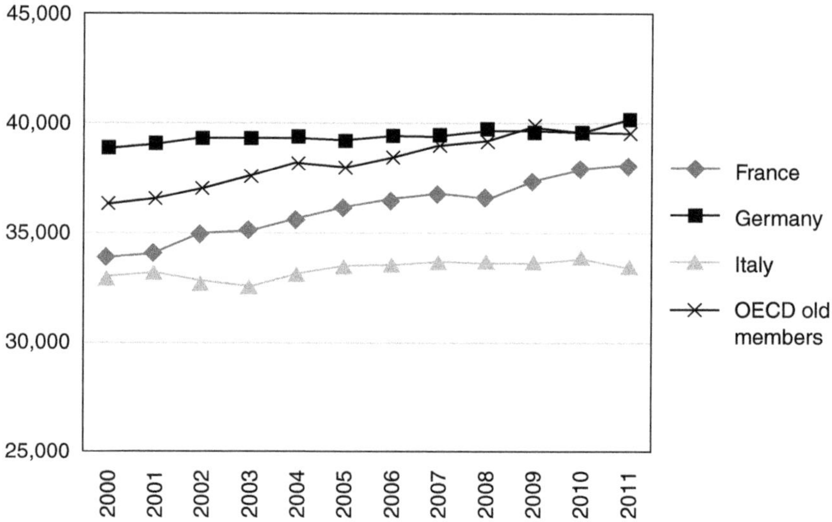

Figure 6.4 Italian stagnant wages (source: own elaboration on OECD (2012)).

and to the inequality that weakened consumption and the effective demand in the economies. The decline of the wage is at the same time in strong correlation with the process of financialization which took place some 30 years ago in the USA and in Europe (Tridico, 2012a). In brief, the argument is that the aggregate demand, which was not sustained by appropriate wages, and by productive investments, used the channels of financialization and credit to sustain consumption. This consumption resulted in the end to be unstable and not able to guarantee long term support to the aggregate demand, in particular after the burst of the bubble in 2007 and the financial sector squeezed the credit for both investments and consumption.

Figure 6.5 above includes agriculture, housing costs for families and some limited forms of independent work. It is therefore an inclusive measure for wage share. Despite that, data are clearly showing a decreasing trend, and the figure for Italy is even more dramatic. When we include only dependent work remunerations, the results are even worse.

Figure 6.6 above shows data for income from dependent work and from capital. A clear drop in the wages occurred during the 1990s, the time of the main labour market reforms (1993 and 1997), from 53 per cent to 46 per cent. During the 2000s wages were more or less stable. During the same period, and until the middle of the 2000s, i.e. before the current crisis, profits increased much more, hence income distribution worsened. Profits, coherently with our assumptions concerning the impact of the 1993 agreement and of the introduction of labour flexibility which compressed wages, increased in particular in the second half of the 1990s from 37 per cent to above 40 per cent, and after remained more or less stable.

Besides, the aggregate demand was also weakened by the decreasing of the public expenditure in the economy, in Italy, more than in other European

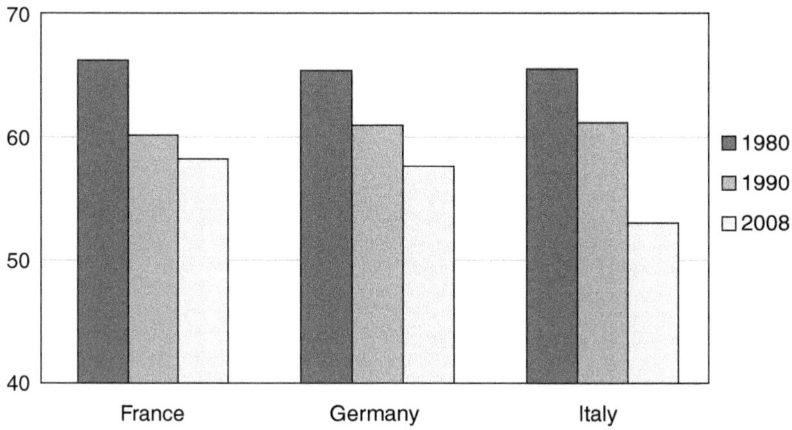

Figure 6.5 The declining of wage shares in the economy (source: OECD (2008); ILO (2010)).

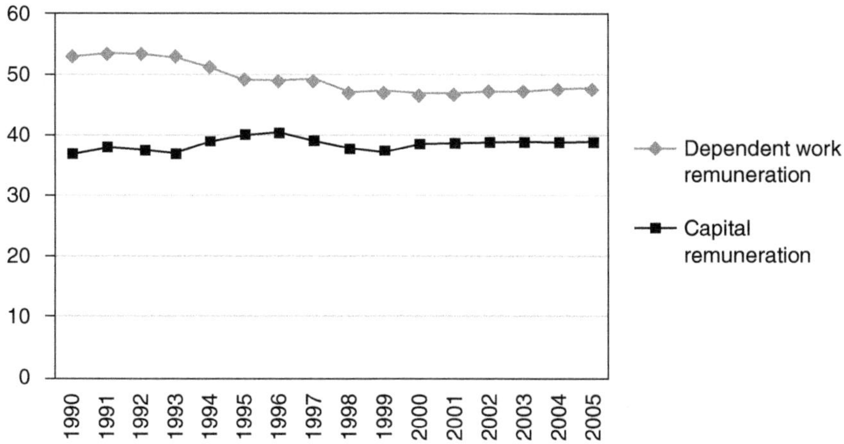

Figure 6.6 Labour and capital in Italy 1990–2005 (source: own elaboration on Istat data, 2010).

Notes

The sum of the factors of production labour and capital will be 100 considering also indirect taxes (between 10 and 15 per cent) and capital gains from abroad (around ±2 per cent). The 'capital remuneration' is here the net operating surplus and indicates the percentage remunerating the capital.

countries: while in Germany and in France, the other two biggest Eurozone economies, public expenditure increased in the last 20 years, in Italy public expenditure decreased as Figure 6.7 below shows.

Such a decrease affected in particular the social expenditure. Moreover, its level was already lower than EU partners such as France and Germany (not to

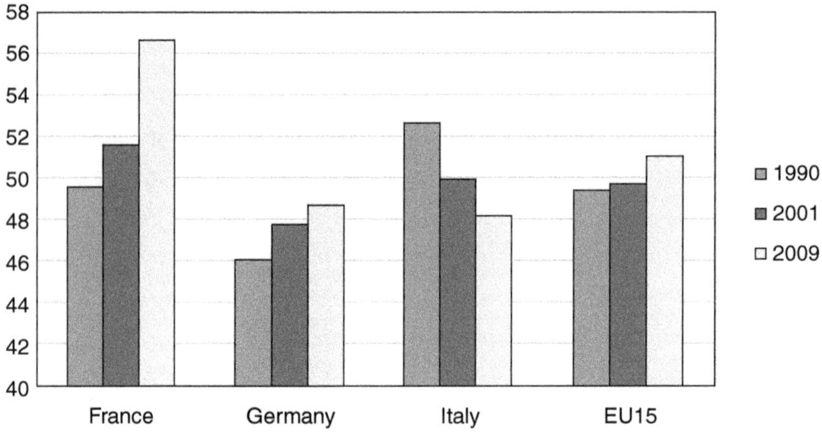

Figure 6.7 Indirect wage, total public expenditure (source: IMF, 2012).

mention Scandinavian countries which have traditionally higher levels of welfare), where social expenditure is around 55 per cent (on total government expenditure) or around 25 per cent of GDP, while in Italy the corresponding figures are approximately 50 per cent and 23 per cent (Figure 6.8). Such a reduction meant a decrease in the indirect wages, and a further weakening of the purchasing power of workers and the middle class who live mainly off direct and indirect wages.

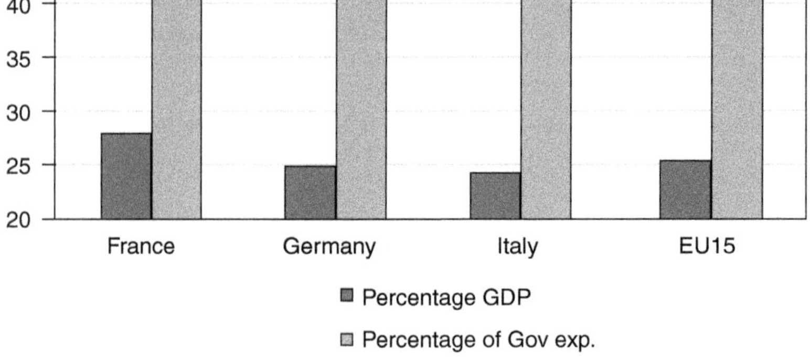

Figure 6.8 Indirect wage, social expenditure (source: own elaboration on OECD (2012)).

Beside that, active and passive labour policies, i.e. job search programmes and subsidies to the unemployed, are notably lower in Italy than in other European countries (Figure 6.9). Such a situation affects negatively both the employment rates (because the unemployed are not adequately supported in finding a job and in matching the labour supply) and the consumption level, since people without an income cannot consume, and stabilizer mechanisms, in particular in recession time, cannot operate.

All of these data have a direct consequence on the worsening of the income distribution which in Italy has taken a very bad path in the past 20 years (Lilla, 2005). The income Gini coefficient has in fact increased tremendously in Italy from around 29 per cent in 1990 to more than 35 per cent in 2009, being dangerously higher than Germany, France and many other EU and OECD countries (Figure 6.10).

The correlation between inequality and flexibility is clear. In the last two decades inequality has increased along with labour flexibility as Figure 6.11

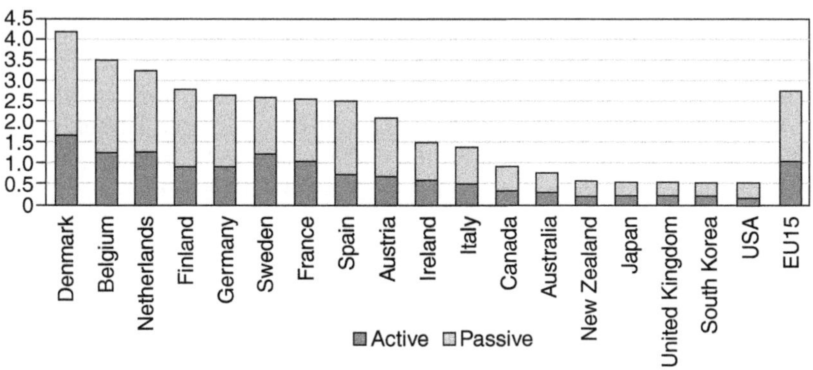

Figure 6.9 Labour policies and unemployment subsidies (source: own elaboration on OECD (2012)).

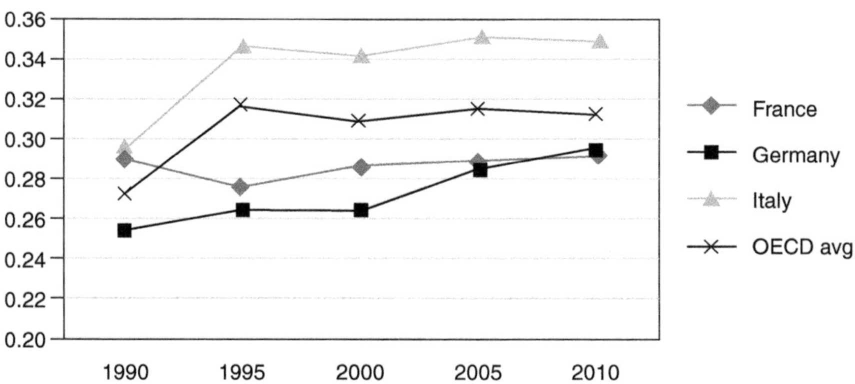

Figure 6.10 Income inequality (source: own elaboration on OECD (2012)).

below shows. In particular, Italy is collocated among the countries with higher inequality and lower EPL (higher labour flexibility), along with Anglo-Saxon, Baltic and Mediterranean countries, which we can define as liberal competitive market economies or hybrid market economies (in the case of the Mediterranean countries). In contrast, Continental and Scandinavian countries, which represent more of a European Social model, coordinated and oriented towards a social market (Amoroso and Jespersen, 2012; Tridico, 2012a) have lower levels of inequality and higher levels of EPL (lower labour flexibility). The two poles here are Germany and the UK, and Italy appears clearly in the UK quadrant.

In such a situation, inevitably, consumption levels fell sharply. Today, the level of Italian consumption is similar to its own level from more than 30 years ago, in 1979. It decreased continuously from 1990, in parallel with the *flexibilization* of the labour market, the decline in the wage share, the decline of the direct and indirect wages and the increase of inequality. It is today one of the lower among the EU15 and far below that of France and Germany (Figure 6.12).

A further weakening of the aggregate demand occurred in Italy with the reduction of the investment level, which fell below, in the last ten years, that of France and Germany (Figure 6.13). Today, in recession time, with scarce and exogenous investments, credit restrictions and rationing policies implemented by banks, after the financial crisis of 2007–09, the situation worsened further: firms cannot finance their investments, innovation will continue to be lacking, productivity will continue not to grow, and aggregate demand will be further depressed.

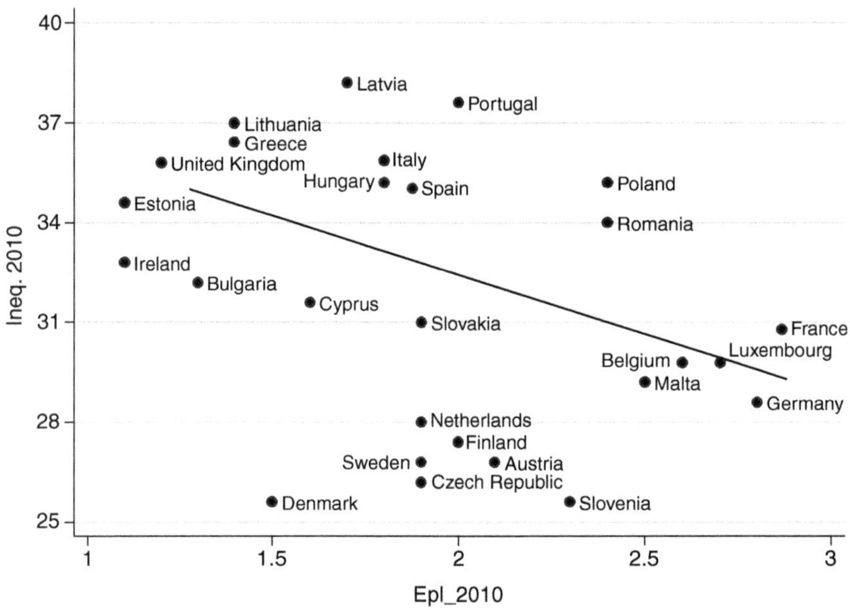

Figure 6.11 Correlation scatter inequality and EPL (source: own elaboration on OECD data).

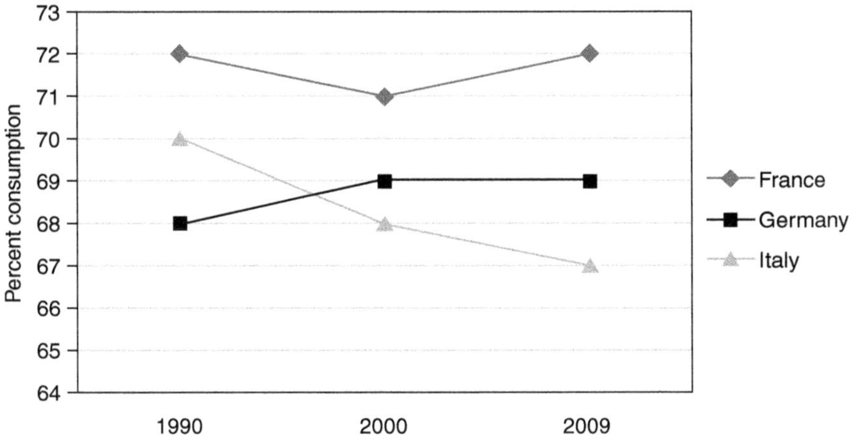

Figure 6.12 The decline in the consumption level (source: own elaboration on Penn World Table 7.1 data).

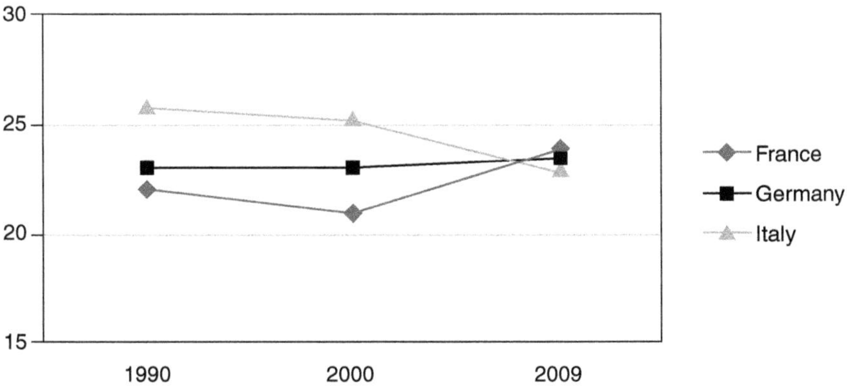

Figure 6.13 The decline in the investment level (source: own elaboration on Penn World Table 7.1 data).

If we go more in the details of the national accounts (Table 6.1), the elaboration of the data (source : OECD) reveals something very interesting. Italy more than France and in particular more than Germany lost a decade (2000–2010) in terms of development and was stagnating in the previous one. Data from Italy concerning the growth dynamics of the main components of the GDP, are systematically below the ones of its main partners. In particular the contribution to growth of Consumption (C) – a crucial element of the aggregate demand – was only 0.3 per cent in the last decade, the lowest not only among the three countries but among OECD countries, and one of the lowest performance since the Second World War. A similar story concerns the Investment (I) contribution to growth and the Public expenditure (G) contribution to growth. The scarce growth dynamics

Table 6.1 National accounts: contribution to growth

		1990–95	*1996–2000*	*2001–2011*	*Average 1990–2011*	*Cumulative growth 1990–2011*
France	C	0.7	1.4	0.9	1.0	3.0
Germany	C	1.5	0.9	0.3	0.9	2.7
Italy	C	0.6	1.5	0.3	0.8	2.4
France	I	0.0	0.8	0.2	0.3	1.0
Germany	I	0.7	0.5	0.0	0.4	1.2
Italy	I	0.0	0.7	0.0	0.2	0.6
France	G	0.5	0.3	0.4	0.4	1.1
Germany	G	0.5	0.3	0.2	0.3	1.0
Italy	G	0.0	0.2	0.2	0.1	0.4
France	Exports	1.2	2.1	0.5	1.2	3.7
Germany	Exports	1.2	2.4	2.3	2.0	5.9
Italy	Export	1.4	1.0	0.4	0.9	2.8
France	Imports	−0.8	−2.0	−0.7	−1.2	−3.5
Germany	Imports	−1.3	−2.2	−1.6	−1.7	−5.1
Italy	Imports	−0.8	−1.4	−0.5	−0.9	−2.6

Source: own elaboration on OECD data.

of the main components of the GDP may confirm (or at least is not contrasting) our hypothesis: the fall in the demand is a consequence of a fall in the Consumption and in the Investment. The biggest role among the GDP components, in terms of contribution to growth, is played by the Exports (E) whose cumulative contribution during the whole period 1990–2011 was higher than other components, but still inferior to the one of France and Germany. This result is not surprising in our approach and it is consistent with the idea that internal demand is declining. The economic policy in the last 15–20 years was not supporting internal demand, and international competitiveness was aimed only by devaluating labour costs through labour flexibility and pressure on wages which were stagnating. In the end, however, exports were no longer enough to carry out aggregate demand and support a positive GDP dynamics. Labour productivity was also not increasing because capital intensive investment was lacking.

As a result of this, the GDP dynamics in Italy over the last 15 years has been stagnating, and, when the recession hit Italy in 2009, it was deeper, and consequentially, the recovery will be more difficult to occur in the given situation. In fact, it does not appear that policies implemented during the recession time, in the last 3–4 years, were inverting the above recalled dynamics. Quite the opposite: the labour market was further liberalized with a new Law introduced by the Ministry of Labour in June 2012 mentioned above (Law no. 92/2012). The austerity measures introduced by the Monti Government and before by the Berlusconi Government decreased the public expenditure and targeted exclusively to balance the budget, with an obvious consequence of reducing further the national expenditure without remarkable results in terms of growth, recovery and not even in terms of Debt/GDP reduction. In fact the measures targeting the reduction of Debt were basically reducing the national revenues and the GDP, thus worsening further the Debt/GDP ratio.

The Italian decline appears clearly in Figure 6.14: in almost 15 years Italy lost, in comparison with the EU, 20 percentage points of GDP. Italy used to be a richer country, with an average GDP above the EU15 (the richest club), and today it is far below this average level. Its GDP equals the average GDP of the EU at 27 countries. The comparison with Germany highlights the two different paths since 2002: while Germany is sloping upwards, Italy continues to decline. Furthermore, while the EU15 including France are still keeping their relative wealth, Italy has already lost it.

In brief and in symbols, all that can be expressed simply in the following textbook equation:

$$AD\ (C+I+G)\downarrow \rightarrow GDP\downarrow \qquad (2)$$

It is not trivial to state that the lack of expansion of aggregate demand causes a further decline in the productivity, following the well known Sylos Labini model that we will explore further in the next section.

When we test a simple model comprised by the relevant variables whose data were listed above, we obtain the expected results. The model which was tested, among the 27 Member States of the European Union, considers a so called

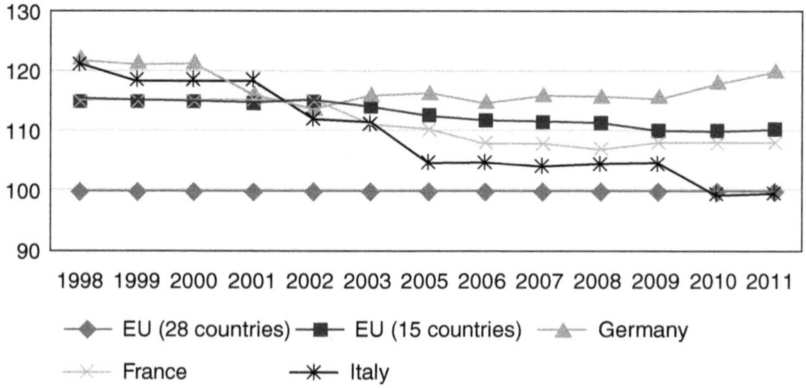

Figure 6.14 The Italian decline (source: own elaboration on Eurostat (2012) data).

Performance Index (I) as a dependent variable, which is nothing more than an algebric sum of GDP growth (g) in 2007–2012, employment change (n) for the same period and unemployment level (u). The independent variables are inequality (gini coefficient), temporary work (share over the total employment) and the EPL. Both the OLS model with 27 observations (which include average values of the relevant variables for the period 2007–2012), and the GLS model of a Panel (with 162 observations), built with the series of each year from 2007 to 2011 (which are the most relevant years of crisis in Europe) gave very interesting and consistent results which confirm our model (Table 6.2).[2]

$$PI(+n-u)=a+b1EPL-b2TW-b3Ineq+e \quad (3)$$

Table 6.2 Regression table, cross-country

OLS Model
Dep Var.: PI (2007–12)

Variable	*Coeff. (stand errors)*	P-*values*
EPL_2008	8.147022 (1.95968)	*
Temporary work 2008	–0.1638903 (0.1295744)	**
Inequality 2008	–0.696365 (0.2433367)	***
Constant	–4.865248 (9.95968)	
R-squared=0.6413		
Adj R-squared=0.5945		
Prob>F=0.0000		
Number of obs=27		

Source: own elaboration.

Note
Significance level:
* within 1%; ** within 5%; *** within 10%.

4 From lack of competition to productivity decline

Besides the issues explained above, the other problem that emerges in Italy is the presence of strong rigidity, and a lack of competition and protection in the goods market. This seems to be the main cause of low productivity dynamics that has characterized the Italian economy for more than a decade as firms prefer a labour intensive investment strategy rather than a strategy of technological innovation and investments expansions, in contradiction with what was agreed with the July 1993 agreement (Fadda, 2009; Nardozzi, 2004). This is because of the relatively cheaper real wages (in fact guaranteed by the downward pressure of labour flexibility), and protections they may enjoy in the goods market, scarcely competitive.

An interpretation of this is offered by the Sylos Labini model and several contributions which follow his approach (Sylos Labini, 1993, 1999; Tarantelli, 1995; Blanchard and Giavazzi, 2003; Tronti, 2005) and in some way refer to classical or Keynesian schemes. This approach explains that the lack of competition in the goods market is the main cause for the low dynamics of labour productivity. Basically, what happens is that a highly flexible labour market, which reduces labour costs through wage pressure, accompanied by a protected goods market and scarcely competitive as the Italian one, encourages firms not to innovate and not to invest, but to still enjoy competitive advantages and increasing profits through wage moderation (Torrini, 2005). This is contrary to what had been established with the agreement of July 1993 where, through a 'political exchange' trade unions accepted a wage moderation in exchange for an incomes policy (i.e. more welfare) and for a strong strategy of productive investments in advanced sectors. This exchange did not take place and productive investments have not grown as Figure 6.15 below shows (Tronti, 2005).

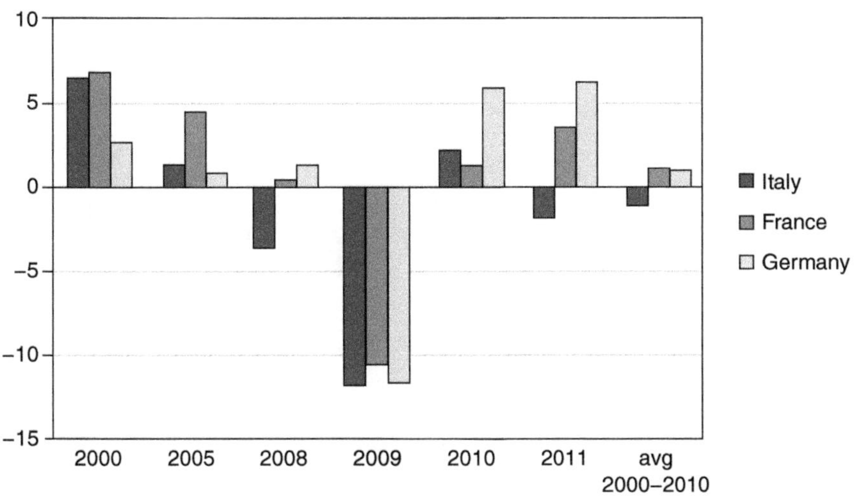

Figure 6.15 The decline in investment changes (source: own elaboration on OECD (2012)).

In contrast, wage moderation and a lack of competition in the goods market has led to the growth of rents, dominant positions and profits for firms, which were able to maintain thus through the pressure on labour, at least temporarily, international competitive positions (Fadda, 2012).

However, de-industrialization is not a determining phenomenon in advanced economies, as the case of Germany shows clearly. In Germany (and other EU partners), the share of the industrial sector grew in the last decade, from 25 per cent to 26 per cent while in Italy it declined from 24 per cent to 19 per cent which corresponds to a fall of around 15 per cent in the value added of the whole industrial sector, as Figure 6.16 below shows.

At the industrial level, the withdrawal of the State from economic activities and the privatization process did not bring more industrial investments. This process simply caused a further squeeze of the Italian economy and in particular the reduction of the industrial sector. The empty space left in manufacturing has simply never recovered. This meant a further reduction of the Italian industrial share in Europe and in the world and the disappearance of large and important firms (Gallino, 2003). Obviously this issue has to be analysed in the context of globalization and of the division of labour which occurred in the last two decades. Hence, the uncompleted liberalization and privatization processes left Italy with a smaller industrial share, and with many protected areas, not subject to competition. Such as the retail sector, protected by regulations and legal technicalities in the wholesale distribution, dominated by a few large monopolies; the agricultural sector subsidized through the EU Common Agricultural Policy; the energy sector which is dominated by a few large private companies that enjoy the benefits of being State owned for a long period of time, and then recently privatized but not fully liberalized therefore still enjoying subsidies,

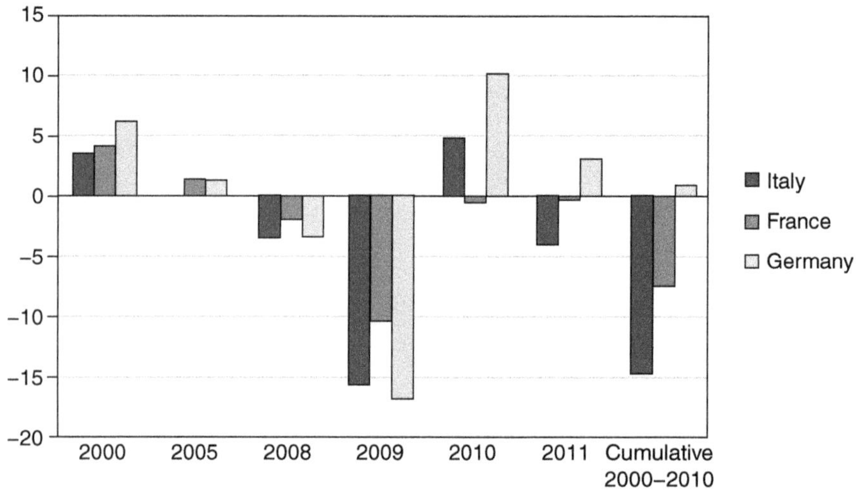

Figure 6.16 The industrial decline (source: own elaboration on OECD (2012)).

support and protections; very few large private companies operating in strategic sectors, such as transport and communications, less exposed to international competition, subsidized often in an opaque way through lobbying pressures. Besides that, R&D at national level did not increase substantially, and the gap in comparison with EU and other partners is increasing consistently (Figure 6.17).

Clearly, all this is at the expense of productivity gains, which are strangled by a lack of expansion of aggregate demand, a price increase in the cost of labour per unit of output, and a lack of investment, especially in technologically advanced sectors. This result is also supported theoretically, if we assume that the productivity depends on the combination of the so called Smith's effect (expansion of demand, with reorganization and division of labour) and Ricardo effect (investments that replace labour with capital-specific technological change). Through this approach, we can observe a negative relationship between productivity and labour flexibility, as Kleinknecht *et al.* empirically demonstrated in several contributions (Kleinknecht and Naastepad, 2005; Kleinknecht *et al.*2006, 2013). The following equation, taken from Sylos Labini (1999), presents the determinants of labour productivity according to this approach:

$$\Delta\pi = a + b\Delta Y + c(CLUP - P) + d(W - P_{MA}) + e\Delta I \tag{4}$$

The change in labour productivity ($\Delta\pi$) depends positively on changes in the product (ΔY), the change in investment (ΔI) and the differences of the variables in parentheses, where P is the price index, P_{MA} the prices of machines and $CLUP$ is the unit labour costs, that is the cost of labour per unit of output, i.e. the ratio between the change in wages and the rate of productivity growth. If the $CLUP$ grows faster than the consumer price index, companies, having a lower margin of profit, will be forced to save labour, and will do capital-intensive investments, or will reorganize the workforce within the company. Thus, if wages rise more than prices of machinery firms will prefer to increase investment labour saving

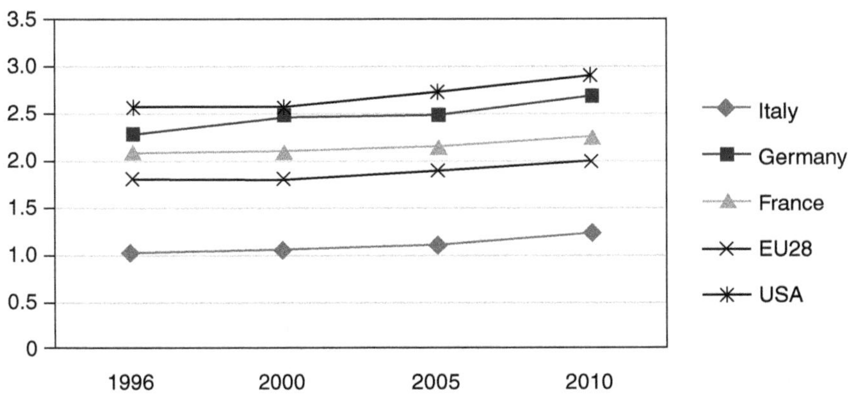

Figure 6.17 The gap in R&D (source: own elaboration on OECD (2012) and Eurostat (2012) data).

because this is cheaper than the employment of new workers, hence productivity will increase. Later, this will also bring about higher employment. This indeed also implies that if wages do not grow properly with respect to the price of machinery, investments are not properly stimulated, entrepreneurs will essentially look for advantageous positions, and the competition will rely primarily on wage moderation. This picture is a good example of what has happened in Italy since 1993 (Tronti, 2005; Sylos Labini 2003; Lucidi, 2006; Tridico, 2009), in which beside a modest employment growth and strong wage moderation, there was a negative trend and stagnant productivity (Figure 6.18). In fact, by definition we have:

$$GDP = Y = L\Pi \text{ (L = labour employment and } \Pi \text{ = average productivity)} \rightarrow \Delta y = \Delta l + \Delta\pi \quad (5)$$

Now, if L (the employment) increases, and the GDP does not grow, the stagnation of GDP is to be found in the poor productivity performance P. However, it could also be the opposite: that because GDP does not grow, productivity is stagnant. In both cases there is a problem of negative interaction between GDP and productivity, related to Smith's effect and to its negative relation with flexibility.

To conclude, if we come back to the equation (2), we can add to it another component, the productivity, and we will observe easily that following the Sylos Labini approach, the contraction of the aggregate demand not only reduces the GDP but does not allow for productivity gains with further negative effects on the GDP, as follows:

$$AD\ (C+I+G)\downarrow \rightarrow GDP\downarrow \rightarrow productivity\downarrow \rightarrow GDP\downarrow \quad (6)$$

Therefore, the pressure on wages and the labour flexibility ended up to be detrimental twice for the GDP growth: (1) via the reduction of the aggregate demand as we saw in the previous section and (2) via the negative effect on the productivity growth.

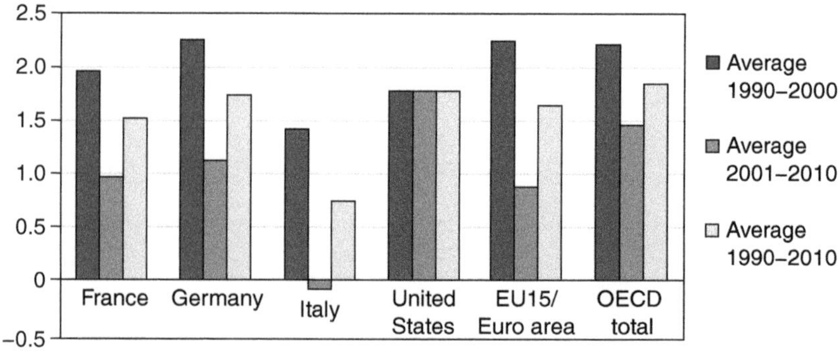

Figure 6.18 Labour productivity (source: own elaboration on OECD (2012)).

5 Discussion

As we saw, during the last decade in almost all the OECD countries, including Italy, labour flexibility, calculated through the reduction of some indices of rigidity of the labour market, increased. One can also observe modest increases in employment rates (Figure 6.19). These increases in labour flexibility were coupled very often with a reduction in labour costs and therefore also with wage flexibility. As a result, the new jobs created are characterized by dissatisfaction and low working efficiency caused precisely by the pressure on the wages, the low incentives that low-paid workers receive, the instability felt by the worker in the job place, and by the poor social security contributions. This can be interpreted also through the efficiency wage approach, where unstable and low-paid jobs push workers to put little effort into their work. Moreover, this does not guarantee that firms and workers invest in training and education in order to improve the quality of human capital, with lower results in terms of productivity, *ceteris pairibus*, by the economic system (Salop, 1979; Shapiro and Stiglitz, 1984).

More specifically, in Italy, until 2007–2008, i.e. before the crisis, there was an increase of employment in the tertiary sector, fragmented and disorganized, poorly motivated and low paid. The result was the lower productivity of the Italian economy. In the end, the only factor partially positive is the modest increase of employment which was negatively offset by the negative labour productivity and by the reduction of the wage share in the GDP. This brought about the reduction of the purchasing power of workers and the lack of a positive dynamic in the aggregate demand and therefore in the GDP.

The lack of sustained economic growth and the current economic crisis resulted in lower levels of employment which contributed to the increase in the unemployment. Until the beginning of the crisis in 2007–2008, most new jobs recorded in Italy, which reached a historically low unemployment rate in 2006 of about 6.5 per cent, were low-paid jobs, with real wages lower than those needed to maintain purchasing power adequate to price levels. Semi-employment contributed to the increase of employment. Since capital-intensive investments

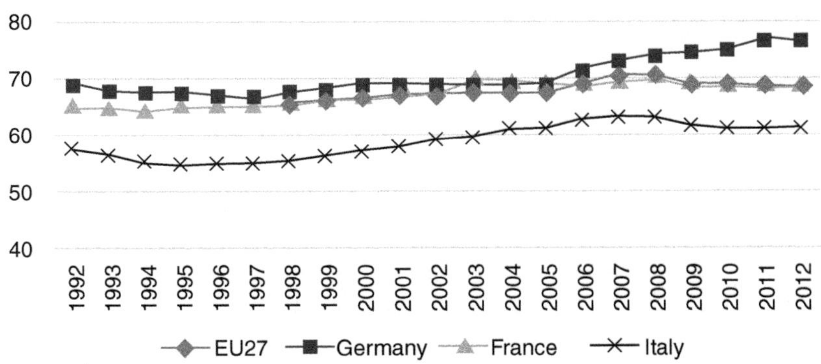

Figure 6.19 Employment trends (source: own elaboration on Eurostat data).

were lacking, industrial production was stagnant or declining, the advanced technological sector was almost inexistent and therefore the Italian economy lost competitiveness in comparison with the EU partners.

These low wages, often accompanied by insecurity, poor incentives and awards for employees, decreased the efforts and thus the efficiency of workers in the job places. The lower real wages, and thus the minimization of costs, rational behaviour on the part of the individual employer, did not lead to an increase in the productivity of the system or to an increased production. It led, on the contrary, to an increase in profits, which often are not converted into new investments, but on the contrary, increased dominant positions of some rent-seeking firms, and increased portfolio movements of speculators and investors. This allowed for accumulation of extra profits by firms, and worsened income distribution. However, the economic system has not had beneficial effects, and accordingly has not realized efficient situations in terms of productivity and economic growth.

The current crisis has only worsened the situation of the labour market and it is the final outcome of an economic decline that originated much earlier at least 15 years ago, as we originally claimed.

These sources are mainly marked by the attempt to introduce, in the early 1990s, a new economic and social model which changes industrial relations, reduces virtuous and automatic mechanisms of income distribution, compresses wages, and encourages firms to save income and to accumulate extra profits and rents rather than to invest in innovation. Furthermore, the State assumes, eventually, the burden of paying the cost of flexibility, as it has to guarantee to firms the freedom of fire and hire as they wish in a labour flexibility regime. This of course will result in an additional burden on the state budget. With the current recession, the first jobs to be cut and lost were flexible, that is, those which arrived at maturity of the contract or whose projects were not renewed, with damage to both employment (with an unemployment rate which has returned to levels of the early 1990s, that is around 10–12 per cent (Figure 6.20) and layoffs

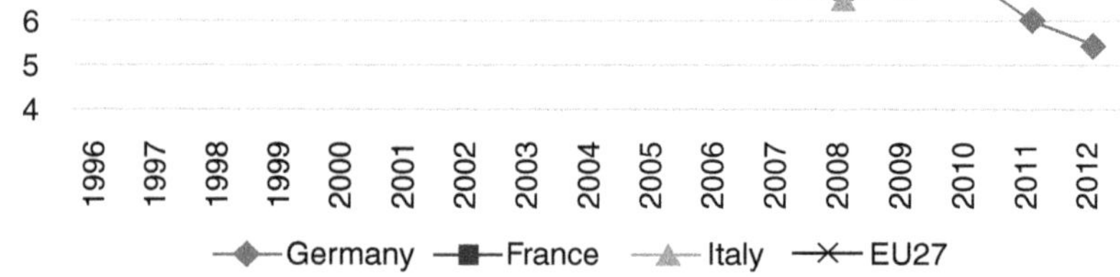

Figure 6.20 Unemployment trends (source: own elaboration on Eurostat data).

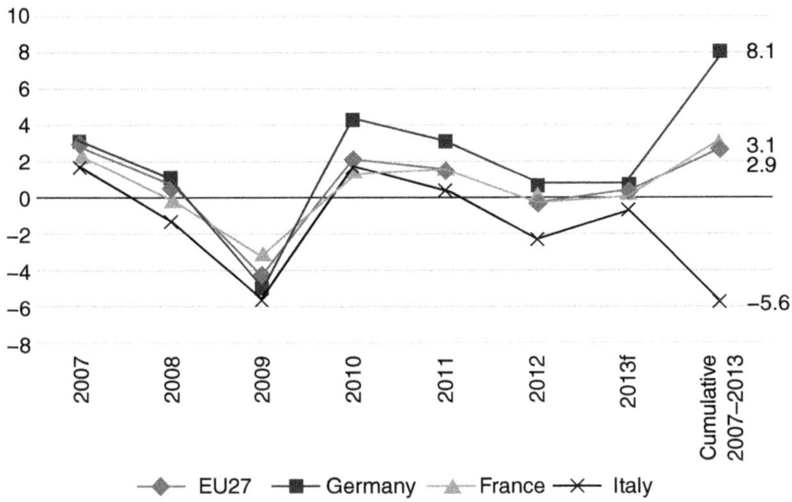

Figure 6.21 GDP performance during the crisis (source: own elaboration on Eurostat data. Forecast for 2013).

that will reach a total of 1 billion working hours lost at the end of 2012), and to income, with consumption levels down to those of 30 years ago.

In conclusion, the country seems plagued today by a triple negative combination: (1) low productivity, (2) low employment and (3) low dynamics of the GDP (Figure 6.21). That labour flexibility is not the right way to increase productivity and income has been announced several times by many Keynesian economists and beyond. However, the initial modest increase in employment was far more than offset by the low dynamics of labour productivity and by the stagnation of GDP even before the current crisis. Today there is a greater consensus among labour economists in particular that in the past 15 years labour policies and development policies were mostly neglected, not integrated and not targeting the same objectives, and this has led to an increase in rents from firms that have mainly exploited the low labour costs to remain competitive, rather than make investments and create innovation in order to increase labour productivity, which could then result in a more consistent GDP growth (Fadda, 2005). Firms, with the current crisis, lost even the benefit of cheap labour cost since they are still burdened by a relatively high taxation, and a continued decline in sales. Thus, in the current situation the economic system deals with low net wages (the lowest in the EU15) and lack of innovation and technology investments: the worst combinations according to one of the most significant Italian economists, who recently passed away, Sylos Labini, whose Keynesian approach would be very useful to Italy today.

6 Conclusion

I have argued, in this chapter, that the current crisis is the final step of a much longer decline which started after the recession 1992–1993. The decline is a consequence of institutional changes, policies and institutions implemented between the beginning of the 1990s and the beginning of the 2000s and which involved mainly labour market reforms (i.e. the 1993 July agreement and the introduction of labour flexibility) coupled with a partial privatization process, and an uncompleted and inefficient liberalization process. These policies and changes, which were mainly created in order to follow the Washington Consensus, to implement in Italy a very market-oriented economic model and to meet the Maastricht criteria, caused from one side income inequality, lower consumption, industrial decline and weaker aggregate demand. From another side they brought about lower productivity dynamics, since Italian firms implemented mainly labour intensive investments, trying to get advantages from cheaper (and flexible) labour and to reduce costs, without innovative investments. In the end, these two forces brought about economic decline and lower GDP dynamics, with a loss for the Italian GDP of more than 20 per cent in comparison with the average of the EU. Moreover, they cause today deeper recession and slower recovery in the current crisis in comparison to the main European economies.

An econometric exercise, for the period of the crisis (2007–12) confirms the expected results: among the 27 EU Member States, performance in terms of GDP growth and labour market is negatively affected by variables such as inequality index, labour flexibility (EPL) and temporary work, which are clearly consequences of labour policies and income distribution institutions.

Notes

1 An earlier version of this chapter was published in the *International Journal of Applied Economics*.

2 A similar work was done, for a panel, and for the 27 EU members all together during the period 2007–2011 by Tridico (2012b). That model included also control variables and produced similar results.

References

Amoroso, B. and Jespersen, J. (2012), *L'Europa oltre l'Euro. Le ragioni del disastro economico e la ricostruzione del progetto comunitario*, Firenze: Castelvecchi.

Banca d'Italia (2012), *Bollettino Economico* no. 70, October 2012.

Barba, A. and Pivetti, M. (2009), Rising Household Debt: Its Causes and Macroeconomic Implications: Along-Period Analysis, *Cambridge Journal of Economics*, 33(1): 113–137.

Blanchard, O. and Giavazzi, F. (2003), Macroeconomic Effects of Regulation and Deregulation in Goods and Labour Markets, *Quarterly Journal of Economics*: 118(3): 879–906.

Boyer, R. (2009), Come conciliare la solidarietà sociale e l'efficienza economica nell'era della globalizzazione: un punto di vista regolazioni sta, *Argomenti*, 1(gennaio/maggio): 5–31.

Brancaccio, E. and Fontana, G. (2011), The Global Economic Crisis (Introduction), in E. Brancaccio and G. Fontana (eds) *The Global Economic Crisis: New Perspective on The Critique of Economic Theory and Policy*, London: Routledge.

Cazes, S., Boeri, T. and Bertola, G. (1999), Employment Protection and Labour Market Adjustment in OECD Countries: Evolving Institutions and Variable Enforcement, ILO Employment and Training Papers, 48.

CNEL (2007), *Liberalizzazioni e Privatizzazioni*, Roma.

Draghi, M. (2007), *Relazione annuale della Banca d'Italia*, Rome.

Eurostat (2012), Structural Indicators, online database, at URL: http://epp.eurostat.ec.europa.eu/portal/page/portal/europe_2020_indicators/headline_indicators.

Fadda, S. (2005), Per una integrazione tra politiche del lavoro e politiche di sviluppo, *Argomenti*, 14/2005.

Fadda, S. (2009), La riforma della contrattazione. Un rischio e una proposta circa il secondo livello, *Nel Merito.com, Relazioni industriali* – 19 giugno.

Fadda, S. (2012), Salari e produttività: una relazione complessa, *Nel Merito.com, Lavoro* – 2 marzo.

Fitoussi, J.P. (2005), Macroeconomic Policies and Institutions, *Rivista di Politica Economica*, Novembre–Dicembre (Settima Lezione 'Angelo Costa', 19 Gennaio 2006).

Fitoussi, J.P. and Saraceno, F. (2010), Inequality and Macroeconomic Performance, OFCE/POLHIA no. 2010-13, Paris, 13.

Fitoussi, J.P. and Stiglitz, J. (2009), The Ways Out of The Crisis and the Building of a More Cohesive World, The Shadow GN, Chair's Summary, LUISS Guido Carli, Rome, 6–7 May.

Gallino, L. (2003), *La scomparsa dell'Italia industriale*, Torino: Einaiudi.

ILO (2010), Global Wage Report 2010/11, *Wage Policies in Time of Crisis*, Geneva.

IMF (2012), International Monetary Fund, World Economic Outlook online Database, October, at URL: www.imf.org/external/pubs/ft/weo/2012/02/weodata/index.aspx.

Istat (2010), Conti ed aggregati economici delle Amministrazioni Pubbliche *SEC95* – Anni 1980–2009.

Kleinknecht, A. and Naastepad, C.W.M. (2005), The Netherlands: Failure of a Neoclassical Policy Agenda, *European Planning Studies*, 13(8): 1193–1203.

Kleinknecht, A., Naastepad, C.W.M. and Storm, S. (2013), Labour Market Rigidities Can Be Useful. A Schumpeterian View, in S. Fadda and P. Tridico (eds), *Financial Crisis, Labour Market and Institutions*, London: Routledge.

Kleinknecht, A., Oostendorp, M.N., Pradhan, M.P. and Naastepad, C.W.M. (2006), Flexible Labour, Firm Performance and the Dutch Job Creation Miracle, *International Review of Applied Economics*, 20(2): 171–187.

Kok Report (2004), *Facing the Challenge: The Lisbon Strategy for Employment and Growth*, Report from The High Level Group, chaired by Wim Kok, Office for Official Publications of the European Communities, Luxembourg.

Levrero, E.S. and Stirati, A. (2005), Distribuzione del reddito e prezzi relativi in Italia 1970–2002, *Politica economica – Rivista di studi e ricerche per la politica economica*, 3/2005, 401–434.

Lilla, M. (2005), Disuguaglianze salariali in Italia: nuove evidenze dai microdati SHIW, *Politica economica – Rivista di studi e ricerche per la politica economica*, 1/2005, 71–102.

Lucidi, F. (2006), *Is There a Trade-off Between Labour Flexibility and Productivity Growth? Preliminary Evidence from Italian Firms*, Università di Roma La Sapienza, mimeo.

Miniaci, R. and Weber, G. (1999), The Italian Recession of 1993: Aggregate Implications of Microeconomic Evidence, *Review of Economics and Statistics*, 81(2): 237–249.

Nardozzi, G. (2004), *Miracolo e declino. L'Italia tra concorrenza e protezione*, Roma-Bari: Laterza.

Nickell, S. (2008), Unemployment and Labor Market Rigidities: Europe versus North America, *Journal of Economic Perspectives*, 11(3): 55–74.

OECD (2008), *Employment Outlook*, Paris.

OECD (2012), *Economic Outlook*, online statistics at: http://stats.oecd.org/.

Penn World Table 7.1 (2012), Database of the Center for International Comparisons of Production, Income and Prices University of Pennsylvania.

Rodrik, D. (2004), *Rethinking Growth Policies in the Developing World.* Cambridge, MA: Harvard University Press.

Rodrik, D. (2008), *One Economics, Many Recipes: Globalization, Institutions, and Economic Growth*, New York and London: W.W. Norton.

Rossi, F. and Sestito, P. (2000), Contrattazione aziendale, struttura negoziale e determinazione decentrata del salario, *Rivista di Politica Economica*, Ottobre–Novembre, pp. 129–184.

Salop, S. (1979), A Model of the Natural Rate of Unemployment, *American Economic Review*, 69(1): 117–125.

Shapiro, C. and Stiglitz, J. (1984), Equilibrium Unemployment as a Worker Discipline Device, *The American Economic Review*, 74(3): 433–444.

Stockhammer, E. (2013), Financialization, Income Distribution and the Crisis, in S. Fadda and P. Tridico (eds), *Financial Crisis, Labour Market and Institutions*, London: Routledge.

Sylos Labini, P. (1993), *Progresso tecnico e sviluppo ciclico*, Bari: Laterza.

Sylos Labini, P. (1999), The Employment Issues: Investment, Flexibility and The Competition of Developing Countries, *BNL Quarterly Review*, 52(210): 257–280.

Sylos Labini, P. (2003), Le prospettive dell'economia mondiale, *Moneta e Credito*, 56(223): 267–295.

Tarantelli, E. (1995), *La forza delle idee. Scritti di economia e politica*, Roma-Bari: Laterza.

Torrini, R. (2005), Quota dei profitti e redditività del capitale in Italia: un tentativo di interpretazione, *Temi di Discussione*, no. 551, Banca d'Italia, Roma.

Tridico, P. (2009), Flessibilità e istituzioni nel mercato del lavoro: dagli economisti classici agli economisti istituzionalisti, *Economia & Lavoro*, 43(1): 113–139.

Tridico, P. (2012a), Financial Crisis and Global Imbalance: Its Labor Market Origins and the Aftermath, *Cambridge Journal of Economics*, 36(1): 17–42.

Tridico, P. (2012b), The Impact of the Economic Crisis on the EU Labour Larket: A Comparative Perspective, *Working Papers* no. 153, Department of Economics, University 'Roma Tre', Rome.

Tronti, L. (2005), Protocollo di luglio e crescita economica: l'occasione perduta, *Rivista Internazionale di Scienze Sociali*, 2.

Tronti, L. and Ceccato, F. (2005), Il Lavoro atipico in Italia: caratteristiche, diffusione e dinamica, *Argomenti*, 14.

Williamson, J. (1990), What Washington Means by Policy Reform, in J. Williamson (ed.), *Latin American Adjustment: How Much Has Happened?* Washington DC: Institute for International Economics.

Part II

Exit perspectives and development strategies

7 Should we cut the welfare state in order to get out of the crisis?

Some methodological considerations

Sebastiano Fadda

Introduction

Nearly all the recommendations concerning the structural reforms needed to 'overcome the crisis' that come from EU officials, when not explicitly mentioning the cutting down of social expenditure, are patent euphemisms for the same concept. The endless repetitions of the need to cut the welfare state down to size have become so insistent and pervasive that they have nearly reached the status of a self-evident truth about which no discussions or questions seem to be allowed.

The downsizing is advocated for social expenditure as a whole, and therefore it concerns all public programmes regarding health, education and training, housing, unemployment benefits, old age, maternity, invalidity, family allowances and so on in all of the three forms that they may take: income transfers; benefits in kind through the provision of personal and social services; price subsidies for some goods and services.

The attitudes towards such programmes may be considered rooted in three different general cultural orientations (Esping Andersen 1990) which still are relevant in shaping the structure of the welfare state: the liberal one (which advocates the minimum involvement of the government in welfare programmes considered only as a residual for desperate situations); the 'corporatist' (which is founded on a contributory basis involving employers and employees); the social democratic (based on a universal provision of income transfer and welfare services). Onto this typology, the typology developed by Titmus may be projected, which specifies three different targets of the welfare systems: the first is merely to cover residual cases, the second is to help the achievement of industrial efficiency, and the third is to implement a redistribution in order to give capitalism a human face. More recent studies (Pontusson 2005) simplify the typology into two broad categories: 'social market economies' and 'liberal market economies'. Notwithstanding this variety of cultures and typologies (which may be further differentiated in more detail), the pressure towards a general reduction of the welfare state seems to affect all of them on the grounds that this is not only a condition to get out of the present crisis but also a condition to improve general economic performance.

The claims about the necessity, not to say the inevitability, of cutting down the welfare state must, nevertheless, be put under discussion and the alleged reasons in favour of this policy must be passed under close scrutiny. The alleged reasons can be grouped into three arguments. First: due to heavy public debt, such welfare expenditures have become unsustainable; second: in the context of globalization, high levels of social expenditure are detrimental to competitiveness; third: welfare systems are as such inefficient by their nature and in most cases also ineffective. Let's consider separately each of these arguments.

1 Budget unsustainability

Whether public expenditure on welfare is sustainable under budget constraints (which are becoming more stringent for European countries given the various fiscal, six and two packs that have been imposed onto them) is a question that cannot be solved only by having knowledge of the budget constraints. As everybody can see, facing the problem of sustainability of social expenditure implies at the same time facing the problem of sustainability of any other public expenditure with which social expenditure is in competition for alternative use of scarce budgetary resources. Public expenditure for defence, or for industrial policy, or for physical infrastructures are under the same budget constraints. In addition to the budget constraints, a kind of (explicit or implicit) preference function must be known in order to make efficient choices about the allocation of the available resources; i.e. to determine the internal composition of public expenditure. In fact the problem is two-faced: one is connected to the ratio of social spending to public expenditure, the other is connected to the ratio of public expenditure to GDP.

In any case, what should be considered as the maximum level of public expenditure allowed by the budget constraint is an open question. The EU parameters and the stability pact do not fix a limit to the absolute level of public expenditure: they simply set a limit to the ratio of public debt or public deficit to GNP. It's obvious that this ratio can be respected whatever the level of public expenditure provided that the fiscal revenue be set accordingly. Therefore this question turns into the one of what level of taxation can be bared against the provision of goods and services by the state. And this is a problem we shall deal with later on.

A conventional way of setting the budget constraint for welfare expenditure is to adopt a maximum ratio between that and GNP. Social expenditure should not exceed, say, 25 per cent of GNP; obviously, exceeding this limit while at the same time respecting a constant ratio of total public expenditure to GNP and keeping constant the fiscal revenue would be possible only at the price of reducing other categories of public expenditure. If this choice were made, the growth of social expenditure would still be sustainable.

Nevertheless, establishing a particular ratio of social expenditure to GNP as a guideline for the size of welfare expenditure, looks as a job to be both arbitrary and full of ambiguities. Consider two countries which have substantial differences in per capita income: if the same quota of GNP were devolved to social expenditure this would result in a very different amount of social expenditure in absolute terms in the two countries. On the other hand, a same amount of per capita social spending would result in a higher share of welfare expenditure in the country with lower per capita income. Should we conclude that the lower income country is spending 'too much' on welfare, or that the higher income country is spending 'too little'? It is clear how this ambiguity can throw substantial doubts on some conclusions drawn from rough international comparisons of such data. Such comparisons do, however, show a great variety of ratios of welfare expenditure to GNP.[1] Which one should be adopted as a guideline?

We can make two main conclusions. First: that setting a limit to public expenditure as a percentage of GNP is an arbitrary choice based on a political decision about how much of goods and services is to be produced by market forces and how much is to be provided by the state through taxation once a maximum level of indebtedness is endogenously or exogenously established. Second: that such a limit, once set, is not sufficient to determine the size of social expenditure: the share of this in the internal composition of public expenditure depends again on the set of preferences of the policy makers. Therefore, given some objective factors which may cause an increase in social needs (such as the ageing of the population, the increasing life expectancy, the increase in long-term unemployment, the growing inequality in income distribution), and given a maximum ratio of public expenditure to GDP, whether this will lead to an increase in social expenditure or to a decrease in per capita social services depends on the set of values and preferences of the policy makers. These preferences are indeed at the base of the internal composition of public expenditure. One more observation should be added. Given the elasticity of social needs to the cycle,[2] the ratio of social expenditure to GNP could well show counter-cyclical behaviour; which would mean that, on one hand, social expenditure would act as an automatic stabilizer but, on the other, that an unbearable strain could be put on public budgets in the downturn of the cycle.[3] This dynamic, though, is not possible anymore under the rules of the recent European fiscal compact, which acts in itself as an automatic de-stabilizer.

2 Globalization and competitiveness

The second argument is based on the problem of competitiveness in the frame of globalization.[4] It is argued that the welfare state as such (and not by virtue of its inefficiency or ineffectiveness) is a cause of loss of international competitiveness, because the resources employed for its financing could be better left in private hands to be used for productive investments. Besides, the corresponding lowering of taxation and fiscal wedge would allow for a reduction of unit costs of production, for the benefit of international price competition. In the first place, one could object that a similar lowering of taxation could be obtained by a reduction in other categories of public expenditure and that the reduction of social services may exert a strong pressure towards wage increases which could counterbalance the supposed original reduction in unit costs of production. But more severe objections can be raised.

First of all, competitiveness is a relative concept. That means that if one country adopts such measures of downsizing the welfare state in order to get an advantage through a kind of 'social dumping' it is okay, but if all the countries adopt the same measures the competitive advantage fully disappears, the relative conditions of countries remain the same and all of them are simply left with a lower degree of social protection. By the way, trying to gain competitiveness through these measures could have the side effect of a negative incentive towards engaging in gaining competitiveness by increasing productivity through investments in innovation. But these measures could have another serious drawback. In the long run, all the saving in social expenditure could be offset by an increase in costs due to the loss in social cohesion, political stability, social capital and also human capital. Worth considering in this regard is the concept of 'guard labour' put forward by Jayadev and Bowles (2006). Their idea is that the loss of social cohesion, the increase in social conflict and political instability due to cuts in social security would require a great amount of labour devoted to keep law and order and to the maintenance of social rules and institutional stability. So what seems to be gained by reducing the social spending is subsequently lost by spending for those goals.

Finally, as a matter of fact, the empirical evidence does not show a negative correlation between level of social protection and economic performance; in many cases, such as Sweden, Denmark and the Low Countries, there is a strong positive relationship.[5] It can be added that the 'size' of the social expenditure is not the right variable to regress against the economic performance: it is its structure, not its size, that is the most influential factor, supposing anyway that a causal relation can be ascertained. Identical sizes of social expenditure may come out of a high level of average benefits and a low number of recipients or vice versa, and substantially different kinds of conditional qualifications may be required for accessing the benefits, and the contingencies towards which the benefits are directed may also be very different. All these will produce different impacts on the economic performance even if the size of expenditure is the same.

Another fundamental aspect must be emphasized in this regard. By now the doubt is widespread about the ability of the level of GDP to represent the degree of 'economic performance'. It would suffice to adopt some indicators of social wellness in an algorithm devised to weigh the traditional indicators of GDP (for instance, using the Gini coefficients to correct the measure of GDP, as Maddison (2003) did following the Sen (1976) suggestion, or taking account of the European Social Indicators approved by the European Council of Laeken 2001[6]) in order to have a radical change in the terms of the problem and obtain (almost by definition) an immediate positive relationship between social protection and GDP. Perhaps this is the fundamental cultural change that is needed in order to frame properly the relationship between welfare state and economic performance.

3 The 'inefficiency' of the welfare state

This problem has to be split in two parts. The first is the one of consistency with the allocative efficiency of the free market; the second is related to the internal efficiency of the system in terms of cost minimization.

As for the first problem, let's have no doubts: the welfare state is a plain violation of the allocative mechanism of the market. In fact, it consists of the use of political and administrative power in order to modify the working of the market mechanism for the sake of achieving three goals: (1) to ensure a minimum level of income to individuals and families independently of their position in the market; (2) to insure individual and families against some fundamental risks, such as illness, old age, invalidity and unemployment; (3) to provide all citizens, without any discrimination based on income or social position, the best quality of an agreed set of social services.[7] Clearly, a reduction of the welfare state would be unavoidable in the presence of at least one of the following conditions: (1) if the above set of goals was no longer considered valid; (2) if public programmes were unable per se to achieve those goals; (3) if those goals could be achieved at lower costs by private initiatives.

Having said this, let's consider the general perspective of 'forcing' and violating the market mechanism in order to achieve those goals. Usually this perspective is justified with the existence of market failures relatively to public goods, merit wants, externalities, increasing returns to scale, information asymmetries and income distribution issues. Nevertheless, two problems of great relevance still seem to be in support of relying totally on the market mechanism: the first is the one of public sector failures; the second is the negative impact on the freedom of choice of individuals and on the labour supply.

In fact, the answer of the public sector to market failures cannot be considered satisfactory in absolute terms. Several factors have to be evaluated and checked in operative terms to establish empirically whether the violation of the market mechanism leads to satisfactory results. Bureaucratic inefficiency of public monopolies, negative 'internalities', adverse selection and moral hazard, agency problems, and flaws in the process of decision making for public choices are some of the elements to be considered in this regard. The devastating role of opportunistic behaviour of 'agents' against the 'principal' is particularly visible in the public health sector as in other sectors linked to direct provision of social services. The extension of the so called 'X inefficiency' is also under everybody's eyes. Nevertheless, it is surely possible to implement institutional devices capable of reducing, if not eliminating altogether, these phenomena. The use of 'vouchers', the introduction of systems of 'regulated competition' within a frame of integration between public and private, effective mechanisms of control and quality evaluation are all possible measures to cope with those failures of the public sector. Therefore, the existence of such failures cannot be considered a valid argument against the welfare state, but rather a valid argument against the inefficient and often corrupted management of the public sector by public managers and politicians.

The second problem is that of restricting the freedom of choice of individual consumers through a strong 'paternalistic' role of the state and that of a negative impact on labour supply and individual initiative and effort. As Marsland (1994) puts it, the welfare state, even if fiscal sustainability were granted, 'is fraudulent in itself, because it has from the beginning deceived the people into expecting something for nothing, as of right'. Actually, talking about 'consumer's sovereignty' as opposite to state paternalism looks rather like telling tales, since 'consumer's sovereignty' exists only in textbooks and not in reality. Freedom of choice is always constrained by the production decisions of both public and private sectors. To a great extension this problem reduces itself to a question of 'degree' and of flexibility of the intervention of public programmes.

As for the negative effect of welfare state on the labour supply, it has now become almost commonplace to state that unemployment benefits or any kind of income support have the effect of reducing the supply of labour and inviting people to live on subsidies rather than engage in productive activity. To begin with, it should be noted that at the present time the problem in the labour market is not one of supply but rather one of demand; nevertheless if we think that labour supply is a function not only of wages but also of non-labour income and wealth, it is beyond doubt that increasing the latter would reduce labour supply. But this may be considered true only if the income effect is not offset by the substitution effect and if subsidies are not accompanied by conditionalities linked to full participation in programmes of active labour policy. It is certainly true that according to the job search models, the acceptance of a job proposal may be delayed if the cost of waiting is lowered, but the provision of income subsidies could, through a coordinated system of active labour policies, turn this effect into an advantage by allowing a better allocation of human resources and supporting a high degree of flexibility in the labour market, useful for restructuring the productive system in order to improve productivity and competitiveness. The well known models of 'flexicurity' may be considered able to catch this opportunity.

A general problem that has to be considered in regard to these aspects is the one of the extension of the access to welfare services. The question is whether to make the welfare provisions universally available to everybody or to restrict them on the basis of some kind of 'means test'. It may be thought that a universal access to social services of good quality, although able to grant all citizens a basic standard of life, is unable to counterbalance the income inequality, while an access discriminated on the basis of the level of income would be more coherent with this target. In fact, the means test criterion seems to be the favourite at the present time, since it is widely applied to several services, such as education in universities, kindergartens, medical services and so on.[8] The above statement is surely based on elements of truth, but paradoxically it must be admitted that discrimination of access on the basis of individual income could turn into a stronger negative incentive towards the supply of labour and the individual effort in economic activity. In addition, it may become a positive incentive towards fiscal fraud and would reveal itself to be absolutely meaningless in those contexts in which fiscal fraud and fiscal evasion are so widespread as to render completely unreliable the income database on which the access discrimination would be based. On the opposite side, if the fiscal weight were correctly distributed on the basis of real incomes and if the universal social services were totally financed by the tax revenue, a counterbalance of the unequal income distribution would automatically occur by the fact that the different users of the same services would contribute differently to their financing due to the different individual levels of taxation.[9]

We can conclude that the validity of the goals assumed by the welfare state is not undermined by the above objections. The remaining two questions have to be explored. First: are social programmes still able to achieve the goals set for the welfare state? If the State cannot reach those goals, a reform of the welfare state becomes necessary, particularly when the social expenditure shows an increasing trend. The first thing to do in order to verify whether this situation occurs is to clearly define the precise set of goals to be attributed to the welfare state. The definition of the welfare state given at the beginning of this chapter is too generic; in fact it is exactly what 'risks' are to be covered and what fundamental services are to be provided that has to be established. Surely it is not possible to cover everything 'from cradle to grave'; a selection must be made, and in doing this it's necessary to avoid the mistake of attributing to welfare those expenditures which are needed for achieving the fundamental objectives of economic policy, that is economic growth, full employment, price stability and balance of payment equilibrium. Public expenditures devoted to the achievement of these goals are directed exactly at avoiding those 'states of nature' which require the provision of social services, and therefore it would be meaningless to compute them as 'social expenditure'. Once the set of goals has been clearly defined, an evaluation must be made about the degree of their achievement. This is what belongs to the 'effectiveness' aspect of the welfare state, which should be constantly put under monitoring in order to implement a reform of the system (quite independently of its fiscal sustainability), whose result could well imply either a reduction or an increase of the expenditure.

The second question is whether those goals of the welfare state can be achieved privately by the free market at lower cost. The choice between direct provision of social services by the state and relying on market solutions seems at present to be shifting in favour of market solutions, particularly with regard to coverage of the risk of illness, invalidity, old age and unemployment. Private insurances seem to be a good substitute for social services. But this solution has to cope with two severe drawbacks. The first is the weakness of paying demand for some services which are to be considered nevertheless socially relevant and desirable. This demand is strongly influenced by income distribution, and the building of a sufficient demand would probably require almost unrealistic redistributions of income. On the other hand, on the supply side, it is doubtful whether these sectors would provide rates of returns high enough to attract private investments. With reference to this last aspect, a second problem crops up: adverse selection and discrimination in the choice of individuals for whom to accept to cover the risks. Obviously, older people would be discriminated against in health insurance, and some other categories of people would be discriminated in other areas. It is true that some solutions to this problem could be envisaged along the lines of the Dutch experience: making insurance compulsory for all citizens and at the same time imposing on all insurance companies not to make any discrimination on any basis, be it health, age, level of income or whatever else. This would certainly ensure a universal coverage and would eliminate the problem of adverse selection. But one should wonder what the difference is between a similar system, in which the financing of the insurance is imposed onto all the citizens through a compulsory insurance contract of a private nature, and the welfare system in which the financing of the insurance is also compulsorily imposed onto all the same citizens through tax payments. If the fiscal system was fair and efficient, the public 'insurance' of the welfare state would clearly be preferable because the weight of financing it would be more equally distributed among the individuals in a way proportional to the individual levels of income. But even in the case of unfair fiscal systems joined with high rates of fiscal evasion, the private choice should not be preferred because it would generate a double distortion. A preference for the private system would be justified only if under this system the cost of providing the same services should be lower. And here another problem comes to the fore: are the private providers of such services more successful than the public sector at minimizing the unit costs of production?

4 The unit costs of social services

Actually, there are no reasons to believe that the provision of social services by the private sector is always able to minimize the cost of production in comparison to the provision by the public sector. On the other hand, there are no reasons either to believe the opposite.[10] The empirical evidence seems to show that the key role in this comparison is played not by the nature (public or private) of the provider, but by the degree of competition in the sector. The degree of competition is an element of the institutional set up. The institutional set up, in turn, is the whole of the formal and informal rules that shape the behaviour of economic agents and that therefore influence the level of productivity and consequently the cost of production of social services. All this plays an important role, because it is, after all, the unit costs of welfare services that determine the quantity and quality of the services that can be provided for a given size of welfare expenditure, or, alternatively, determine the size of welfare expenditure needed for a given quantity and quality of services. As everybody knows, different countries show huge differences in these variables and in these conditions. Still, the control of unit costs of production of welfare services is the first variable to be considered when thinking about reforming the welfare system and is preliminary to any evaluation of fiscal sustainability of social expenditure.

The increase of the degree of competition, both among public structures and among public and private sectors, is thus the first element which would favour the reduction of the unit costs of production of social services. Nowadays, growing connections between rent-seeking politicians and rent-seeking civil servants are bound to make this process increasingly difficult; in addition, the usual attitudes of bureaucrats push towards a strengthening of monopolistic power; finally most privatization processes have turned to be a simple transfer from public monopolies to private monopolies with no effect on the liberalization of the markets. When this happens, the growth of welfare expenditure in most cases has nothing to do with providing more or better services, but is simply a way of financing structures and bodies whose only goal is to keep themselves alive and enjoy monopolistic rents.

If competition is the most influential factor in regard to the efficiency in the provision of welfare services, the second one is the managerial capability of the public administration personnel. The typical objective elements which are at the basis of the so called 'X inefficiency' of the public administration are often strengthened by the lack of managerial ability and organizational capacity of individuals and institutions. There is a strong correlation between the lack of these capacities and the performance of the welfare systems, as can be seen through a comparison of different countries. When this happens, quantity and quality of welfare services on one side and welfare expenditure on the other are bound to move perversely in opposite directions: the increase of the latter is paralleled by a decrease of the former. The productivity growth and the consequent reduction of unit costs of social services does not depend entirely on the provision of good institutional architecture shaped by clever 'institutional designers'; it also depends on the behavioural patterns of the agents, on the culture and training of the civil servants, on the criteria adopted by the evaluation activity (in the cases in which it takes place). Therefore a great need and a great opportunity emerges in this regard for all the possible programmes and initiatives directed at 'capacity building', particularly in those countries where such deficiency is at the root of the inefficiency of the welfare system.

5 Another problem...

At this point we can draw the conclusion that none of the arguments in favour of a reduction of the welfare state holds true: not the budget sustainability, nor the competitiveness argument, nor the inefficiency one. But this is not the end of the story. Supposing that the best allocation of public expenditure has been reached and that perfect efficiency rules the provision of social services, a great question remains open: how far are taxpayers ready to pay for the financing of the welfare state? This is a quite different problem from that of international competitiveness or budget sustainability; it deals with sustainability of the fiscal burden from the point of view of the citizens taxpayers. Once admitted (and some reservations can be raised about this) that public indebtedness has to be reduced in order to overcome the financial and real economic crisis, the extent to which this impacts on the welfare expenditure is mediated in the first place by the internal composition of the public expenditure. Appropriate redistributions among its components might avoid the need to cut social expenditure. Obviously, as it has been said, such decisions are strictly dependent on the set of preferences of the policy makers, or of the citizens if they are perfectly represented, and therefore belong to the field of political choices. Political choices could also decide to cut social expenditures even if no reduction in public expenditure and in public indebtedness was required, just with the aim of redistributing the budget to the advantage of other categories of expenditure on the basis of value judgements about the relative importance of them. But once the availability of resources for social expenditure is determined within a given budget, new resources could be raised through increasing taxation. And here comes the point: how much are people willing to pay for the financing of the welfare state? This depends to a large extent on the prevailing culture and set of values, and it cannot be denied that at the present time the pressing of politicians of most influential countries in the European Union and the pressing of international financial institutions and corporations has shifted the public opinion rather against the welfare state, but there are three other factors relevant in determining this willingness: one is the income distribution and the distribution of the fiscal burden, the second is the perceived degree of fairness and effectiveness of social expenditure, and the third is the perceived degree of efficiency in the production of social services. Acting along these lines is necessary in order to make socially acceptable the financing of the welfare state without cutting it down to size. The advocated 'reforms' of the welfare state, instead of being a 'euphemism' for its reduction, should be interpreted as moves towards improvements in these three factors. In fact the first factor implies a move towards a reduction of income inequality and towards reform of the fiscal system in order to avoid fiscal evasion and to obtain a more equal distribution of fiscal pressure. The second factor implies steps towards cancelling those distortions in the access, distribution and use of social services that betray the goals of the welfare state and have negative effects on the working of the economy. The third factor implies actions in order to eliminate all waste in the production of social services due both to involuntary inefficiency and to voluntary twisting of the process of production as a result of rent-seeking behaviour.

6 In place of conclusion

Four main general conclusions can be drawn from the above considerations. First, the cost of the welfare state could be reduced to a certain extent without reducing the quantity and quality of the services through significant improvements in the efficiency of their production. Second, the increasing demand for social services due to the above mentioned objective factors could be partially met through the gains obtained with the improvements in efficiency. Third, the residual demand whose satisfaction would imply an increase in social expenditure could be financed through a change in the internal composition of the public expenditure. Fourth, the remaining possible increase in public expenditure could be financed through an increase in the fiscal revenue subject to the condition that the three factors mentioned in the previous paragraph are adequately dealt with.

These four conclusions, coupled with the lack of validity of the three main arguments in favour of downsizing the welfare state that have been previously discussed, lead me to say that, contrary to popular opinion, cutting down the welfare system is not necessary either for getting out of the crisis or for improving economic performance. This is not to say that reforms are not needed; on the contrary, they are a must precisely in order to avoid cutting down the welfare system, which, as it has been suggested (Aiginger 2008), would be able to foster growth and improve the economic performance if substantial institutional changes were implemented to increase its effectiveness and its efficiency. The main reforms should consist of measures to increase effectiveness and reduce unit costs of social services; but the lack of such reforms (due to resistance of institutional nature) actually nurtures the mental, or ideological, attitude against the welfare state.

Appendix

Annex 7.1 Government social spending: total public social expenditure as a percentage of GDP

	2005	*2006*	*2007*	*2008*	*2009*	*2010*	*2011*	*2012*	*2013*
Australia	16.5	16.5	16.4	17.8	17.8	17.9	18.2	18.8	19.5
Austria	27.1	26.8	26.3	26.8	29.1	28.9	27.9	27.9	28.3
Belgium	26.5	26.0	26.0	27.3	29.7	29.5	29.7	30.5	30.7
Canada	16.9	16.9	16.8	17.6	19.2	18.7	18.1	18.1	18.2
Chile	10.1	9.3	9.4	9.6	11.3	10.8	10.4	10.2	
Czech Republic	18.7	18.3	18.1	18.1	20.7	20.8	20.8	21.0	21.8
Denmark	27.7	27.1	26.5	26.8	30.2	30.6	30.6	30.8	30.8
Estonia	13.1	12.7	12.7	15.8	20.0	20.1	18.2	17.6	17.7
Finland	26.2	25.8	24.7	25.3	29.4	29.6	29.2	30.0	30.5
France	30.1	29.8	29.7	29.8	32.1	32.4	32.0	32.5	33.0
Germany	27.3	26.1	25.1	25.2	27.8	27.1	25.9	25.9	26.2
Greece	21.1	21.3	21.6	22.2	23.9	23.3	24.4	24.1	22.0
Hungary	22.5	22.8	23.0	23.1	23.9	22.9	21.9	21.6	21.6
Iceland	16.3	15.9	15.3	15.8	18.5	18.0	18.1	17.6	17.2
Ireland	16.0	16.1	16.7	19.7	23.6	23.7	23.3	22.4	21.6
Israel	16.3	15.8	15.5	15.5	16.0	16.0	15.8	15.8	15.8
Italy	24.9	25.0	24.7	25.8	27.8	27.7	27.5	28.0	28.4
Japan	18.6	18.5	18.8	19.8	22.2	22.3			
Korea	6.5	7.5	7.7	8.4	9.6	9.2	9.1	9.3	
Luxembourg	22.8	21.8	20.3	20.8	23.6	23.0	22.6	23.2	23.4
Mexico	6.9	7.0	6.9	7.4	8.2	8.1	7.7	7.4	
Netherlands	20.7	21.7	21.1	20.9	23.2	23.4	23.4	24.0	24.3
New Zealand	18.1	18.9	18.6	19.8	21.2	21.3	21.4	22.0	22.4
Norway	21.6	20.3	20.5	19.8	23.3	23.0	22.4	22.3	22.9
Poland	21.0	20.8	19.7	20.3	21.5	21.8	20.5	20.6	20.9
Portugal	23.0	23.0	22.7	23.1	25.6	25.4	25.0	25.0	26.4
Slovak Republic	16.3	16.0	15.7	15.7	18.7	19.1	18.1	18.3	17.9
Slovenia	21.1	20.8	19.5	19.7	22.6	23.6	23.7	23.7	23.8
Spain	21.1	21.1	21.3	22.9	26.0	26.7	26.4	26.8	27.4
Sweden	29.1	28.4	27.3	27.5	29.8	28.3	27.6	28.1	28.6
Switzerland	20.3	19.3	18.6	18.5		20.6	19.5	18.8	19.1
Turkey	9.9	10.0	10.5	10.7	12.8				
United Kingdom	20.5	20.3	20.4	21.8	24.1	23.8	23.6	23.9	23.8
United States	16.0	16.1	16.3	17.0	19.2	19.8	19.6	19.7	20.0
OECD – Total	19.7	19.5	19.2	19.9	22.1	22.1	21.7	21.8	21.9

Source: own elaboration on OECD Social Expenditure Statistics (database).

Annex 7.2 Government social spending per head: total public social expenditure per head, at current prices and PPPs

	2003	*2004*	*2005*	*2006*	*2007*	*2008*	*2009*	*2010*
Australia	5,517.9	5,734.6	5,795.8	6,107.7	6,404.1	6957.4	7,130.6	7,288.5
Austria	8,647.4	9,019.8	9,129.9	9,791.1	9,996.2	10,643.8	11,308.1	
Belgium	8,041.9	8,265.0	8,544.8	8,912.7	9,271.4	10,103.3	10,912.0	
Canada	5,417.7	5,698.3	6,023.3	6,294.8	6,485.8	6,799.1	7,326.9	
Chile	1,261.4	1,249.1	1,275.5	1,283.0	1,372.8	1,477.7	1,740.7	1,733.3
Czech Republic	3,734.6	3,812.2	3,977.7	4,261.2	4,618.6	4,680.8	5,303.6	
Denmark	8,610.1	9,084.2	9,204.9	9,764.9	9,977.9	10,670.9	11,564.0	
Estonia	1,739.9	1,987.2	2,164.2	2,434.2	2,751.0	3,492.3	3,965.9	
Finland	7173.5	7784.2	8031.3	8544.5	8930.6	9642.4	10506.9	
France	8,178.4	8,480.4	8,902.5	9,377.0	9,845.9	10,169.2	10,799.5	
Germany	7,872.3	8,061.8	8,492.4	8,770.6	8,916.4	9,368.7	10,013.4	10,146.7
Greece	4,489.3	4,784.5	5,148.4	5,720.3	5,978.1	6,575.7	7,015.4	
Hungary	3,448.9	3,501.7	3,816.8	4,169.8	4,359.0	4,729.6	4,822.3	
Iceland	5,438.9	5,853.1	5,719.3	5,685.9	5,672.4	6,237.3	6,782.0	
Ireland	5,476.9	5,930.8	6,230.0	6,826.6	7,605.3	8,391.9	9,385.9	9,598.1
Israel	4,025.4	3,977.2	3,784.1	3,916.9	4,084.7	4,262.4	4,380.2	4,579.7
Italy	6,601.2	6,764.1	7,029.0	7,586.8	7,929.2	8,609.2	8,966.0	
Japan	5,027.6	5,329.0	5,709.2	5,943.7	6,286.7	6,589.2	7,209.2	
Korea	1,090.2	1,311.6	1,482.4	1,813.1	2,010.9	2,252.9	2,609.6	2,685.7
Luxembourg	13,956.2	15,279.9	15,593.7	17,121.9	17,156.4	18,573.9	19,555.8	
Mexico	734.4	760.6	862.2	957.6	999.1	1,134.8	1,183.1	1,227.5
Netherlands	6,749.5	7,053.2	7,279.5	8,275.5	8,614.6	8,953.9	9,525.5	
New Zealand	4,213.2	4,326.5	4,555.6	5,104.4	5,306.1	5,765.8	6,201.9	6,331.3
Norway	9,432.7	9,871.3	10,283.0	10,914.6	11,435.2	12,137.5	12,742.1	
Poland	2,672.5	2,783.7	2,898.3	3,131.7	3,300.0	3,655.1	4,070.2	
Portugal	4,274.7	4,408.0	4,923.9	5,271.3	5,499.6	5,759.2	6,371.9	
Slovak Republic	2,342.8	2,409.6	2,636.0	2,939.7	3,281.5	3,654.2	4,231.1	
Slovenia	4,426.4	4,726.0	4,953.0	5,297.5	5,312.5	5,736.2	6,130.5	
Spain	5,118.5	5,401.4	5,775.3	6,415.1	6,878.2	7,571.6	8,350.5	
Sweden	9,153.2	9,592.6	9,506.5	10,156.1	10,517.9	10,908.8	11,134.7	
Switzerland	6,725.6	6,973.5	7,187.5	7,550.2	7,958.3	8,436.6		
Turkey			1,124.7	1,293.2	1,460.9	1,606.1	1,851.1	
United Kingdom	6,001.8	6,538.9	6,837.0	7,136.3	7,287.2	7,744.3	8,365.9	
United States	6,127.1	6,398.9	6,700.0	7,101.1	7,471.5	7,894.0	8,713.3	9,204.1
OECD – Total	5,433.4	5,712.4	5,927.3	6,347.1	6,614.7	7,091.9	7,604.9	

Source: own elaboration on OECD Social Expenditure Statistics (database).

Annex 7.3 Total public expenditure as a percentage of GDP (average 2007–2012)

Low (below 40%)		*Medium (40%–49%)*		*High (50% and above)*	
Korea	30.5	Japan	40.1	Hungary	50.0
Switzerland	33.3	United States	40.5	Austria	51.0
Slovak Republic	37.8	Luxembourg	41.8	Greece	51.5
Estonia	39.3	Israel	42.6	Belgium	52.1
		Czech Republic	43.0	Sweden	52.2
		Norway	43.1	Finland	53.4
		Poland	43.5	France	55.3
		Spain	44.4	Denmark	55.9
		Germany	45.6		
		Slovenia	47.1		
		Ireland	47.1		
		United Kingdom	47.9		
		Portugal	47.9		
		Netherlands	49.1		
		Iceland	49.5		
		Italy	49.8		

Source: own elaboration on OECD database.

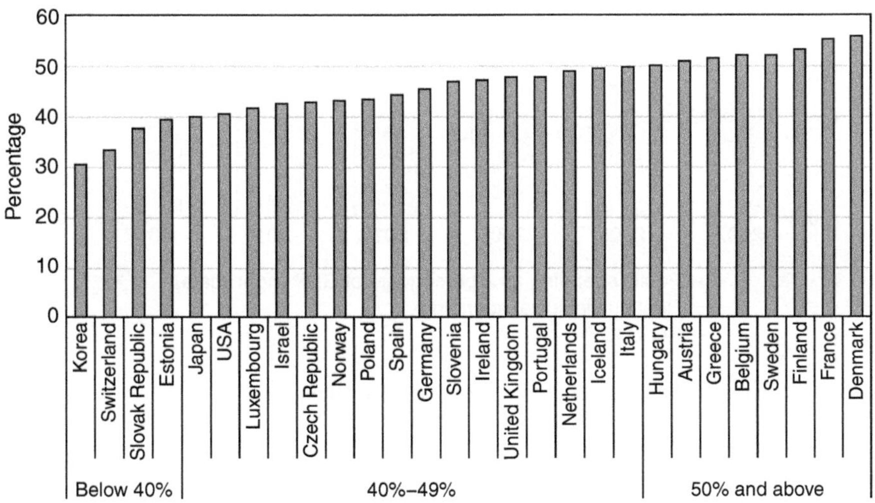

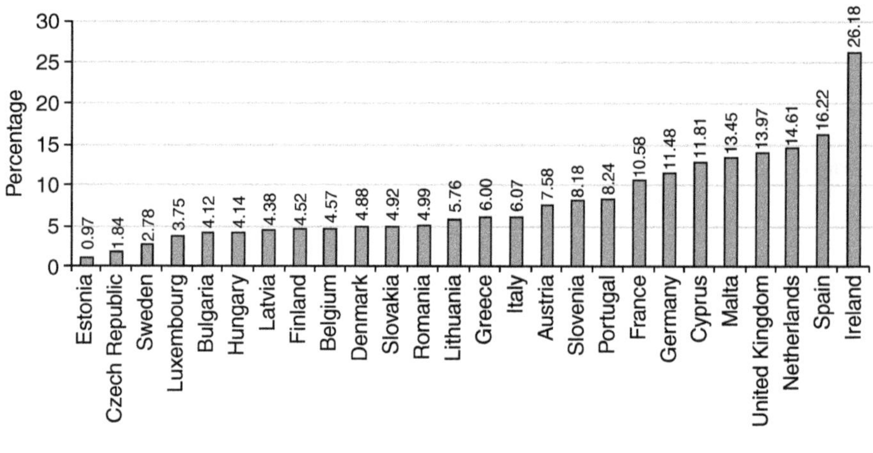

Annex 7.4 Means-tested social protection benefits as percentage of total social benefits – 2011 (source: own elaboration on Eurostat Statistical database).

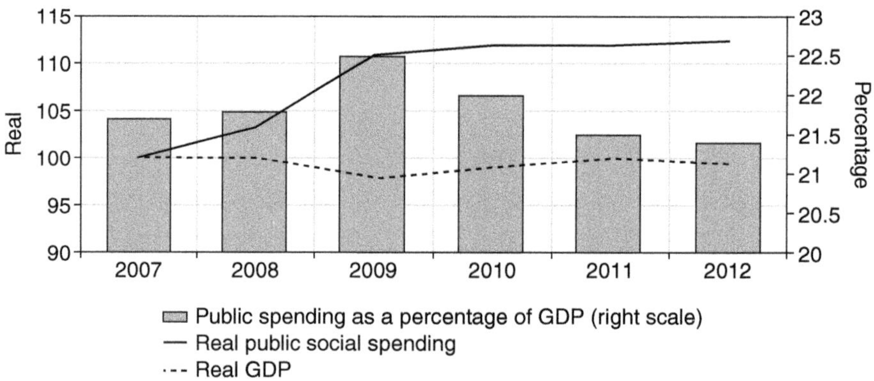

Annex 7.5 Real public social spending and real GDP (Index 100 in 2007) on the left axe; public social spending as a percentage of GDP on the right axe (source: own elaboration on OECD data).

Notes

1 For such comparisons see Annexes 7.1 and 7.2.
2 See Annex 7.5.
3 These aspects are explored to a great depth in Darby and Melitz (2008).
4 For a wider discussion about the impact of globalization on social expenditure, see Sykes *et al.* (2001) and Dreher *et al.* (2008).
5 See Sachs (2006: 42): 'On average, the Nordic countries outperform the Anglo-Saxon ones on most measures of economic performance. Poverty rates are much lower there, and national income per working-age population is on average higher.'
6 See, for details about these indicators, Atkinson *et al.* (2002).

7 The definition adopted by the OECD is:

> Social expenditure is the provision by public (and private) institutions of benefits to, and financial contributions targeted at, households and individuals in order to provide support during circumstances which adversely affect their welfare, provided that the provision of the benefits and financial contributions constitutes neither a direct payment for a particular good or service nor an individual contract or transfer. Such benefits can be cash transfers, or can be the direct ('in-kind') provision of goods and services. Social expenditure is 'unrequited': it does not include 'market transactions', i.e. payments in return for the simultaneous provision of services of equivalent value.
>
> (Glossary of statistical terms, OECD Statistical Portal)

8 For an idea of the percentage of the means-tested social benefits of total benefits see Annex 7.4.

9 A way of measuring the redistribution effect of the welfare systems is measuring the 'net social wage', that is the difference between the benefits received and the taxes paid by the whole population of the working class. See and Shaik (2003) and Fazeli and Fazeli (2012).

10 For a deep, critical analysis, of advantages and disadvantages of private social expenditure, see Pearson and Martin (2005).

References

Aiginger, K. (2008), *Performance Differences in Europe: Tentative Hypotheses on the Role of Institutions*. WIFO Working Paper, REPEC/IDEAS, University of Connecticut.

Atkinson, A. B., Cantillon, B., Marlier, E. and Nolan, B. (2002), *Social Indicators: The EU and Social Inclusion*, Oxford, Oxford University Press.

Darby, J. and Melitz, J. (2008), *Social Spending and Automatic Stabilizers in the OECD*, Economic Policy, CEPR.

Dreher, A., Sturm, J.-E. and Ursprung, J. W. (2008), The impact of globalisation on the composition of government expenditures: Evidence from panel data, *Public Choice*, 134.

Esping Andersen, G. (1990), *The Three Worlds of Welfare Capitalism*, Princeton, Princeton University Press.

Fazeli, R. and Fazeli, R. (2012), The welfare state and the market economy: The American and German experiences of social policy, *Ekonomska Istrazivanja*, 25.

Jayadev, A. and Bowles, S. (2006), Guard labour, *Journal of Development Economics*, 79.

Maddison, A. (2003), *The World Economy: Historical Statistics*, Paris, OECD.

Marsland. D. (1994), *Freedom, Self-reliance and Welfare Reform*, paper for the conference 'Future of the Welfare State', 21–29 January, Alton (UK).

Pearson, M. and Martin, J. (2005), *Should We Extend the Role of Private Social expenditure?* IZA Discussion Paper No. 1544.

Pontusson, J. (2005), *Inequality and Prosperity: Social Europe versus Liberal America*, Ithaca, Cornell University Press.

Sachs, J. (2006), Welfare states beyond ideology, *Scientific American*, November.

Sen, A. (1976), Real national income, *Review of Economic Studies*, 43.

Shaikh, A. (2003), Who pays for the 'welfare' in the welfare state? A multicountry study, *Social Research*, 70.

Sykes, R., Palier, B. and Prior, P. M. (2001), *Globalization and European Welfare States: Challenges and Change*, Basingstoke, Palgrave.

8 The future of the euro

Vincent Duwicquet, Jacques Mazier, Pascal Petit and Jamel Saadaoui

Introduction

The euro crisis illustrates the deficiencies of adjustment mechanisms in a monetary union characterized by a large heterogeneity. Exchange rate adjustments being impossible, few alternative mechanisms are available. Nevertheless, fiscal policy could play an active role. In a federal state like the USA its stabilization coefficient is around 20 per cent (Italianer and Pisani-Ferry, 1992). But there is no equivalent in the European case. Well-integrated capital markets, with portfolio diversification and intra-zone credit, have been proposed as a powerful adjustment mechanism by the 'international risk sharing' approach. Intra-zone credit and capital income from international portfolios would have stabilization coefficients around 20–30 per cent each (Asdrubali and Kim, 2004). These results have been used during the 2000s by proponents of liberal economic policies in the EU to promote deeper financial integration without having to develop a federal budget (European Commission, 2007; Trichet, 2007). However, the theoretical basis and the results appear highly questionable (Clévenot and Duwicquet, 2011).

Consequently, relative wage and price flexibility are proposed in order to take the place, at least partially, of exchange rate adjustments. Actually these mechanisms allow only a very slow and partial return to equilibrium with an important cost in terms of growth and employment and with large differences between countries, due to huge structural specificities. They are more inefficient when they are implemented simultaneously in interdependent countries, as is the case in the eurozone, especially in the Southern European countries (Mazier and Saglio, 2008). This situation reflects a simple diagnosis. At the level of the whole eurozone, the current account is close to equilibrium and the fiscal deficit is smaller than in many other OECD countries. The euro is close to its equilibrium parity. But intra-European imbalances are huge. The euro is strongly overvalued for Southern European countries, France included, and largely undervalued for Northern European countries, especially Germany (Jeong *et al.*, 2010). These overvaluations slow growth and induce fiscal and current deficits in the South while undervaluations boost growth in the North via exports, especially towards the rest of the eurozone, and deficits are reduced. This situation is equivalent to implicit positive transfers in favour of the North and negative transfers at the detriment of the South, which are largely ignored in the public debate.

The chapter is organized as follow. In the first part, we give a new evaluation of these exchange rate misalignments inside the eurozone, using a FEER approach, and we discuss the structural character of these misalignments. In the second part, we analyse the deadlock of the actual European institutional framework and propose two alternative exit strategies, a first step towards a fiscal federalism or, on the opposite, a new monetary regime based on a multi-euro system.

Intra-European exchange rates misalignments

A structural heterogeneity

Since the beginning of the 2000s, we have observed a surge of current account imbalances inside the eurozone in spite of a rather balanced current account for the whole area. On the one side, Northern European countries have accumulated huge current account surpluses and on the other side, Southern European countries have run important current account deficits. These evolutions reflect, at least partially, the increasing heterogeneity of exchange rate misalignments inside the eurozone. After 2009, current account deficits of Southern European countries have been reduced because of restrictive policies and internal devaluations. In this section, we give new estimations of Fundamental Equilibrium Exchange Rates (FEERs) based on the methodology introduced by Williamson (1983) for ten European countries over the period 1994–2012 (see Table 8.1). The FEER is defined as the exchange rate prevailing when the economy simultaneously reaches the external equilibrium and the internal equilibrium for all the trading partners. This measure was derived from a standard world trade model in which all the variables are endogenous except the external equilibrium (sustainable current account) and the internal equilibrium (full utilization of the productive potential). The external equilibrium is estimated with panel regression techniques. The internal equilibrium is reached when the output gap is closed (see Jeong *et al.* (2010) for further details). In this new estimation the underlying current account is obtained by taking into account the delayed effects of past exchange rate variations (in *t-1* and *t-2*), as was done in the previous estimations, but also the effects of domestic output gap on imports and foreign output gap on exports, as has been proposed by Bayoumi and Faruqee (1998). This second correction is more significant in the present period due to the size of the output gaps since 2008.

Since the early 2000s, we have observed a sharp increase of the heterogeneity of misalignments in the eurozone (Table 8.1) with a split within the eurozone between some countries increasingly undervalued (like Germany, Austria, Netherlands and Finland) and others increasingly overvalued (like Greece, Portugal, Spain and France). On average between 2005 and 2010, Germany, Austria, the

Table 8.1 Misalignments in real effective terms (in %)

	EU	*FRA*	*GER*	*ITA*	*SPA*	*AUT*	*FIN*	*IRL*	*NLD*	*PRT*	*GRC*
1994	−3.4	3.1	−10.5	9.2	0.6	−3.1	−1.7	3.8	0.8	4.3	13.9
1995	1.2	1.4	−9.4	11.2	8.8	−8.3	7.2	3.8	0.8	7.0	1.3
1996	4.2	3.9	−4.8	9.4	−4.6	−9.2	9.3	0.8	0.4	−11.3	−12.5
1997	3.5	15.2	−3.2	8.2	−0.8	−8.8	16.9	0.6	1.8	−19.3	−12.7
1998	0.6	15.4	−5.2	5.1	−1.4	−3.5	17.4	−0.8	−2.2	−18.5	−8.4
1999	2.0	19.5	−8.1	1.8	−6.9	−2.9	17.6	0.4	−0.7	−23.7	−17.8
2000	0.1	7.4	−8.4	−0.7	−10.0	1.1	21.4	−2.2	−3.7	−28.7	−25.2
2001	6.9	7.6	−3.5	−1.2	−13.0	−3.5	22.2	−5.4	−6.4	−34.3	−24.3
2002	6.6	2.4	3.5	−4.2	−12.9	9.8	23.0	−6.2	−8.2	−27.4	−22.4
2003	2.2	−3.0	2.2	−6.9	−13.6	2.9	12.0	−6.8	−3.0	−23.8	−11.8
2004	6.6	−5.7	9.0	−1.9	−22.0	1.2	12.7	−7.2	−1.1	−33.8	1.0
2005	1.8	−11.2	11.6	−1.2	−30.7	3.8	5.5	−7.3	1.6	−44.2	−4.6
2006	0.3	−8.8	16.5	−0.7	−34.0	7.9	9.4	−5.1	6.1	−42.5	−5.1
2007	0.1	−12.8	18.4	−0.3	−42.0	10.4	11.5	−11.1	3.1	−33.8	−7.4
2008	−2.6	−19.8	14.3	−5.7	−46.7	12.6	4.5	11.1	0.0	15.9	−10.1
2009	0.6	−11.6	16.3	−2.0	−21.4	7.2	−0.4	−2.5	2.1	−35.4	−0.4
2010	1.6	−8.9	20.2	−3.2	−21.5	9.8	3.4	8.1	8.4	−26.8	−11.5
2011	8.2	−15.4	16.9	−4.1	−19.5	6.9	−7.3	3.9	6.6	−22.1	−46.2
2012	14.1	−14.1	19.9	4.3	−1.3	7.8	−5.2	13.0	7.1	2.7	−15.9

Source: authors' calculations. A positive (negative) number indicates an undervaluation (overvaluation) expressed in per cent of the observed value.

Note

Forecasts for 2012 based on IMF WEO October 2013; See Jeong *et al.* (2010) for a complete description of the model of world trade and the methodology used to compute ERMs.

Netherlands and Finland have been undervalued by 13 per cent while Greece, Portugal, Spain and France have been overvalued by 23 per cent. These intra-European exchange rate misalignments reflect a strong structural heterogeneity between European countries at almost all the levels (nature of the international specialization, size and productivity of the firms, R&D effort, and qualification of the labour force). They are at the heart of the current problems of the eurozone.

However, since the beginning of the eurozone crisis in 2010, a reduction of misalignments is observed for most of the Southern European countries. The Irish, Spanish, Italian and even Portuguese euros seem no more overvalued in 2012. But the Greek and French euros remain overvalued around 15 per cent and the German euro undervalued around 20 per cent. These movements have been mainly driven by large real effective devaluations in Ireland, Spain, Portugal and Greece, as shown in Figure 8.1 with the evolutions of the relative unit labour cost (ULC), i.e. real effective exchange rates based on ULC. These politics of internal devaluation are very painful and have led to a deep recession in Greece, as in other Southern European countries, with a reduction of current deficits mainly due to the shrinking of imports, but with limited improvement of public finance.

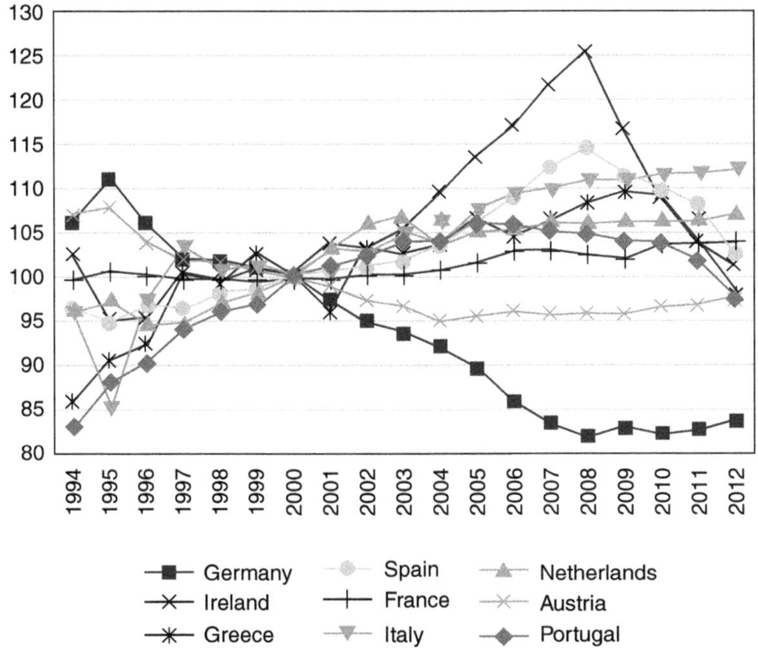

Figure 8.1 REERs based on unit labour cost (relative ULC) (source: authors' calculations based on European Commission data, basis 100 in 2000).

These evolutions can be analysed in more detail using other indicators of real effective exchange rates based on nominal unit wage cost (Figure 8.2) and export price deflator (Figure 8.3). In spite of large wage cut adjustment in Greece, the Greek euro remains overvalued and the export price competitiveness is very deteriorated. This implies that the Greek export firms have used the wage cuts mainly to increase their margins without improving their price competitiveness. To a lesser extent the Portuguese and Spanish firms have implemented the same strategy, but with more success on the export shares for Spain, which can be explained by non-price competitiveness factors. On the opposite, wage and employment adjustments have been very large in Ireland and have been accompanied by an improvement of export price competitiveness which is reflected in a slight undervaluation. Italy has faced a drift of its relative ULC and export price competitiveness without any attempt to adjust it in the recent period. The limited overvaluation of the Italian euro reflects non-price competitiveness factors. Apart from the French case which will be analysed in more detail below, Germany is the last country to be examined. From 2000 to 2008 sharp wage and productivity adjustments have led to a large reduction of the German relative unit labour cost which has been preserved during the crisis. Export price competitiveness has also been improved, although to a lesser extent than the relative

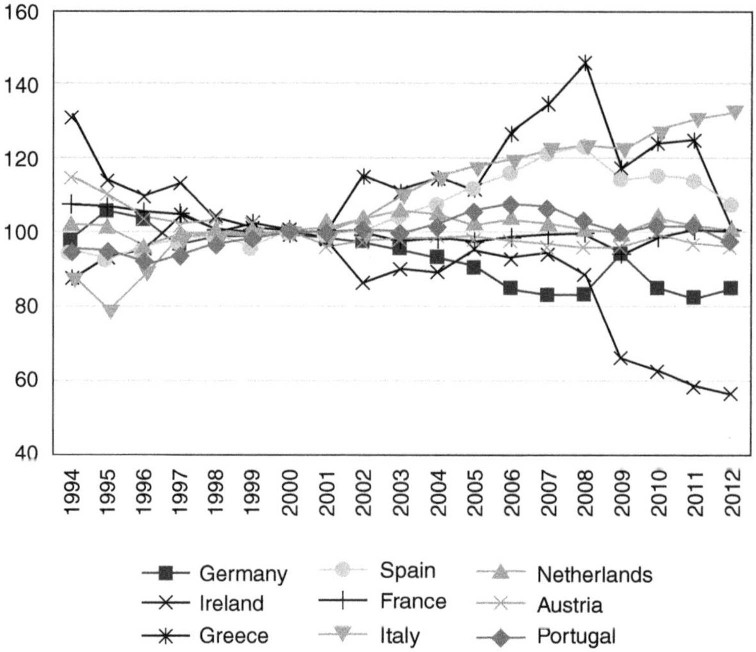

Figure 8.2 REERs based on unit wage cost (relative unit wage cost) (source: authors' calculations based on European Commission data, basis 100 in 2000).

ULC which has allowed a consolidation of the export margin of the German firms.

The French case is interesting. French relative ULC and unit wage cost have followed an intermediate path without large drift, but without cost adjustments. Facing this evolution, export margins have been regularly reduced to preserve, and even improve, export price competitiveness. This has not been sufficient to avoid an increasing overvaluation of the French euro, due to the weakness of non-price competitiveness.

Another way to illustrate these issues is to compare two estimations of the relative ULC, one measured in level using purchasing power parity (RULC), the other measured with the equilibrium exchange rate (FEER) and corresponding to an equilibrium value of the ULC (RULC*). These indicators have been estimated for France and Germany (Figure 8.4). They show that the French RULC has remained for almost thirty years close to one, i.e. that the French unit labour cost was at a level close to the ULC of the main partners. In that sense it could be said that there was no problem of cost competitiveness, in spite of a slight drift during the 2000s.

A more precise analysis leads to a different diagnosis. At the end of the 2000s the French RULC was very close to the German one, in contrast with what was observed during the 1990s when the German RULC was quite a lot higher than

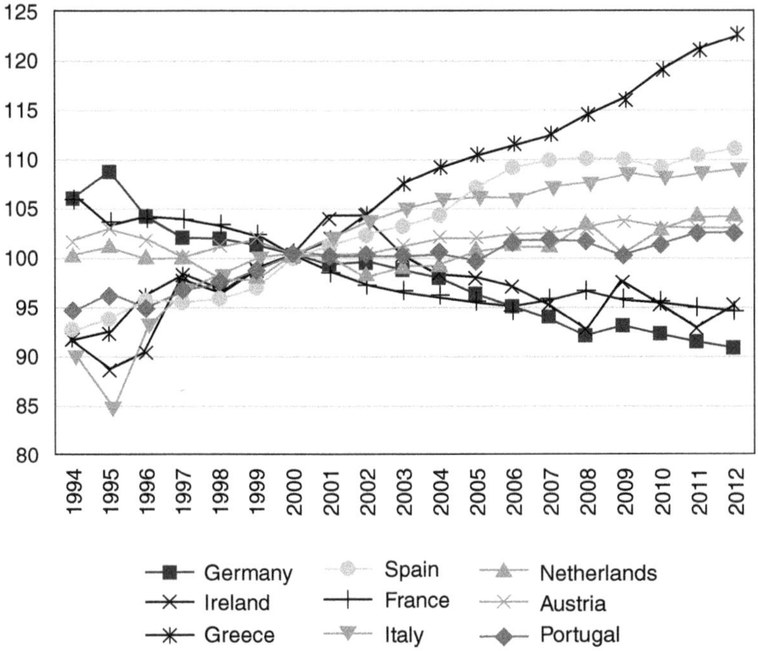

Figure 8.3 REERs based on export price deflator (export price competitiveness) (source: authors' calculations based on European Commission data, basis 100 in 2000).

the French one. The French firms had at that time a cost advantage in contrast with the German firms which suffered a cost disadvantage. It helped the French firms to survive and compensate for their insufficiency in the matter of non-price competitiveness while the German firms partly compensated their cost disadvantage by non-price competitiveness advantage. Consequently, the overvaluation of the deutschmark (changed to the German euro in 1999) remained limited. At the end of the 1990s the French RULC was under its equilibrium value, which illustrated the undervaluation of the franc (changed to the French euro in 1999). During the 1980s and 1990s the equilibrium value of the French ULC has appreciated progressively, which was reflecting some effort to restructure the manufacturing sector, but also the declining position of its main competitor, the German economy, which was engaged during the 1990s in a painful reunification.

During the 2000s the reverse has been complete. The German equilibrium (RULC*) has appreciated, thanks to industrial restructuration (mainly with delocalization in Eastern Europe) and cost adjustments, which has led to a large undervaluation of the German euro. In sharp contrast, the French equilibrium (RULC*) has experienced a depreciation because of a deindustrialization process and declining investment and R&D. Without cost adjustments, as has been seen,

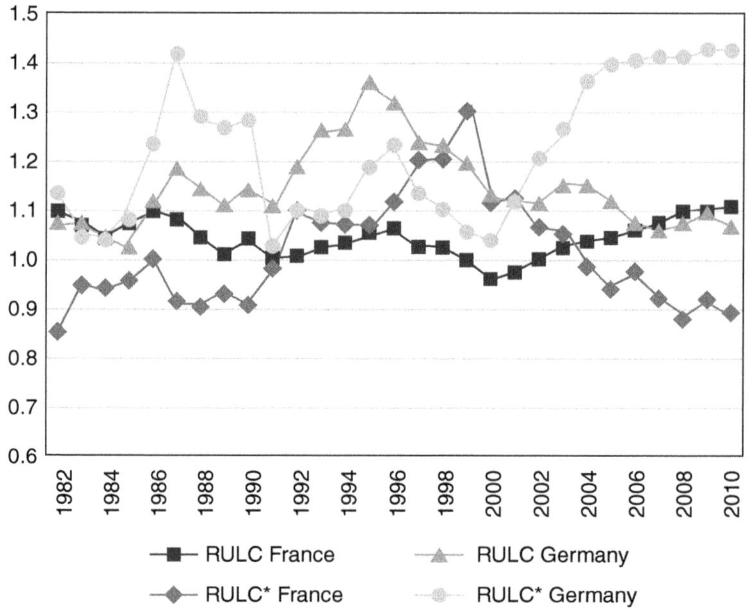

Figure 8.4 Level (RULC) and equilibrium relative unit labour cost (RULC*) (source: authors' calculations based on Eurostat Istat data, basis 100 in 2000).

and, in spite of the reduction of the export margins, a structural overvaluation of the French euro has appeared.

The French economy is clearly in an impasse. There are three alternative issues. Like in other Southern European countries, cost adjustments through wage cut and productivity gains could be used. But the social cost is high, their efficiency is limited, they are a long lasting process, they will perpetuate the recession in France and in other European countries. They are not on the agenda of the present government.

The parity of the euro franc could be depreciated. This would mean a complete change in the European monetary regime, which is not impossible but raises many problems.[1] It is not also on the agenda of the present government.

The third solution, which has been adopted, is the 'employment-competitiveness credit tax' (20 billion euros, around 1 per cent of GDP) followed by the 'responsibility pact' in January 2014 (10 billion more of reduction of social contributions). Costs are reduced through tax cuts. This raises, at least, two questions. The target is not clear. If it is improving the competitiveness, the measure is not well calibrated as all the firms, including those of the non-tradable sector like banks and retailers can benefit from the tax cuts. Consequently, the transfer in favour of the tradable sector is too limited, compared with the cost disadvantage which actually prevails. A larger transfer would be necessary but could not be supported by the public finance. If the target is to improve employment, as seems to be more the case with the 'responsibility pact', the past experiences show that efficiency is not warranted and the problem of cost-competitiveness, which cannot be ignored, is not solved. The government is aware of these limits and has completed its 'tools box' by re-launching industrial policy measures (major industrial projects, innovation policy, etc.) to improve non-price competitiveness. This is welcome but takes time (around ten years) to be operational.

The risk is therefore that any target can be reached. The competitiveness problem will remain and financing the current deficit might become more difficult. Tax reduction could have a limited impact on employment, all the more as the profit margins have been reduced during the crisis, especially for the export sector. The financing of the tax reduction will imply public expenditures cuts with a negative impact on activity. More likely will be a long lasting period of stagnation.

Divergence of ERM inside the euro area

In other approaches of equilibrium exchange rate like the Behavioural Equilibrium Exchange Rate approach (BEER), the misalignments are necessarily stationary on the studied period. They correspond to residuals of a long-run relationship between the real effective exchange rates and its long-term determinants. Thus the misalignment is stationary, by definition. In the case of European countries during the period 1982–2011, the hypothesis of exchange rates on average in equilibrium in the studied period (i.e. the misalignment is stationary) seems to be unrealistic since these countries have experienced diverging paths concerning their competitiveness, as evidenced by the evolution of current account imbalances (Figure 8.1).

In the long run and at the world level, the FEERs and the REERs are integrated and cointegrated. In other words, the misalignments are stationary for a large panel of industrialized and emerging countries over the period 1982–2007 (Saadaoui, 2011). Nevertheless for European countries over the period 1982–2011, it seems highly doubtful that the misalignments have been stationary.

In Table 8.2, we implement panel unit root tests proposed by Carrion-i-Silvestre *et al.* (2005) on the series of misalignments of eight European countries over the period 1982–2011. These third generation panel unit root tests take into account structural breaks. The tests give clear-cut results. We reject the null of stationarity at the 1 per cent level. The intra-European ERM is not stationary over the period 1982–2011.

In order to impose any value on the cointegrating vector, we also implement panel cointegration tests proposed by Westerlund (2008). These tests allow for cross-sectional dependence and eventually stationary regressors. In Table 8.3, we can see that we cannot reject null of non-cointegration at the 1 per cent level in all tests. The REERs and FEERs are not cointegrated. These results are in line

Table 8.2 Panel unit root test with structural breaks

Country	*Break dates*	
FRA	1996	
GER	1990	2000
ITA	1992	
SPA	1992	2006
FIN	1992	2002
IRL	1986	2006
NLD	1985	
GRC	1990	
	Quadratic Test (*p*-value)	
Breaks (homogeneous)		12.428 (0.000)
Breaks (heterogeneous)		20.657 (0.000)

Source: authors' calculations.

Notes
The number of break points has been estimated using the LWZ information criteria allowing for a maximum of $m^{max}=2$ structural breaks. The long-run variance is estimated using the Quadratic spectral kernel with automatic spectral window bandwidth selection as in Andrews (1991), Andrews and Monahan (1992) and Sul *et al.* (2003).

We exclude Austria and Portugal for reasons of missing observations. *P*-values in parentheses.

Table 8.3 Panel cointegration tests

DHg	1.565 (0.058)
DHp	1.813 (0.034)

Source: authors' calculations.

Notes
All tests are based on an intercept and the Newey and West (1994) procedure for selecting the bandwidth order. In implementing the Durbin-Hausman tests, the maximum for the estimation of the number of common factors is set to 5. The *p*-values are based on the asymptotic normal distribution. *P*-values in parentheses.

with those of Duwicquet *et al.* (2013) and reflect unsustainable evolutions of competitiveness in the eurozone over the studied period.

What about fundamental equilibrium exchange rates from a post Keynesian perspective?

As pointed out by Officer (2012), the Purchasing Parity Power (PPP) approach, introduced by Cassel (1918), is indeed a monetarist approach as changes in relative prices (a nominal variable) affect the nominal exchange rate but not the real exchange rate. In the long run, nominal variables do not affect real variables in this approach. Thus, we have a dichotomy between the real sphere and the monetary sphere.

We can classify the different approaches of equilibrium exchange rates thanks to the criteria of Officer (2012). Approaches in which real variables are not affected by nominal variables can be labelled as monetarist and approaches in which nominal variables affect persistently real variables can be regarded as non-monetarist.

In the case of the FEER approach, the current account expressed in nominal terms affects persistently the real effective exchange rate. An increasing current account deficit will induce downward pressures on the real effective exchange rate. Thus the FEER approach can be regarded as a non-monetarist approach.

Furthermore, Cline and Williamson (2012) indicate that the FEER approach may be characterized as 'path dependent'. An increasing depreciation will produce an undervalued currency only in the case where the fundamental rate does not observe a stronger depreciation. Path dependency can be defined in this way: the initial situation will affect the evolution of exchange rate misalignments in the following periods (Cline and Williamson, 2012).

In the light of the post-Keynesian tradition, the FEER approach has two important features. The FEER approach is non-monetarist (absence of dichotomy between the real sphere and the monetary sphere) and admits hysteresis (this approach requires any assumption on the stationarity of misalignments, the exchange rate can or cannot revert to its fundamental value as in Duwicquet *et al.* (2013)).

Davidson (2004) argues that the only analytical difference between Williamson's FEER and market fundamentalists is the speed of adjustment of the real exchange rate towards its fundamental value. According to Davidson, market forces are not able to reach this equilibrium rate. Our empirical results are in line with the point of Davidson. They indicate a huge divergence in the eurozone. Some countries are increasingly undervalued and other countries are increasingly overvalued. The case of the eurozone is very interesting as it illustrates in a very striking way the failure of market forces to reach the FEER.

As market forces are unable to reach FEERs, we need a new economic and financial architecture in the euro area (see Mazier and Petit (2013) for some new proposals) in order to help overvalued countries affected by mass unemployment and sluggish growth to achieve their external adjustments without putting a huge strain on aggregate demand in the eurozone.

Alternative exit strategies for the eurozone

These exchange rate misalignments have important consequences for overvalued countries. They experienced a reduction of their growth rates and an increase of public and external deficits. Conversely, undervalued countries benefit from implicit advantages in terms of price competitiveness. These advantages allow growth performances to be enhanced and public and external deficits to be reduced. These monetary misalignments imply a variation of relative costs in favour of Northern countries and at the detriment of Southern countries (at the end of the last decade, this variation of relative costs represented more than +5 per cent of GDP for France and Spain and about –12 per cent for Germany).

This deterioration in terms of cost competitiveness due to an overvaluation of the euro has been investigated in the case of the French economy in the Gallois report on competitiveness (2012).

This report offers a quite complete description of the difficulties faced by the French industry. Unfortunately, the government measure implemented to tackle these problems, a tax rebate for firms without any requirement, seems to underestimate the extent of the problem (this measure represents about 1 per cent of French GDP whereas an effort of 5 per cent of French GDP is required to offset the competitiveness loss induced by the overvaluation of the euro) and the nature of the problem (as the tradable sector is not specifically targeted). The 'pacte de responsabilité' enacted in January 2014 perpetuates the same kind of flawed strategy.

The European 'pressure cooker'

The eurozone is clearly in a deadlock. The strategy of European governments is based on two main pillars: first, a generalization of austerity programmes to achieve internal devaluations and reduce public deficits; second, the implementation, by successive steps and under the constraint, of a new financial architecture aimed at providing funds to countries which experience episodes of financial distress. This strategy is at best hazardous. Indeed, the economic slowdown produced by these measures, particularly in Southern countries, reduces public debt sustainability. This strategy can be understood only from the double perspective of the Northern countries and the 'European elite' i.e. the dominant classes and the European technocracy. The first group has suffered from the economic slowdown in Southern countries but has succeeded in stabilizing growth and employment since the onset of the euro crisis. The second group uses the crisis context to promote more and more liberal reforms and reinforce its position.

The underlying idea that financial measures (eurobonds and debt mutualization, unlimited purchase of bonds by the ECB, European Stability Mechanism and a larger role for the European Investment Bank) are sufficient to overcome the euro crisis, is not really convincing. An increase of intra-European credit to Southern countries from private banks of other countries in the eurozone, or from the European Investment Bank, or the European Stability Mechanism, or even the ECB, could be a way to ease the pressure on interest rates and to reduce the debt burden. This could allow a modest recovery which offsets partially the negative effects induced by the overvaluation of Southern countries. But this kind of measure does not solve the competitiveness problems of countries within the eurozone.

The euro crisis is deeply rooted in structural macroeconomic imbalances resulting from heterogeneity of eurozone economies and divergent evolutions since the beginning of the 2000s. Structural policies have to be implemented in order to increase the non-price competitiveness of Southern countries (industrial policy, research, education, infrastructures). These policies are complex and their total effect can be measured only after an extended period of time. During this period, the public debt and external debt remain at high levels. In the current institutional background (explicitly in the European mechanism of stability in particular), this leads to a reinforcement or a perpetuation of restrictive budgetary policies, inconsistent with the structural policies aforementioned and which maintains economic stagnation.

Eurobonds could be seen as useful tools to implement more long-run structural policies as public debts are pooled beyond a specific threshold, 60 per cent of GDP for instance, where eurobonds are issued to finance national public debts. This scheme allows the burden of national debt to be transferred to the supranational level and thus avoiding austerity programmes. However, this kind of system requires a strong control of national public finance by the European authorities with the creation of a European Debt Agency. Northern countries fear that Southern countries would not use this new room for manoeuvre to improve their international specialization, but to implement laxist policies oriented towards domestic consumption and thus benefit from permanent financial support from more competitive countries. This is the main reason that explains the reluctance of Germany to use a scheme based on a massive issuance of Eurobonds.

In this context, a financial federalism is not sufficient. Even if these measures are useful, and sometimes necessary, they are not able to solve problems induced by the macroeconomic heterogeneity of the eurozone. Intra-zone credits bring only temporary relief. Transfers should be made between members of the eurozone to settle the problem. The debt restructuration of heavily indebted countries is one of the most prominent examples of the above proposition. After the Greek partial default in July 2011, we still fear a new debt restructuration. This successive debt restructuration is viable only if the largest economies of the North of the eurozone have to bail out the smallest economies. But the cost of bailing out the largest economies would be too high. This shows the non-viability of this process.

In the short to medium run, we can fear a cumulative slowdown of economic growth in the eurozone. The risks of a persistent stagnation are now obvious with an increasing divergence between Northern and Southern countries of the eurozone.

In this context, a break-up of the eurozone cannot be excluded in an episode of financial distress where a Southern country would be forced to leave the euro to avoid social unrest. This break-up would have disastrous consequences such as capital flights, cumulative devaluations and large disruption in the domestic banking system. A new systemic crisis could lead the eurozone into a new deep recession. In order to avoid such an apocalyptic scenario, the ECB and Germany have reduced their constraint a little and will continue to do so, but without addressing the underlying problems faced by the eurozone.

Scenarios and simulations

These scenarios, the suck-down and stagnation, the euro break-up, towards fiscal federalism and the multi-euro scenario, have been described using the Cambridge Alphametrics Model (CAM) in the AUGUR project analysing Europe in the world in 2030 (see Cripps *et al.*, 2013, Eatwell *et al.*, 2014 and Mazier *et al.*, 2013 for the main results).

Other simulations have been made using Stock Flow Consistent (SFC) model of the eurozone to illustrate adjustments with different institutional frameworks: increasing intra-European financing, euro bonds, fiscal federalism, multi-euros regime (see Duwicquet *et al.* (2013, 2014); Mazier and Valdecantos (2014)).

Alternative policies

In order to exit from the stalemate and avoid a break-up, alternative policies have been previously and extensively discussed but they are complex to implement. We need to draw the lines of a European growth strategy instead of being trapped in inefficient austerity strategies. A set of regulatory measures in the financial sector should be adopted in order to limit the financial excess observed during the 1990s and the 2000s. This growth strategy should rest on the potential of countries with an undervalued currency and a lesser public indebtedness, and particularly Germany, through wages increase in the short run. This implies that Germany should accept a higher inflation target in order to participate in real exchange rate adjustment. At the level of the European Union, economic growth should be reignited by investment in strategic sectors (education, research, green technologies, and suburbs renovation) financed by a large European loan and by credit lines granted by the European Investment Bank. The consolidation of public finance will be the product of new fiscal resources. These new fiscal resources will come, on the one hand, from the recovery and, one the other hand, from the cancellation of tax rebates granted since 1990 to capital incomes and to wealthier households. But we need to go further by using and coordinating national resources. The coordination of economic policies and the 'European economic government' face national interests and the fact most of the social and political issues are settled at the level of national spaces. For more than twenty years, many people have called for a greater political integration and a coordination of economic policies. The notion of 'European economic government' has been specially promoted by the successive French governments. But, the European history has shown that coordination is too complex from an institutional point of view to be fully efficient. This statement is even stronger if we talk about coordination of wages at the European level even when national wage policy does not exist in many European countries. We need to acknowledge this last point. The 'European economic government' can only be achieved through explicitly federal institutions. It is useless to wait for a mythical European coordination.

First scenario: fiscal federalism

We propose two alternative scenarios. The first one is based on a federal budget with a progressive implementation limited to about 5 per cent of eurozone GDP at the medium term. This budget will be financed thanks to new taxes on saving and capital incomes and firms' profits in order to limit the effect of fiscal competition. Taxes on financial transactions will contribute to limit speculative movements and a tax on CO_2 emissions to preserve the environment. This budget will help to introduce some stabilization mechanisms through a system of budgetary insurance (for a relatively modest cost, about 0.3 per cent of eurozone GDP). A European Social Fund (about 0.5–1 per cent of eurozone GDP) would finance social transfers to help some countries to reach social standards, differentiated by countries and defined by large sectors. This will reinforce the sentiment of belonging to a European community.

European structural policies would be rehabilitated in terms of research (about 0.4 per cent of eurozone GDP), in terms of large technological and infrastructure programmes (about 1 per cent of eurozone GDP), in terms of regional development where the European experience can be considered as important (about 0.5 per cent of eurozone GDP). Finally, the issuance of Eurobonds would contribute to finance European investment projects and would induce a debt service limited to 0.7 per cent of GDP in the long run (with a ceiling of 20 per cent for the European debt). This federal scenario has an uncontestable economic consistency. Its main problem is its feeble political credibility. The European people does not exist and there is a very limited solidarity between the different members of the union. We also need to acknowledge this last point and be realistic.

Second scenario: a multi-speed eurozone

The second scenario takes into account reluctances or impossibilities of increasing the European budget and the difficulties of implementing coordinated policies. It leads us to examine a multi-speed eurozone where the new monetary regime includes a reintroduction of national currencies, eventually linked to an 'external euro'. This more flexible eurozone is characterized by:

The implementation of a new monetary regime in Europe where national euros are reintroduced with the possibility of periodical adjustments of intra-European parity when a fundamental disequilibrium is detected. This new monetary regime could be organized according to two distinct schemes:

The *first scheme* would be based on a simple reintroduction of national currencies with a system of exchange rate managed in several ways (a return to the European Monetary System; or an exit of Northern countries from the euro area, with a floating currency for these countries, and the preservation of the euro for Southern countries).

The *second scheme* would preserve some institutional elements of the present euro area. It would be based simultaneously on a common 'external euro', floating and managed by the ECB, and on national euros, non-convertible at the international level, linked to the 'external euro' with a grid of fixed but adjustable parities. National Central Banks would have an account in euros in the ECB representing the total amount of cumulated current accounts and capital flows with the rest of the area. The ECB would play the role of a clearing union, but only up to a certain point. Beyond this threshold, the intra-European parity of the country would have to be modified.

An absence of a federal budget, i.e. the preservation of its current level (1 per cent of Europe's GDP) would ensure the continuation of some interventions in the sectors of agriculture and research. European regional policies will not be pursued as monetary adjustments are now possible. Structural national policies, mainly industrial policy and regional policy, will regain some room for manoeuvre facing a less dominant European competition policy. Some specific cooperation could be implemented to develop some targeted projects.

Social models will remain heterogeneous without institutional convergence (no European minimum wage, diversity of pension scheme and country-specific trade unions). Nevertheless, a partial convergence will be allowed thanks to catching-up effects and a stronger growth.

This scenario of a more flexible eurozone faces one of the most important challenges that has been revealed by the crisis. It offers a real answer to the macroeconomic imbalances induced by the heterogeneity of the eurozone's members thanks to possibilities of adjustments of intra-European parities. However, this scenario has its own caveats. We can identify a series of three potential problems.

First, instability factors cannot be ignored but can be reduced thanks to the introduction of capital controls (mandatory reserves on deposits and assets in foreign currency, tax on financial transactions). These measures have only a relative efficiency and the key element is the credibility of the parity fixed by Southern monetary authorities.

Second, the management of the external debt in euros is a sensible question. The reimbursement of this debt induces, either, a loss for foreign creditors in the case of a reimbursement in a (depreciated) new currency or in national euros, or, an additional cost for domestic countries that have devalued, if they settle their external debt in euros. An international arrangement, indeed largely intra-European as a large part of the debt is held by Europeans, should be a way to overcome this difficulty. Devaluing countries must have the possibility of reimbursing their debt in their new (devalued) currency. Furthermore, if we take into account the high levels of indebtedness of Southern countries, a debt restructuration seems to be necessary or else inevitable. This will induce an additional cost for creditor countries and their banks. This effort is a necessary condition to move forward.

Finally, achieving a transition towards a new monetary regime is not an easy task. An array of efficient and relevant measures must be prepared to avoid an apocalyptic scenario with capital fights, cumulative devaluation and a commercial war. In some cases, these measures could mean a temporary closure of private banks in order to implement the new monetary regime. Southern countries should rapidly control imported inflation. The exit from a deadlock is, sometimes, not an easy thing.

Note

1 This is discussed in other papers (Mazier, 2014; Mazier and Valdecantos, 2014).

References

Andrews, D.W.K. (1991). 'Heteroskedasticity and autocorrelaction consistent covariance matrix estimation', *Econometrica* 59, 817–858.

Andrews, D.W.K. and Monahan, J.C. (1992). 'An improved heteroskedasticity and autocorrelation consistent autocovariance matrix', *Econometrica* 60, 953–966.

Asdrubali, P. and Kim, S. (2004). 'Dynamic risksharing in the United States and Europe', *Journal of Monetary Economics* 51(4): 809–836.

Bayoumi, T., and Faruqee, H. (1998). 'A calibrated model of the underlying current account.' IMF Occasional Paper 167.

Carrion-i-Silvestre, J.L., del Barrio-Castro, T. and López-Bazo, E. (2005). 'Breaking the panels: an application to the GDP per capita', *Econometrics Journal* 8(2): 159–175.

Cassel, G. (1918). 'Abnormal deviations in international exchanges', *The Economic Journal* 112: 413–415.

Clévenot, M. and Duwicquet, V. (2011). 'Partage du risque interrégional', *Revue de l'OFCE* 119(4): 5–33.

Cline, W. R. and Williamson, J. (2012). 'Updated estimates of fundamental equilibrium exchange rates', *Peterson Institute for International Economics Policy Brief* 12–23.

Cripps, F., Duwicquet, V. and Mazier, J. (2013). 'Les scénarios européens', in *L'économie mondiale en 2030: ruptures et continuité* (J. Mazier, P. Petit and D. Plihon, eds). Paris: Economica.

Davidson, P. (2004). 'The future of the international financial system', *Journal of Post Keynesian Economics* 26(4): 591–605.

Duwicquet, V., Mazier, J. and Saadaoui, J. (2013). 'Désajustements de change, fédéralisme budgétaire et redistribution', *Revue de l'OFCE* 127: 57–93.

Duwicquet, V., Mazier, J. and Saadaoui, J. (2014). 'Interest rates, eurobonds and intra-European exchange rate misalignments: the challenge of sustainable adjustments in the eurozone', presented during the international workshop 'Full employment in Europe, with or without the Euro?' University of Grenoble.

Eatwell, J., McKinley, T. and Petit, P. (eds) (2014). *Challenge for Europe in the World 2030*. Farnham: Ashgate.

European Commission (2007). *Quarterly Report on the Euro Area*, no. 3.

Gallois, L. (2012). *Rapport au Premier Ministre: Pacte pour la compétitivité de l'industrie française*, November, Paris.

Italianer, A. and Pisani-Ferry, J. (1992). 'Systèmes budgétaires et amortissement des chocs régionaux: implications pour l'Union économique et monétaire', *Économie Internationale* 51(3): 49–69.

Jeong, S.-E., Mazier, J. and Saadaoui, J. (2010).'"Exchange rate misalignments at world and European levels: a FEER approach', *Économie Internationale* 121(3): 25–58.

Mazier, J. (2014). 'Le futur de l'euro', in *Changer l'Europe* (Les économistes atterrés). Paris: Les Liens qui Libèrent Editions.

Mazier, J. and Petit, P. (2013). 'In search of sustainable paths for the eurozone in the troubled post-2008 world', *Cambridge Journal of Economics* 37(3): 513–532.

Mazier, J. and Saglio, S. (2008). 'Interdependency and adjustments in the European Union', *International Review of Applied Economics*, 22(1).

Mazier, J. and Valdecantos, S. (2014). 'A multi-speed Europe: is it viable?' *CEPN Working Paper* 2014–03.

Mazier, J., Petit, P. and Plihon, D. (eds) (2013). *L'économie mondiale en 2030: ruptures et continuité*. Paris: Economica.

Newey, W.K. and West, K.D. (1994). 'Automatic lag selection in covariance matrix estimation', *Review of Economic Studies* 61, 631–653.

Officer, L. H. (2012). 'Purchasing power parity in economics history', in *The Handbook of Exchange Rates* (J. James, I. W. Marsh and L. Sarno, eds). Hoboken, NJ: John Wiley and Sons.

Saadaoui, J. (2011). 'Exchange rate dynamics and fundamental equilibrium exchange rates', *Economics Bulletin* 31(3): 1993–2005.

Sul, D., Phillips, P.C.B. and Choi, C.Y. (2003). 'Prewhitening bias in HAC estimation'. Cowles Foundation Discussion Paper No. 1436.

Trichet, J.-C. (2007). 'Le processus d'intégration européenne', President Speeches, ECB.

Westerlund, J. (2008). 'Panel cointegration tests of the Fisher effect', *Journal of Applied Econometrics* 23(2): 193–233.

Williamson, J. (1983). *The Exchange Rate System*. Washington, DC: Peterson Institute for International Economics.

9 Consumption and credit for households in the run-up to crisis and in the efforts to overcome recession[1]

Maria Lissowska[2]

1 Introduction

The financial crisis which arose in the US in 2008 is still the most important event and the major condition affecting economies today. However, the interpretation of its underpinnings is not simple, and neither has been the impact of the efforts to come back to the 'normal path' of economic development. If the sources of the crisis are limited to the behaviour of the financial sector, it may seem easy to repair this situation, perhaps introducing better regulation to ensure economic recovery. However, the consecutive stages of crisis in Europe have shown that curing one disease (defaulting banks) may bring about another (sovereign debt) followed by depressed demand which hampers growth.

In the present chapter I will present a complementary input to the reasons for the crisis, namely indicating the excessive rise of indebtedness of households. This process may be well illustrated in the extreme case of post-transition countries (new Member States of the European Union), where growing inequality and poverty together with consumerism may be indicated as a reason for rapidly growing debt, mostly in the form of consumer credits. Indebtedness enabled by foreign financing amplified the possibilities for consumption, but, when easy credit vanished, it deepened the recession.

I will further compare these dynamics with those of Western European countries. While starting from higher levels of household debt, they developed predominantly mortgage credits in the run-up to crisis, with less direct, but visible impact on consumption. Countries with a higher rise of indebtedness were also systematically subject to deeper falls in consumption after the crisis. Thus, the sharply growing indebtedness of households could be an important reason for the fast, but unsustainable rise in consumption, in Western European countries similar to (but to a lesser degree) the case of Central and Eastern Europe.

Finally, I will reflect on the possible role of enabling recovery by promoting household debt, seen by some as pointing to the detrimental insufficiency of demand. However, a repetition of the scenario from before the crisis does not seem likely.

2 Hypotheses on the role of consumption and household credit in the run-up to the crisis

The standard interpretations of the financial crisis of 2008 focus on the destabilizing outcome of innovations in the banking sector, in particular of securitization (Shin 2009). Securitization amplified the usual business cycle that emerges periodically, boosted by over-optimism and leading to excessive lending.

According to the financial accelerator model of Bernanke *et al.* (1998) during the ascending phase of the business cycle company profits rise together with their net worth which may then be used as collateral. This decreases the cost of external borrowing for these firms and makes banks speed up lending. When risk increases and the net worth of companies starts to decrease in the slowdown phase, both the cost of external finance rises and the value of collateral that firms can provide declines. Both factors limit the opportunity for contracting external finance. Thus the financial accelerator acts in a pro-cyclical manner. In this approach both demand for credit from companies and the propensity of banks to lend somehow mechanically follow the changes of prices and rewards.

Another insight into the role of credit decisions in economic cycles is provided by the Financial Instability Hypothesis of Hyman Minsky (1992). This hypothesis does not focus exclusively on companies, as the financial accelerator model does, but includes all types of borrowers. To model the credit cycles, Minsky distinguishes between different types of borrowers: those that may meet their contractual obligations from their cash flows (hedge borrowers), and those that cannot meet either principal or even interest payments (speculative and Ponzi borrowers). The major element driving the credit cycle upwards is that during periods of stability risk aversion lowers, both in terms of loosening credit standards by lenders, and of loosening the supervision and regulation requirements to the banks. This leads to excessive lending, and to a greater degree to speculative and Ponzi borrowers. Excessive demand created by credit results in an excessive rise in asset prices. Thus 'stability inherently creates instability', claims the first Minsky hypothesis.

Minsky's second hypothesis states that the reaction of authorities to inflation by imposing money constraints puts a stress on speculative borrowers who find themselves unable to meet their commitments and forces them to sell assets. This leads to a collapse in asset values. Thus a point of flip between self-reinforcing expansion and contraction appears, a Minsky Moment.

This model explains very well the situation in the American mortgage market in the first decade of the twenty-first century. The initial element was that of lowering interest rates by the FED in the beginning of the 2000s, entailing credit availability and lowering credit standards. This led to a boost in demand for housing and housing prices. But an additional element was that of securitization, having decisive consequences for both increasing the availability of credit and lowering lending standards.

It should be underlined, that in some way, increasing the possibilities to extend loans thanks to securitization was at the origin of a supply pressure on crediting, in particular in the US. When the prime borrowing sector became saturated, lenders turned to the subprime sector (Shin 2009). Thus profit-seeking enabled by rising leverage caused a deterioration in the quality of assets which were the basis of securitization. The same profit-seeking by the owners of banks (who wished to gain in spite of low basic interest rates) led to speculation on highly rewarding (but risky) products of securitization based on the non-transparent packaging of loans.

In the particular case of Europe, and specifically in the case of the Euro area, the common monetary policy applied by the ECB (low interest rates) confronted with different inflation rates provided for negative real interest rates in some countries, boosting borrowing. The system of supervision over the banks proved to be too weak to stop banks encountering insolvency risk (Hellwig 2008).

This interpretation neglects however the underlying situation, role and decisions of economic agents – in particular households – in the run-up to crisis. It does not explain why they decided to borrow. Excessive borrowing could, finally, lead to over-indebtedness.

There is however another trend in literature pointing to the impact of the changes on the labour markets and in the proportions between actual and expected welfare.

It is well known from statistics that since the beginning of the 1980s the proportion of wages in the value added was falling worldwide. This trend is explained by the speed-up of technological progress from the middle of the 1980s requiring flexible adjustments of employment and the deteriorating negotiating position of workers (Ellis and Smith 2007). The additional factor impacting on the change of proportion between wages and profits was globalization which increased the availability of cheap labour from emerging countries (and impacted by the competitive pressure of imports of cheap goods and by immigration) and thus making capital relatively rare, and sectoral changes towards the sectors with a lower proportion of wages, like finance (De Serres *et al.* 2001; Guscina 2006). Other research, however, indicates the strong impact of welfare state retrenchment, of the decreasing power of trade unions and liberal policies and also the growth of the financial sphere on decreasing the weight of wages in value added (Jayadev 2007; ILO 2008; Stockhammer 2013).

Tridico (2012) added a new element to the explanation of the decreasing trend of wages in value added. Namely, he argued that the increase of financialization (measured as a value of market capitalization in stock exchanges reported to GDP) exerted pressure for liberalization, resulting among others in wage reduction and increased flexibility in the labour market.

As can be seen from Table 9.1, the trend in the decreasing share of labour in value added was present in many (but not all) European countries and in Europe as a whole in the previous decade, and even earlier, until the crisis (when the trend was temporarily inverted), and it re-started in 2011 with austerity policies. The weakening of this proportion in the years 1995–2000 was particularly frequent in post-transition countries.

Table 9.1 Compensation of employees in value added

Country	*1995*	*2000*	*2008*	*2011*
European Union (28 countries)	–	0.562	0.545	0.554
European Union (15 countries)	–	0.565	0.552	0.559
Belgium	0.570	0.571	0.574	0.578
Bulgaria	0.455	0.4	0.410	0.444
Czech Republic	0.436	0.446	0.463	0.474
Denmark	0.604	0.613	0.653	0.647
Germany	0.607	0.607	0.556	0.566
Estonia	0.556	0.5	0.565	0.528
Ireland	–	0.44	0.511	0.463
Greece	–	0.375	0.404	0.400
Spain	0.533	0.553	0.539	0.534
France	0.580	0.580	0.579	0.593
Italy	0.460	0.441	0.464	0.472
Cyprus	0.480	0.466	0.497	0.503
Latvia	0.538	0.469	0.564	0.455
Lithuania	0.385	0.438	0.495	0.446
Luxembourg	0.521	0.519	0.521	0.527
Hungary	0.571	0.524	0.544	0.536
Malta	0.522	0.49	0.508	0.507
Netherlands	0.567	0.566	0.558	0.570
Austria	0.594	0.568	0.539	0.548
Poland	0.458	0.465	0.434	0.412
Portugal	0.544	0.560	0.574	0.567
Romania	0.417	0.438	0.475	0.386
Slovenia	0.652	0.596	0.580	0.597
Slovakia	0.440	0.472	0.398	0.414
Finland	0.567	0.545	0.562	0.593
Sweden	0.602	0.624	0.615	0.602
United Kingdom	0.576	0.611	0.593	0.604

Source: own calculations based on Eurostat data from the table: http://appsso.eurostat.ec.europa.eu/nui/show.do?dataset=nama_gdp_c&lang=en.

As to the consequences of the rising proportion of capital gains, according to some views it could underpin positive long-term consequences in terms of strong investment and job creation reducing unemployment (De Serres *et al.* 2001). It is however underlined in other studies that the impact of changes of both labour and capital gains on the scale and type of demand is far from obvious (Naastepad 2006).

The other kinds of consequences of pro-capital economic policy (profits at the expense of wages) were studied along the lines of a post-Keynesian approach by Lavoie and Stockhammer (2012). They claimed that income distribution is important for growth, both due to its impact on demand and on supply (labour productivity effects). They gave a number of arguments for the negative or positive growth effects of the rising or falling proportion of wages. They claimed, however, using the results of econometric studies and simulations, that in the majority of countries growth is actually wage-led. Thus the positive effects of pro-capital income distribution may be assured only due to debt (sustaining consumption) or exports (sustaining total demand). In their view, the contemporary global economy is based on a symbiosis between debt-led countries (such as the US) relying on financial inflows from other countries and export-led ones (China). This mode of growth, with conflict between the policy and growth regime, is unstable and unsustainable.

Tridico (2012) underlines the impact of the decreasing trend of wages on instability of growth, and also on the occurrence of the financial crisis of the last decade. Namely, unstable jobs and poor wages in the framework of consumerism (strong in the US, but also present in Europe) encouraged households to borrow.[3] This helped to sustain consumption, but at the cost of instability. In support of his argument Tridico quotes not only the growing level of indebtedness of US households, but also the higher inequality of income compared to consumption, made more equal by credit. Unsustainable consumption boosted by credit unavoidably led to financial crisis. As for Europe, the pressure of firms for labour market flexibility led also to a financial burden on governments obliged to provide social support to the unemployed.[4]

The explanation for the growth of consumption to income ratio before the financial crisis in the US (and then of its sharp fall after the crisis) provided by Cynamon and Fazzari (2013) links it to the rising inequality of incomes. The proportion of incomes of the top 5 per cent was rising which would normally imply a fall in the consumption to income ratio (due to the lower propensity of the rich to consume). However, due to the availability of credit, it resulted more in a high growth of debt-to-income for the poorer part of the population, enabling them to increase consumption. Cynamon and Fazzari underline the impact of the behavioural features of consumers (their tendency to stick to previous spending patterns and 'conspicuous' consumption, mimicking the rich, as postulated by Veblen in his book *The Theory of the Leisure Class: Study of the Evolution of Institutions*). The rise of household debt was however unsustainable and contributed to the fall in consumption after the crisis, making recovery difficult.

The objective of this chapter is to clarify what the role of the growing indebtedness of households in speeding up growth of consumption in the run-up to crisis was and in what way it could have contributed to the unsustainability of this growth. The role of household debt (and the underpinnings of its growth) will be shown first in the drastic example of post-transition countries. It will be then verified to what degree the role of household debt was relevant for the other countries of the European Union. Finally, the role of evolution of household debt during the recession in European countries and the possibility of speeding-up growth through consumer credit channels will be discussed.

3 The particular case of growing indebtedness in post-transition countries[5]

The evolution of post-transition country members of the EU before and after the financial crisis is a good illustration of the role of consumption and debt in raising the vulnerability of those countries.

3.1 Growth of consumption and of incomes

The countries of Central and Eastern Europe that have undertaken the transition to a market economy, and further accessed the European Union, constituted a particular case among European countries. As seen in Table 9.2, until 2008 all post-transition countries enjoyed rapid growth in GDP. This brought about fast convergence per capita in GDP, expressed in Purchasing Power Standard units, to the level of the countries of the European Union. Consumption per inhabitant also converged quickly to the level of EU15.[6]

According to general interpretation, this fast growth was due to a boost of entrepreneurship after the transition to the market economy, to the integration with the global economy (and in particular, with the European Union on the eve and after accession), and to substantial flows of Foreign Direct Investment (see discussion in Myant and Drahokoupil 2011: 299–312). However, the fast growth experienced until 2008 terminated in a deep fall in all (except two – Poland and Slovakia) post-transition economies after 2008.

This is not the only puzzle that can be disclosed beneath the 'success story' of post-transition countries. There was also inconsistency between growth of consumption and of earnings. While consumption per inhabitant rapidly converged to the EU15 level, the level of wages (average annual earnings in industry and services) still lagged behind. As the data for the EU15 are unavailable (and also for some post-transition countries), the level of wages will be compared in Table 9.4. to the Netherlands, where the household consumption per inhabitant is only 1–2 per cent higher than in the EU15.

One could try to explain this apparent inconsistency by the influence of the 'black market' (part of incomes not officially declared) which is known to be higher in post-transition countries than in Western Europe. However, the available studies suggest that earnings in the unofficial economy are by far lower than those in the 'official' one (*Praca*, 2005). Even if we take into account that part of the additional earnings in some professions (doctors) was undeclared, it could hardly explain the size of the gap between wages and consumption. To some degree the reason for the discrepancy between convergence of consumption and of earnings could also be remittances from people working abroad. As for social transfers, they are smaller as reported to GDP compared to the EU15 countries, so could hardly contribute to the improvement in the convergence to EU15 measured by consumption as compared to that measured by earnings.

The data quoted above suggest that there could be other structural reasons underpinning the discrepancy between growth of earnings and of consumption. In the following I will clarify the reasons for this discrepancy, in particular the growing levels of household debt. I will also assess the impact of those structural features of the growth of welfare on the vulnerability of economic growth in these countries.

Table 9.2 Growth and convergence of GDP and consumption

Country	*Cumulated GDP growth 2008/1995*	*GDP per inhabitant, in PPS, as percentage of EU15*		*Consumption per inhabitant,[a] as a percentage of EU15*	
		1995	*2008*	*1995*	*2008*
EU15	1.337	100.0	100.0	100.0	100.0
Bulgaria	1.590	27.3	39.2	7.6	18.7
Czech Republic	1.562	65.9	72.8	21.0	43.4
Estonia	2.214	30.9	62.2	10.5	39.8
Latvia	2.295	27.1	52.7	9.5	39.8
Lithuania	2.227	30.6	58.0	8.6	39.8
Hungary	1.488	44.2	57.6	17.1	34.3
Poland	1.808	36.9	50.7	16.2	35.5
Romania	1.593	28.1	44.2	8.6	26.5
Slovenia	1.728	64.2	81.8	45.7	58.4
Slovakia	1.901	40.9	65.3	13.3	41.0

Sources: own calculations based on Eurostat data from the tables: http://appsso.eurostat.ec.europa.eu/nui/show.do?dataset=nama_gdp_k&lang=en; http://appsso.eurostat.ec.europa.eu/nui/show.do?dataset=nama_gdp_c&lang=en

Note

a Final consumption of households and non-profit institutions serving households (NPISH).

Table 9.3 Increase/decrease of GDP 2009–2011

Country	*Cumulated change of GDP in %*
EU15	–0.9
Bulgaria	–3.5
Czech Republic	–0.5
Estonia	–5.7
Latvia	–13.4
Lithuania	–8.5
Hungary	–4.0
Poland	+10.1
Romania	–5.8
Slovenia	–6.9
Slovakia	+2.4

Source: own calculations based on Eurostat data from the table: http://appsso.eurostat.ec.europa.eu/nui/show.do?dataset=nama_gdp_k&lang=en.

Table 9.4 Consumption per inhabitant vs average earnings in post-transition countries, as a percentage of the Netherlands

Country	*Annual gross earnings*		*Final consumption of households per inhabitant*	
	2008	*2010*	*2008*	*2010*
Bulgaria	8.4	9.7	19.3	19.0
Latvia	20.1	17.9	40.4	33.5
Hungary	23.6	21.2	34.2	31.6
Romania	n.a.	12.7	26.7	24.1
Slovakia	21.9	23.2	41.6	44.3

Source: own calculations based on Eurostat data from the tables: http://appsso.eurostat.ec.europa.eu/nui/show.do?dataset=nama_gdp_c&lang=en; http://appsso.eurostat.ec.europa.eu/nui/show.do?dataset=earn_gr_nace2&lang=en.

Table 9.5 Expenditure on social protection as a percentage of GDP

Country	*1995*	*2000*	*2008*
EU15	20.9	19.3	18.4
Bulgaria	n.a.	12.7	11.2
Czech Republic	16.0	18.0	12.5
Estonia	10.8	11.0	11.6
Latvia	12.7	12.5	9.6
Lithuania	n.a.	12.0	12.3
Hungary	17.6	15.4	17.8
Poland	n.a.	n.a.	15.6
Romania	10.2	10.5	12.4
Slovenia	n.a.	17.9	15.9
Slovakia	14.4	16.0	10.2

Source: Eurostat data from the table: http://appsso.eurostat.ec.europa.eu/nui/show.do?dataset=gov_a_exp&lang=en.

3.2 The role of household debt

Different analyses of the crisis that took place in post-transition countries underline that its roots were in vulnerabilities created (or persisting) during the previous phase of fast growth. The fall in growth of post-transition countries after 2008 is attributed to exogenous factors. For example EBRD (2010) points out that sudden declines in output in the fourth quarter of 2008 were mostly impacted by the crisis in advanced countries. While the integration of post-transition countries with the rest of the world (through trade, financial flows, migration and remittances) that followed their transition to a market system boosted their pre-crisis growth, it also created significant vulnerabilities.

The confirmation that the type and speed of growth seen by post-transition countries in the late 1990s and early 2000s contributed to their vulnerability is common in the analyses of crisis. Already the IMF report (IMF 2009: chapter 1) points to the dependence of this growth on foreign-financed credit, additionally often extended in foreign currencies, and on foreign capital flows as the principal factors of exposure to the sudden stop of funding. The later analysis of Gardo and Martin (2010) identifies additional vulnerabilities present in all or in most post-transition countries in their phase of fast growth: credit/deposit ratios in banks rapidly rising, widening current account deficits, in some countries also the limited margin of manoeuvre of policy due to fixed exchange rates. The trade balance position is also indicated as an important factor of differentiation of the impact of the crisis on Eastern European countries by Pisani-Ferry *et al.* (2010), besides the growth (but not size) of credit as a crucial driver and also the deepening effect of a fixed exchange rate regime. As Table 9.1 shows, in post-transition countries the proportion of wages was substantially lower during all the post-transition period than in EU15 (with the notable exception of Slovenia). This table shows also that in almost all those countries for which data are available the proportion of compensation of employees decreased from 1995 till 2000, or till 2005 (as was the case in Slovakia). The proportion of the compensation of employees increased in all the countries (except Poland, Slovenia and Slovakia) over the period 2000–2008. Till 2000 the population thus received a systematically lower proportion of the fruits of growth and the growth of incomes was delayed compared to the growth of the value added. It means also that the proportion of profits in gross value added in post-transition countries was higher than on average in EU15 and it tended to increase. Low taxation of corporate profits, in particular in the Baltic States, should be underlined also.

The statistical data reveal rapidly growing levels of household indebtedness (both consumer and mortgage credit) in post-transition countries. Growth of the percentage of credit reported to disposable income proxies the contribution of credit to potential rise of consumption. This figure (in percentage points) is reported in the last column of Table 9.6. It is clear that debt allowed households in post-transition countries a much more substantial growth of consumption that in the countries of Western Europe.[7]

Table 9.6 Indebtedness of households and NPISH – debt as a percentage of disposable income

Country	*2000*	*2008*	*Change 2000–2008 in percentage points*
Euro area (18 countries)	74.92	95.17	+20.25
Czech Republic	13.33	49,65	+36.32
Estonia	15.01	91.91	+76.90
Latvia	8.55	70.78	+62.23
Lithuania	2.20	44.89	+42.69
Hungary	9.57	62.24	+52.67
Poland	9.79	48.03	+38.24
Slovenia	23.36[a]	42.38	+19.02
Slovakia	6.80	35.37	+28.57

Source: Eurostat data from the table: http://epp.eurostat.ec.europa.eu/tgm/table.do?tab=table&init=1&plugin=1&language=en&pcode=tec00104.

Note
a 2002.

I wish to show that growing indebtedness, allowing growth of consumption above this of incomes (and also enabling growth of housing sector) was underpinned by flows of external finance to those countries, but also by the pressure of needs on households. Those needs could be real but also imaginary (to follow the standards of richer people).

All post-transition countries received substantial inflows of foreign credits, as illustrated in Table 9.7. It was underlined by the analyses of crisis quoted above as the major reason of vulnerability of those countries.

Table 9.7 Inflow of foreign credits as percentage of GDP

Country	*Average 1995–2008*	*Standard deviation 1995–2008*	*Indicator of variation 1995–2008*	*Average 2009–2011*
Bulgaria	5	6	108	–2
Czech Republic	3	3	114	0
Estonia	9	7	75	–6
Latvia	15	10	67	–3
Lithuania	6	4	72	–6
Hungary	4	6	134	1
Poland	2	2	131	2
Romania	4	3	75	3
Slovenia	7	7	102	–7
Slovakia	4	6	162	5

Sources: own calculations based on Eurostat data from the tables: http://appsso.eurostat.ec.europa.eu/nui/show.do?dataset=bop_q_c&lang=en;http://appsso.eurostat.ec.europa.eu/nui/show.do?dataset=nama_gdp_c&lang=en.

It should be underlined that those credits were obviously channelled both to households and to firms. However, the role of households cannot be neglected. Supply of foreign finance alone would not be sufficient to explain such substantially growing indebtedness. It should meet demand on the side of households.

The populations of post-transition countries had reasons for assessing that their needs were not satisfied. One of those was the hopes that were invested in transition (Lissowska and Tridico 2010). Those populations were quickly disillusioned with the reality of transition. One should be reminded that workers in centrally planned economies enjoyed high levels of protection in labour relations and almost nonexistent unemployment.[8] Contrastingly, the transition to a market economy brought about a sharp rise of unemployment and a decrease in employee protection.

Rates of unemployment for post-transition countries are available in the Eurostat database only from the end of the 1990s. As before transition unemployment was almost nonexistent (the right to work was one of the principal rights of citizens and those not working were considered 'social parasites'). Thus Table 9.8. shows the dramatic social shock.

Unemployment was one of the reasons for falling into poverty by some layers of the population. It was also a source of pressure to make labour protection looser and to enable income inequalities. According to Eurostat data reported in Table 9.9, inequality, as measured by the Gini coefficient, was in the mid-2000s systematically higher in new Member States (the overwhelming majority of which are post-transition countries) than in the EU15. However, the degree of inequality tended to stabilize in post-transition countries (or even to decrease in some of them) over the decade, and in particular after the financial crisis. Inequality was particularly deep in the Baltic States, Bulgaria, Romania and Poland. High income inequality radically broadened the layer of the population at risk of poverty.[9] While this percentage in 'old' European Union countries was at the level of 20 per cent, it had reached 40 per cent

Table 9.8 Rate of unemployment in post-transition countries

Country	*1998*	*2000*	*2005*	*2008*
EU15	9.5	7.9	8.3	7.2
Bulgaria	–	16.4	10.1	5.6
Czech Republic	6.5	8.8	7.9	4.4
Estonia	–	13.6	7.9	5.5
Hungary	14.3	13.7	9.6	8.0
Latvia	13.2	16.4	8.0	5.3
Lithuania	8.7	6.3	7.2	7.8
Poland	10.2	16.1	17.9	7.1
Romania	5.4	6.8	7.2	5.8
Slovakia	7.4	6.7	6.5	4.4
Slovenia	12.7	18.9	16.4	9.6

Source: Eurostat data from the table: http://appsso.eurostat.ec.europa.eu/nui/show.do?dataset=une_rt_a&lang=en.

Table 9.9 Indicators of inequality and poverty in 2000s

Country	*Level of Gini coefficient*					*Population at risk of poverty after social transfers*	
	2000	*2005*	*2006*	*2007*	*2008*	*2000*	*2008*
EU15	29	29.9	29.5	30.2	30.7	15	16.3
New Member States (12)	–	33.2	33	31.8	31.3	–	17.3
Bulgaria[b]	25	25	31.2	35.3	35.9	14	21.4
Czech Republic	25[a]	26	25.3	25.3	24.7	8[a]	9.0
Estonia	36	34.1	33.1	33.4	30.9	18	19.5
Latvia	34	36.1	39.2	35.4	37.7	16	25.9
Lithuania	31	36.3	35	33.8	34	17	20.0
Hungary	26	27.6	33.3	25.6	25.2	11	12.4
Poland	30	35.6	33.3	32.2	32	16	16.9
Romania	29	31	33	37.8	36	17	23.4
Slovenia	22	23.8	23.7	23.2	23.4	11	12.3
Slovakia	–	26.2	28.1	24.5	23.7	–	10.9

Sources: Eurostat data from the tables: http://appsso.eurostat.ec.europa.eu/nui/show.do?dataset=ilc_peps01&lang=en; http://appsso.eurostat.ec.europa.eu/nui/show.do?dataset=ilc_di12&lang=en; http://epp.eurostat.ec.europa.eu/tgm/refreshTableAction.do?tab=table&plugin=1&pcode=t2020_52&language=en.

Notes
a 2001.
b break in time series.

(before social transfers) in new Member States by 2005, with particularly high levels in the Baltic States, Bulgaria, Romania and Poland. However, this measure of inequality was highly differentiated from one country to another (with particularly low levels in the Czech Republic and Slovenia) and decreased in a number of countries after 2005, and in particular in the period following the financial crisis.

The actual growth of household incomes was thus limited and in particular very unequal compared to the speed of economic growth. The newly emerging poverty of a big proportion of the population could hardly be compensated for by social transfers, which, as shown above, were weaker in proportion to GDP than in EU15 and, in the majority of post-transition countries, this proportion had decreased in the last decade, at least before the crisis.

As welfare expectations were very high on the eve of transition, the limited growth of incomes could cause frustration. Another factor for frustration could have been the availability of consumer goods, contrasting with acute shortages of supply before transition. Frustration was due not only to expectations which were not met, but also to actual poverty, as revealed by the high percentage of the population in a precarious situation.

Also the structure of needs changed. One reason for that was the withdrawal of the State from granting numerous services, in particular housing. Thus young couples had to look to private investment in apartments.

The above indicated inflow of foreign finance changed the opportunities of households to satisfy needs previously suppressed due to delayed growth of incomes, poverty or shortage of housing. It should be mentioned also that the lending practices of this period (both with respect to consumer credit and to mortgage credit) were aggressive and cared little about the creditworthiness of borrowers. It should be said also that the citizens of post-transition countries lacked sufficient financial education to be fully aware of their actual ability to repay loans.

There is some statistical evidence that income inequality impacts on the propensity to borrow. Namely, other research has confirmed that in Eurozone countries households with lower incomes tend to be more indebted in consumer credit and suffer much higher credit service burdens compared to richer households (Gomez-Salvador *et al.* 2011). It seems that poorer households tend to fill the gap between their income and their needs (or consumption wants) by credit. In the case of post-transition countries this gap could be particularly wide because of rapidly rising income differences (and the incidence of unemployment), expectations of welfare gains boosted by transition and aggressive marketing of consumer goods. It is obvious that transition to a market economy involved big cultural changes and could lead to an excessive propensity to consume and irresponsible borrowing.

The research carried out on Polish households in principle focuses on changes in their borrowing behaviour during transition. It tends however to confirm the existence of the pressure of needs on borrowing. The fact of having high burden of debt is frequent for households on the lowest incomes and with bigger sizes of household. They take consumer credit to satisfy their current (not home ownership) needs. It may be basic consumption needs (food and clothing), financing of fixed costs (like rent), or else financing previous debts. The richest and youngest households however tend to take mortgages under pressure of housing needs. Thus both higher income differentiation and lagging income growth may underpin household decisions to borrow (Bialowolski 2014). This borrowing would have different causes for poorer and richer layers of the population: to satisfy basic needs in the case of poor households, and to invest in housing (in particular, when it was insufficient or of insufficient quality before transition) by richer ones.

It may be concluded that the availability of foreign financial flows was obviously a factor in increasing vulnerability of post-transition economies. However, one of the internal factors underpinning this vulnerability was a particularly high propensity of households to fund their consumption (and housing) by debt. This propensity turned into growth constraint once financial flows were cut back and credits had to be repaid.

4 What is relevant for EU as a whole?

If the rise of household debt fuelling consumption and housing investment was a substantial factor of unsustainability of growth for Eastern European countries, could we say the same for Western European countries? Did it also expose them to higher risk of recession?

According to empirical research (Storm and Naastepad 2012) long-term growth of the majority of EU15 is based on consumption. However, growth of incomes of employees, as indicated in Table 9.1, was in many countries progressively suppressed up to the crisis to the advantage of the growth in profits. Thus, growing indebtedness was necessary to sustain growth of consumption. The question now is to what degree this indebtedness developed in the pre-crisis period and to what degree could it contribute to the vulnerability of Western European economies?

As can be seen from Table 9.10, the level of indebtedness of households in EU countries is very differentiated. What is even more significant, the change in percentage points of the relationship between debt and income between 2000 and 2008 was very different also. This change proxies the role of (net) inflow of credit in potentially financing consumption (meaning to what degree consumption relied on new credit). It should be however taken into account that household debt in Table 9.10 is the total of consumer credits and mortgage credits, the latter not directly financing consumption. Statistics may underestimate the actual level of debt, because it is based only on debt issued by monetary financial institutions (banks taking deposits or financing themselves by covered bonds) without taking into account (at least in some countries) other creditors (other financial institutions or sellers granting credits).

From Table 9.10 stem two conclusions in comparison between Eastern and Western European countries. The degree of indebtedness of households was and is, on average, much higher in Western European countries. But the increase of this indebtedness (and thus reliance of consumption on the net inflow of credit) was higher in Eastern European countries than in the majority of Western European countries. Among Western European economies, the fastest growth of indebtedness of households took place in Denmark, Ireland, Spain, UK, Finland, the Netherlands and Portugal. In those countries the growth of indebtedness of households was as fast as in post-transition countries.

However, it should be taken into account that only a part of household debt, namely consumer credits, could directly feed into consumption. The other part was credits for housing, approximated by mortgage debt in Table 9.11.[10]

The relationship between the whole of consumer credits to income cannot be directly compared to the relationship between mortgage credits and income, because they do not cover the same period of time and the methodology is not the same. We can see that, on average, in Western European countries there was a higher increase in mortgage credit than in Eastern European ones. Thus household credit could exert much more indirect impact (through the growth of the housing sector) than direct, by boosting consumption.

Table 9.12 illustrates growth of another part of household debt, this time only for consumption purposes.

Table 9.10 Gross debt to gross disposable income of households and NPISH (non-profit institutions serving households)

Country	*2000*	*2001*	*2002*	*2003*	*2004*	*2005*	*2006*	*2007*	*2008*	*Change[a] 2000–2008*
Euro area (18 countries)	74.9	75.1	77.2	79.7	83.1	87.8	91.7	94.1	95.2	20.3
Belgium	62.0	58.3	60.3	63.4	66.3	71.1	74.2	76.8	78.8	16.8
Czech Republic	13.3	14.2	19.1	20.5	26.1	31.4	36.5	45.5	49.7	36.3
Denmark	184.0	180.8	187.8	195.8	210.4	232.0	238.1	254.6	261.9	77.9
Germany	106.6	104.7	104.5	103.3	101.8	99.6	97.2	94.2	90.5	–16.2
Estonia	15.0	18.9	24.9	32.9	45.5	60.5	81.1	88.3	91.9	76.9
Ireland	–	–	112.2	126.6	146.7	170.9	191.8	202.8	198.8	86.5[b]
Spain	68.9	72.5	79.3	87.8	99.0	111.0	123.8	129.9	126.6	57.7
France	54.2	54.3	54.8	57.3	60.0	64.9	68.6	72.4	74.7	20.6
Italy	33.7	35.4	37.7	40.3	44.1	48.4	52.8	57.0	58.1	24.4
Latvia	8.6	9.7	14.5	20.7	29.6	48.6	70.9	81.2	70.8	62.2
Lithuania	2.2	2.7	4.8	8.0	13.7	21.2	31.6	44.1	44.9	42.7
Hungary	9.6	12.7	18.6	27.5	32.4	37.9	43.0	50.3	62.2	52.7
Netherlands	151.6	152.8	163.6	179.3	189.6	205.3	218.8	222.3	230.1	78.5
Austria	73.4	75.2	77.1	76.4	79.6	84.1	85.5	85.0	86.5	13.2
Poland	9.8	11.8	17.3	17.8	19.1	21.9	27.0	35.1	48.0	38.2
Portugal	83.8	89.1	96.2	102.2	108.2	113.9	121.9	126.4	127.6	43.9
Slovenia	–	–	23.4	24.6	25.6	29.3	34.4	40.4	42.4	19.0[b]
Slovakia	6.8	9.3	9.2	11.8	13.7	20.4	23.7	30.6	35.4	28.6
Finland	60.8	61.4	65.1	70.1	76.0	85.1	92.4	96.8	97.9	37.0
Sweden	96.2	97.2	100.8	106.9	115.2	123.8	130.4	132.5	136.5	40.3
United Kingdom	99.3	103.9	113.8	123.1	133.6	136.1	143.1	149.6	151.4	52.1

Source: own calculations based on Eurostat data from the table: http://epp.eurostat.ec.europa.eu/tgm/table.do?tab=table&init=1&plugin=1&language=en&pcode=tec00104.

Notes
a change in percentage points.
b compared to 2002.

Table 9.11 Residential mortgage debt as a percentage of gross disposable income of households and NPISH (non-profit institutions serving households)

Country	*Mortgage debt*			*Change of total household debt to income, between 2000 and 2008 in percentage points*
	2002	*2009*	*Change between 2002 and 2009 in percentage points*	
Belgium	43.9	69.7	25.8	16.8
Czech Republic	3.2	21.5	18.3	36.3
Denmark	155.7	213.0	57.3	77.9
Estonia	1.3	7.3	6.0	76.9
Finland	37.6	67.1	29.5	37.0
France	33.8	56.4	22.6	20.6
Germany	78.3	69.8	–8.5	–16.2
Greece	18.6	46.5	27.9	–
Ireland	37.5	158.2	120.7	86.5
Italy	14.3	27.2	12.9	24.4
Latvia	6.3	55.4	49.1	62.2
Netherlands	148.7	218.7	70.0	78.5
Poland	4.6	28.4	23.8	38.2
Portugal	66.1	90.0	23.9	43.9
Slovakia	6.2	23.3	17.1	28.6
Slovenia	12.2	17.1	4.9	19.0
Spain	54.8	94.1	39.3	57.7
Sweden	91.2	150.7	59.5	40.3
United Kingdom	92.1	129.7	37.6	52.1

Source: own calculations based on data from *Hypostat 2011*, EMF Brussels Table 2, p. 11 and Table 9.10, p. 165.

Table 9.12 reveals clearly higher growth of consumer credit in Central and Eastern Europe than elsewhere in Europe (except Greece).

If we now look at the relationship between the speed of growth of indebtedness and of household consumption, before and after the financial crisis, we obtain the following results (Table 9.13).

It should be noted that in the period 2000–2008 for the EU15 consumption grew by 16 per cent and for the period 2009–2010 it decreased by 1 per cent.

As said above, the whole debt, composed mainly of mortgages, could not have a very high impact on household consumption. It is confirmed by the Spearman correlation coefficient between change of total household debt to income and rise of consumption between 2000 and 2008 amounting to 0.43, which is significant but not very high. Conversely, the Spearman correlation coefficient between the change of consumer credit and rise of consumption over the same period is substantially higher, amounting to 0.61. This confirms that consumption in a number of European countries was boosted by consumer credit.

Keeping in mind the statistical imperfection of the figures characterizing household debt, it can be confirmed that sharply growing indebtedness of households, and in particular consumer credit, could be an important reason for the

Table 9.12 Consumer credit outstanding in percentage of household disposable income

Country	*2000*	*2002*	*2004*	*2005*	*2006*	*2007*	*2008*	*2009*	*Change pp. 2000–2008*
EU	13.0	13.2	14.0	14.5	14.6	14.9	14.8	14.4	1.8
Belgium	8.0	8.0	8.1	8.2	8.5	9.0	9.3	9.1	1.3
Bulgaria	–	–	12.4	17.7	18.1	23.9	26.0	26.5	13.6[a]
Czech Republic	1.9	3.2	4.6	5.7	6.5	7.4	8.4	9.0	6.5
Denmark	15.7	13.5	13.7	14.0	15.3	17.9	17.6	15.1	1.9
Germany	15.7	15.1	15.4	14.9	14.3	13.7	13.4	13.5	–2.3
Estonia	0.8	1.7	3.3	4.8	7.5	9.3	9.3	9.3	8.5
Ireland	13.9	16.0	19.2	20.4	19.5	19.7	18.6	18.6	4.7
Greece	5.3	8.6	13.0	15.6	17.9	19.2	21.3	20.3	16
Spain	11.5	11.2	11.4	13.0	14.5	15.3	14.3	12.9	2.8
France	11.9	11.6	12.0	12.3	12.3	12.3	11.9	11.7	0
Italy	4.5	5.1	6.3	7.3	8.3	9.2	9.7	10.2	5.2
Latvia	1.6	2.4	4.3	6.4	8.5	8.4	7.6	7.1	6.0
Lithuania	0.3	0.4	1.8	3.3	4.8	6.1	6.2	5.8	5.9
Hungary	2.2	3.2	5.8	9.1	12.3	16.6	22.7	23.4	20.5
Netherlands	6.2	7.4	9.1	9.3	9.3	8.6	8.6	8.4	2.4
Austria	18.2	16.4	16.2	17.3	14.9	14.2	13.3	12.6	–4.9
Poland	11.1	8.2	8.3	9.6	11.0	13.6	16.8	18.2	5.7
Portugal	9.5	8.3	8.9	8.9	10.4	12.2	13.1	13.3	3.6
Romania	–	–	–	8.6	15.2	20.4	21.6	23.4	13.0[b]
Slovenia	–	–	10.5	10.5	11.6	12.8	12.4	12.6	1.9[a]
Slovakia	–	–	2.5	2.8	4.0	3.8	4.4	4.0	1.9[a]
Finland	4.4	8.6	9.3	10.7	11.3	11.5	11.7	11.7	7.3
Sweden	–	6.6	7.1	7.7	8.4	8.7	8.9	9.1	2.3[c]
United Kingdom	20.6	23.3	25.4	25.8	25.2	25.4	25.5	24.8	4.9

Sources: European Credit Research Institute (ECRI), *Lending to households in Europe, 1995–2009* and Eurostat, *National accounts*, adapted from the original Table 3 in *Research note 4/2010 Over-indebtedness – New evidence from the EU-SILC special module*, European Commission, 2010 (http://ec.europa.eu/social/BlobServlet?docId=9817&langId=en). Responsibility for the adaptation lies entirely with Maria Lissowska.

Notes
a 2004–2008.
b 2005–2008.
c 2002–2008.

Table 9.13 Comparison of the growth of indebtedness and growth of consumption of households

Country	*Change of household debt to income, 2008–2000, in pp.*	*Change of consumer credit to income, 2008–2000, in pp.*	*Index of growth of consumption*	
			2008/2000	*2010/2008*
Belgium	16.8	1.3	1.11	1.03
Czech Republic	36.3	6.5	1.33	1.01
Denmark	77.9	1.9	1.19	0.98
Germany	–16.2	–2.3	1.04	1.01
Estonia	76.9	8.5	1.76	0.83
Ireland	86.5[a]	4.7	1.41	0.95
Spain	57.7	2.8	1.27	0.97
France	20.6	0	1.16	1.02
Italy	24.4	5.2	1.05	1.00
Latvia	62.2	6.0	1.97	0.79
Lithuania	42.7	5.9	1.94	0.78
Hungary	52.7	20.5	1.30	0.90
Netherlands	78.5	2.4	1.07	0.98
Austria	13.2	–4.9	1.12	1.03
Poland	38.2	5.7	1.34	1.05
Portugal	43.9	3.6	1.13	1.00
Slovenia	19.0[a]	1.9[b]	1.28	1.02
Slovakia	28.6	1.9[b]	1.51	0.99
Finland	37.0	7.3	1.30	1.00
Sweden	40.3	2.3[c]	1.19	1.04
United Kingdom	52.1	4.9	1.22	0.98

Sources: own calculations based on Tables 9.10 and 9.12 and Eurostat data from the table: http://appsso.eurostat.ec.europa.eu/nui/show.do?dataset=nama_gdp_k&lang=en.

Notes
a 2008–2002.
b 2004–2008.
c 2002–2008.

fast, but unsustainable rise of consumption, in Western European countries similar to (but to a lesser degree) the case of Central and Eastern Europe.

As to the reasons for indebtedness growing so fast, obviously some factors relevant for Eastern European countries were not present here. The populations in Western Europe did not live through transition, because they were already in market economies. They already had credits before and were more used to financial management of their budgets.

However, the period before 2008 was also particular for Western European economies. They enjoyed high rates of economic growth which, according to the hypothesis of the financial accelerator, brought about general optimism (also of creditors) and easing of lending standards. Deregulation of financial markets was progressing and new financial products emerged, for example zero-interest housing loans, which boosted the willingness to borrow. Interest rates were low (while still higher for unsecured consumer credits) which impacted on positive assessment of future wealth and the capacity for repayment. Finally, a borrowing culture proliferated among households, in spite of previously prudent spending attitudes (Chmelar 2013, 5–6).

Compared to the recently revealed features of the population of the Central and Eastern European countries, Western societies are more egalitarian and (with the exception of Germany and Italy) this feature did not change through the 2000s. However, when studying the data in Table 9.14 below it seems that less egalitarian countries (in terms of Gini coefficient or of the percentage of the population at risk of poverty) had a tendency of higher growth of credit to households. This was the case with Ireland, Spain, Portugal and the United Kingdom. It could be both because of the poorest population contracting credit for everyday purposes, and of the richer people investing in housing.

Thus, some underpinnings of rising household indebtedness are common. In the case of both groups of countries (Western and Eastern European) household debt was enabled by availability, and on relatively low price, of credits. It was also fuelled by consumerism promoted by the industry itself. Selling on credit on the very point of sale became a current commercial practice. The fact that the Consumer Credit Directive[11] which obliged creditors to provide comprehensive information to the consumers and check their creditworthiness was applicable only from 2010 was relevant for all of Europe. In some countries the reason of extensive borrowing was insufficiency (and inadequate quality) of the public housing assets. This obliged households to make housing investment themselves.

5 The role of household debt in recession and in recovery

Growing household indebtedness contributed to rapid growth of the European economies in the period preceding the financial crisis. However, this was precisely one of the reasons of the crisis. The subsequent rescue policy of European governments was directed mainly (while not exclusively) to the banks as agents of public interest. The bail-outs of banks at risk of default led to accumulation of government debt which, in the majority of European countries, was somewhat

Table 9.14 The indicators of inequality and poverty in European countries

Country	*Gini coefficient*		*Population at risk of poverty after social transfers*	
	2000	*2008*	*2000*	*2008*
European Union (27 countries)	–	30.9	–	16.5
European Union (15 countries)	29	30.8	15	16.3
New Member States (12 countries)	–	31.3	–	17.3
Belgium	30	27.5	13	14.7
Bulgaria[a]	25	35.9	14	21.4
Czech Republic	–	24.7	8[b]	9.0
Denmark	–	25.1	–	11.8
Germany	25	30.2	10	15.2
Estonia	36	30.9	18	19.5
Ireland	30	29.9	20	15.5
Greece	33	33.4	20	20.1
Spain	32	31.9	18	20.8
France[a]	28	29.8	16	12.5
Italy	29	31.0	18	18.7
Cyprus	–	29.0	–	15.9
Latvia	34	37.5	16	25.9
Lithuania	31	34.0	17	20.0
Luxembourg	26	27.7	12	13.4
Hungary	26	25.2	11	12.4
Malta	30	28.1	15	15.3
Netherlands	29	27.6	11	10.5
Austria	24	26.2	12	12.4
Poland	30	32.0	16	16.9
Portugal	36	35.8	21	18.5
Romania	29	36.0	17	23.4
Slovenia	22	23.4	11	12.3
Slovakia	–	23.7	–	10.9
Finland	24	26.3	11	13.6
Sweden	–	24.0	–	12.2
United Kingdom	32	33.9	19	18.7

Sources: Eurostat data from the tables: http://appsso.eurostat.ec.europa.eu/nui/show.do?dataset=ilc_di12&lang=en; http://appsso.eurostat.ec.europa.eu/nui/show.do?dataset=ilc_peps01&lang=en; http://epp.eurostat.ec.europa.eu/tgm/refreshTableAction.do?tab=table&plugin=1&pcode=t2020_52&language=en.

Notes
a for Bulgaria and France there was a break in time series.
b 2001.

decreasing before the crisis. Under the pressure of financial markets requesting high interest rates on sovereign debt the so-called exit policies were undertaken. Those policies, aiming at reducing government debt, focused more on reducing public spending than increasing tax revenues.

The reality of post-crisis is deleveraging, among others, of the consumer debt. However, as stems from Table 9.15, the fact and speed of deleveraging is much diversified from one country to another.

Table 9.15 Gross debt to household income in post-crisis period

Country	*2008*	*2009*	*2010*	*2011*	*2012*	*Change in pp. 2012–2008*
European Union (28 countries)	–	–	–	–	–	–
Euro area (17 countries)	95.04	97.64	99.53	98.94	98.43	3.39
Belgium	78.84	79.92	84.28	88.75	89.45	10.61
Bulgaria	–	–	–	–	–	–
Czech Republic	49.65	52.02	53.16	56.14	57.30	7.65
Denmark	261.91	269.92	266.81	266.44	265.65	3.74
Germany	90.47	90.51	88.21	85.76	84.53	–5.94
Estonia	91.91	95.70	92.94	82.66	80.46	–11.45
Ireland	198.77	208.95	205.80	203.05	197.75	–1.02
Greece	–	–	–	–	–	–
Spain	126.59	125.66	128.37	124.60	122.85	–3.74
France	74.73	78.08	80.54	82.36	83.33	8.60
Italy	58.05	62.50	64.99	65.28	65.75	7.70
Cyprus	–	–	–	–	–	–
Latvia	70.78	74.69	73.43	65.88	56.90	–13.88
Lithuania	44.89	45.89	43.07	40.08	37.66	–7.23
Luxembourg	125.81	131.90	134.57	140.45	142.90	17.09
Hungary	62.24	62.92	67.25	63.40	53.99	–8.25
Malta	–	–	–	–	–	–
Netherlands	230.06	243.88	250.70	248.86	250.34	20.28
Austria	86.51	85.96	89.15	89.24	86.44	–0.07
Poland	48.03	48.04	52.23	57.82	53.88	5.85
Portugal	127.60	130.52	128.10	126.53	122.48	–5.12
Romania	–	–	–	–	–	–
Slovenia	42.38	44.71	47.31	46.83	47.08	4.70
Slovakia	35.37	37.08	39.31	42.50	45.06	9.69
Finland	97.87	100.00	102.18	103.99	106.01	8.14
Sweden	136.46	142.04	148.89	148.29	147.19	10.73
United Kingdom	151.40	146.58	139.18	136.20	132.79	–18.61

Source: own calculations based on Eurostat data from the tables: http://epp.eurostat.ec.europa.eu/tgm/table.do?tab=table&init=1&plugin=1&language=en&pcode=tec00104.

In some European countries gross household debt even increased after the crisis. In others it fell slightly. It was, among others, the reality for countries subject to austerity policies (Ireland, Spain and Portugal). On the other hand, households in Estonia, Latvia, Lithuania, Hungary and United Kingdom reduced their debt substantially. It is even more striking because in those countries (except the UK) the absolute level of debt to income was much lower than in Western Europe.

The reasons for differentiation of deleveraging are multiple (Cuerpo *et al.* 2013). One of them is simply that the level of household debt was previously too high or growing too fast. However, it is difficult to assess the degree of debt overhang in individual countries. While some (Cecchietti *et al.* 2011) quote the figure of 85 per cent of debt to income as a critical threshold, there is no evidence of the relationship between the relative level of indebtedness and deleveraging.

Cuerpo *et al.* (2013, 3–15) assess the degree of debt overhang against the income of agents, approximated by GDP at the national level, and against the level of assets as a source of repayment. As an outcome, the degree of deleveraging pressures for individual countries was estimated.

Another approach is that of assessing the constraints on the side of supply of credit and of demand for it. As to the attitude of borrowers, the weak prospects of income increase and growing unemployment discouraged borrowing. The decline of incomes and consumption, due to rising unemployment and wage restrictions, obviously made households less creditworthy and also feeling insecure about their future.

As for supply, the deteriorating financial situation of the banks themselves could influence their prudent lending attitude. Namely, increase of the percentage of non-performing loans, lower profitability and tightening requirements with respect to capital ratio could lead to tightening of lending conditions. The survey on the lending standards of banks carried out by the ECB proves this tightening (Cuerpo *et al.* 2013, 25).

The bank's risk aversion impacted in particular on lending not secured by mortgage, perceived as more risky. However, the assessment of Cuerpo *et al.* (2013) indicates that demand side constraints had an impact in more countries than supply side ones. The factors of deleveraging are symmetrical to previous factors impacting on the rise of debt.

This analysis covers deleveraging in general, without particularly focusing on the elements of household debt. However, in my opinion the structure of household debt had a major role both for the dynamics of consumption and for the speed of deleveraging. It is true that the speed of deleveraging was clearly related to the previous rise of household debt in the pre-crisis period (as can be seen in Table 9.13). But it is also related to the structure of household debt, which is not so frequently noticed. Where the proportion of consumer credit in the overall debt of households was higher, deleveraging was deeper. This is technically understandable, because consumer credit is awarded for shorter duration, so just the refusal (or unwillingness) to roll it over would result in a rapid decrease of debt. This is not so automatically the case with mortgage credit.

Consumer credit, which represents a small proportion of household debt (only 13 per cent in 2009 in the EU on average) speeded up by 150 per cent in Europe between 1995 and 2008, much higher than in the US (Chmelar 2013, 15). This expansion was underpinned by over-optimistic expectations of growth. However, this type of credit is very sensitive to expectations and costs of credit. The fact that the proportion of consumer credit as an overall percentage of household credit was very different from one country to another impacted on the sensitivity of this stock of credit.

Unsecured consumer credit is perceived by creditors as substantially more risky and thus the risk premiums on this credit (and interest rates) are now substantially higher than on mortgage credit.[12] Interest rates on consumer credit are particularly high after the crisis. Costs of consumer credits (measured by Annual Percentage Rate of charge) exceed 10 per cent in the majority of European countries (even in the euro area), in spite of ECB rates at 0.5 per cent, which reduced the willingness to borrow. They are particularly high, even up to 35 per cent in the countries of Eastern and Central Europe.

Such high costs of credit would imply adverse selection of borrowers: only those badly in need of money (thus the poorest, more and more frequent in European countries) would decide to take those credits. It could in particular be the case with non-bank financial institutions (institutions not taking deposits) offering very short-term and very expensive credit to the customers rejected by banks.

Household deleveraging obviously contributed to recession, but it is difficult to assess to what degree. The simulation carried out by the European Commission services on the QUEST model indicate that household deleveraging would contribute to the contraction of GDP of a European economy of an average size by 3 per cent over three years (Cuerpo *et al.* 2013, 36–39). This is due to the contraction of housing investment and consumption, leading to shrinking demand, output and employment. This effect is amplified by the debt-deflation spiral (deflation increases real debt, thus forcing deeper deleveraging). Deflation leads also to an increase in real interest rates, discouraging capital investment. Fall in output, in its turn, deepens public deficit. On the positive side, due to an increase of exports and decrease of imports, deleveraging improves the current account position of the country. Furthermore, extensive deleveraging of the public sector deepens recession.

The problem is now recession. Actual speed-up of economic growth would improve fiscal revenues. But, this growth is lagging. One of the reasons for this persisting depression is insufficient lending and borrowing, in spite of the interest rates of central banks being at historically low levels. As for household debt, Table 9.15 shows that its proportion to incomes has decreased or stabilized. New mortgage lending declined and the stock of mortgage loans increased just by 1.9 per cent in 2011 (compared with 6 per cent on average over the period 2001–2011) (Hypostat 2011). The most flexible part of household debt, consumer credit, decreased by about 5 per cent compared to its maximum in 2007.

While this tendency to deleverage is understandable (the same as recommended to governments nowadays) and proves the higher risk awareness of borrowers, it has contributed to recession. Thus the opinions may be formulated that, to speed up growth and combat recession faster, it would be advisable to promote more lending. However, there are numerous obstacles making both lenders and borrowers unwilling to provide/get credit. The major problem is the existing (while very difficult to assess statistically) over-indebtedness of both companies and households. Discussions are ongoing on the advantages and disadvantages of enabling more flexible bankruptcy procedures for the private sector. With respect to households the challenge is what is left to the household after bankruptcy. Social reasoning would leave sufficient liquidity for living and consuming, while the commercial reasoning of banks is not very concerned about this. One of the opportunities discussed is *datio in solutum* – freeing households of the whole of their mortgage debt in exchange for giving residential properties to the lenders. While such a solution gives a 'new start' to the household, it is criticized as a possible source of moral hazard on the household side.

An obvious reason for discouraging both lending and borrowing are cloudy perspectives of growth and income. On the side of the banks, as said previously, non-performing loans and capital ratio requirements may discourage lending, in particular unsecured. Banks may turn rather to short-term speculative operations.

If promoting lending, the question is now if it should be lending to companies or to households. The current preference is to promote lending to companies, and in particular to SMEs as the biggest job creating sector and particularly disadvantaged by the banks. In this respect even easing of securitization has been proposed (European Commission 2014, 94–126).

Obviously, the role of investment and consumption demand for the economy is not the same. The major argument is that investment creates future money to repay debt, while this is not the case with consumption. It is true, however, that, according to the life cycle hypothesis, debt contracted by younger households (mostly for education and housing) would be repaid from revenues in older age. However, taking into account the empirical observation that growth in the majority of developed countries is wage- rather than profit-led, speeding up household consumption, albeit to overcome recession, should not be neglected.

As to mortgage credit, it is still increasing, although at a slower rate in spite of low interest rates. This type of lending, of a long-term nature, is less flexible. It is true, however, that in the countries subject to a housing bubble (like Spain) the situation is far from being cleared. It seems that there is neither room nor necessity to speed up mortgage credit beyond that linked to the life cycle of wealthy young households.

As to unsecured lending (consumer credit) the willingness to lend is much more limited and attention should be paid to the types of credits offered and the structure of agents on the supply and demand side. Interest rates on consumer credit are high (APR of 5 per cent to 35 per cent from one country to another). In some countries (UK) the speeding up of lending by non-bank financial institutions and having very high costs was revealed (OFT 2012). This kind of lending is clearly focused on people under substantial financial stress and who are moreover financially illiterate. Rolling-on those credits pushes them into an even worse situation. Due to high costs there is a negative selection of those borrowers, in principle very risky. Even a hypothesis of an emerging spiral of increasing risk and negative selection may be formulated: selection biases credit portfolio towards higher risk, which makes for increasing risk margins, sharpening still more negative selection.

Conclusion

It seems that rapidly rising household debt, in particular in the form of consumer credit, contributed substantially to a rise in consumption in the period of run-up to crisis. As in the majority of European countries growth is wage (or rather consumption) led, it contributed to the speed-up of growth. This growth was however unsustainable. One of its underpinnings was rising income inequality in European countries and credit was one of the tools to smooth this inequality. Poorer households were tempted to imitate the style of consumption of the rich and to follow the aggressive marketing practices of sellers. Taking credit was one of the means of 'keeping up with the Joneses'. Thus the willingness of creditors to lend to households and of households to borrow for consumption purposes contributed to the building of the financial crisis.

Speeding-up of consumption by debt was the most pronounced in post-transition countries, where rapidly inflowing foreign finance enabled meeting consumption expectations of the population, on top of softening rapidly increasing layers of poverty. But the Western European countries, while to a lesser degree, did not escape excessive propensity to borrow, both for housing and for consumption purposes. Both the Eastern and the Western European economies where consumption relied on credit, subsequently suffered a fall of consumer credit and of consumption.

If growth is wage-led, would the promotion of household debt help in overcoming recession? This seems to be doubtful, first of all, because of the already high over-indebtedness problem where the offer of very expensive credits risks provoking a rising spiral of risk margins and the negative selection of more and of more risky borrowers. Even if such credit would help people in financial stress in the short term, it cannot replace social remedies.

Notes

1 This chapter was initially prepared for the students of the Summer School of the European Association for Evolutionary Political Economy in Rome, July 2013.
2 The views expressed in this chapter are exclusively of its author and are not binding, in any case, on the European Commission.
3 It should be noted that a number of other conditions contributed to the rise of household borrowing: availability of credit thanks to securitization (Shin 2009), its low price due to lowering interest rates by FED, government policy promoting house ownership.
4 Tridico (2012) also indicates other factors weakening economic growth, namely low real investment and financial speculation to earn higher profits.
5 This section draws on Lissowska (2014).
6 In Tables 9.2 and 9.4 at current prices, for comparability with earnings in Table 9.4.
7 However, one should keep in mind that the figures in this table combine consumer credit and mortgage credit, thus only a part of this (consumer credit) would directly impact on consumption (while the boost of housing would have some indirect impact). The reader is invited to compare the figures in Table 9.6 with the ones in Table 9.11. Rise of mortgage debt (for the countries where the data are available) constituted on average less than half of the growth of household debt.
8 It was not necessarily positive for the economy as such – it provoked an artificial shortage of labour and risk of inefficiency of workers not exposed to any administrative discipline (Kornai 1980).
9 The threshold of the risk of poverty is defined as 60 per cent of the median national equivalized disposable income.

10 In some countries (such as Denmark) different credits, also for consumption, may be secured by mortgage.

11 Directive 2008/48/EC.

12 According to ECB data, the difference in APR on consumer credits as compared to mortgage credits goes from 2 to 10 percentage points (in countries reputated as risky: Czech Republic, Hungary, Latvia, Poland, Slovakia).

References

Bernanke, B., Gertler, M. and Gilchrist, S. (1998). The financial accelerator in a quantitative business cycle formation. *NBER Working Paper* No. 6455, Cambridge, MA: NBER.

Białowolski, P. (2014). Patterns of debt possession in Poland: a multi-group latent class approach. *Bank i Kredyt* 45(2) (forthcoming).

Cecchietti, S., Mohanty, M. and Zampoli, F. (2011). The real effects of debt. *BIS Working Paper* No. 352.

Chmelar, A. (2013). Household debt and the European crisis. *European Credit Research Institute Research Report* No. 13, Brussels.

Cuerpo, C., Drumond, I., Lendvai, J., Pontuch, P. and Raciborski, R. (2013). Indebtedness, deleveraging dynamics and macroeconomic adjustment. *European Economy Economic Papers* No. 177.

Cynamon, B.Z. and Fazzari, S.M. (2013). *Inequality, the Great Recession, and Slow Recovery*. Available at: http://dx.doi.org/10.2139/ssm.2205524.

De Serres, A., Scarpetta, S. and De la Maisonneuve, C. (2001). Falling wage shares in Europe and in United States: how important is aggregation bias? *Empirica* (4).

EBRD (2010). *Transition Report 2009. Transition in Crisis?*. London: European Bank for Reconstruction and Development.

Ellis, L. and Smith, K. (2007). The global upward trend in the profit share. *BIS Working Papers* No. 231, Basel: Bank for International Settlements.

European Commission (2014). *European Financial Stability and Integration Report*, Brussels. Available at: www.ecb.europa.eu/events/conferences/shared/pdf/EC_financial_integration_report.pdf?d8d7b6095ff770bebc48aa6ad25a9542.

Gardo, S. and Martin, R. (2010). The impact of global economic crisis on Central, Eastern and South-Eastern Europe: a stock taking exercise. *ECB Occasional Paper Series* No. 114, Frankfurt: European Central Bank. Available at: www.suomenpankki.fi/pdf/166571.pdf.

Gomez-Salvador, S., Lojschova, A. and Westermann, T. (2011). Household sector borrowing in the euro area: a micro data perspective. *ECB Occasional Paper Series* No. 125, Frankfurt: European Central Bank. Available at: www.ecb.europa.eu/pub/pdf/scpops/ecbocp125.pdf.

Guscina, A. (2006). Effects of globalisation on labor's share in national income. *IMF Working Paper* WP/06/294. Washington, DC: International Monetary Fund.

Hellwig, M. (2008). *Systemic Risk in the Financial Sector: An Analysis of the Subprime-Mortgage Financial Crisis*, Bonn: Max Planck Institute for Research on Collective Goods.

Hypostat (2011). *Hypostat 2011: A Review of Europe's Mortgage and Housing Markets*. Brussels: European Mortgage Federation.

ILO (2008). *World of Work Report 2008: Income Inequalities in the Age of Financial Globalization*. Geneva: International Labour Organization.

IMF (2009). *Global Financial Stability Report: Responding to the Financial Crisis and Measuring Systemic Risks*. Washington, DC: International Monetary Fund.

Jayadev, A. (2007). Capital account openness and the labour share of income. *Cambridge Journal of Economics* (31): 423-443.

Kornai, J. (1980) *Economics of Shortage*, Amsterdam: North Holland Press.

Lavoie, M. and Stockhammer, E. (2012). Wage-led growth: concept, theories and policies. *ILO Working Papers Conditions of Work and Employment Series* No. 41. Geneva: International Labour Organization. Available at: www.ilo.org/wcmsp5/groups/public/--ed_protect/--protrav/-travail/documents/publication/wcms_192507.pdf.

Lissowska, M. (2014). Welfare against growth gains in post-transition countries: what are the consequences for stability? *Economics: The Open-Access, Open-Assessment E-Journal* 8(2014–13). Available at: http://dx.doi.org/10.5018/economics-ejournal.ja.2014-13.

Lissowska, M. and Tridico, P. (2010). Hopes and reality in transition economies. *Rivista Dell'Associatione Rossi-Doria* 4: 7–33.

Minsky, H.P. (1992). The financial instability hypothesis. Working Paper No. 74, The Jerome Levy Economics Institute of Bard College.

Myant, M. and Drahokoupil, J. (2011). *Transition Economies: Political Economy in Russia, Eastern Europe, and Central Asia*. Hoboken, NJ: John Wiley & Sons.

Naastepad, C.W.M. (2006). Technology, demand and distribution: a cumulative growth model with an application to the Dutch productivity growth slowdown. *Cambridge Journal of Economics* 30: 403–434.

OFT (2012). *Payday Lending Compliance review*. Interim report, London. URL: http://80.86.35.165/shared_oft/business_leaflets/consumer_credit/OFT1466.pdf.

Pisany-Ferry, J., Petrovic, P. and Landesmann, M.A. (2010). Whither growth in Central and Eastern Europe. Policy lessons from an integrated Europe. *Bruegel Blueprint Series*, Vol. XI, Brussels: Bruegel. Available at: www.bruegel.org/publications/publication-detail/publication/453-whither-growth-in-central-and-eastern-europe-policy-lessons-for-an-integrated-europe/.

Praca nierejestrowana w Polsce w 2004 r. (2005). Warszawa: GUS.

Shin, H.S. (2009). Securitisation and financial stability. *The Economic Journal* 119: 309–332.

Stockhammer, E. (2013). Why have wage shares fallen? A panel analysis of the determinants of functional income distribution. Conditions of Work and Employment Series No. 35. Geneva: ILO.

Storm, S. and Naastepad, C.W.M. (2012). *Macroeconomics Beyond the NAIRU*, Cambridge, MA and London, England: Harvard University Press.

Tridico, P. (2012). Financial crisis and global imbalances: its labour market origins and the aftermath. *Cambridge Journal of Economics* 36: 17–42.

10 United in diversity

Consequences for common labour market policy in the times of crisis

Jacek Wallusch and Beata Woźniak-Jęchorek

1 Introduction

The theory of employment, and respectively unemployment, clearly remains a central problem in economic analysis. Regardless of their methodological background, the short-run fluctuations in aggregate (un)employment have particularly attracted economists' attention. Labour market dynamics have been explained by a whole variety of factors. Since the works of Hicks (1937) and Modigliani (1944), the present mainstream debates on the theory of employment/unemployment have substantially revolved around rigidities, their validity as a stylized fact, and, in the case of a positive answer, their sources and consequences.

A successful fight against unemployment also remains a central feature of the EU Labour Market Policy. Institutions have been implicitly considered by policymakers, especially after the outbreak of the global financial crisis. Aiming at the unification of the European labour market, the EU faces a dilemma, which is depicted in the struggle between regulation and deregulation. On one hand, a unified labour market constitutes the ultimate goal of the EU labour market policy. On the other hand, however, regional differences among the member countries require country-specific actions.

The newest developments in mainstream labour market theory put emphasis on stickiness and institutions. The former determine the real wage by the mark-up of the representative firm, which depends on the elasticity of demand in product markets. The latter determine the equilibrium unemployment, which in turn keeps the real wage at the level consistent with the mark-up. Persistent unemployment has a structural characteristic that ultimately depends on the institutional arrangement concerning unemployment benefits and employment protection. Obviously, the relationship between unemployment and labour market institutions goes much deeper. Norms, habits, traditions or culture affect the unemployment rate as well. The *science of social provisioning* is in sharp contrast to the *science of choices* (Dugger 1996). Whether or not economics is a study of *social provisioning* and emphasizes the fact that agents collectively secure their standard of living (Power 2004), a large scope of institutions must be covered by a labour market model.

In this chapter we try to provide some additional insight into this problem. We estimate a group of models and trace out the impact of real wage and institutional variables on the unemployment rate. Regardless of the methodological approach, real wage, or a proxy depicting the dynamics of real earnings, has been a standard element of many labour market models. For institutional variables we decided to employ the Kaitz index, gender gap, tax wedge and union density. The status of these variables, however, was much more complicated, as there was no agreement on whether they captured the impact of institutions on the unemployment rate or not.

Our results reveal huge differences between the labour markets in old and new EU countries. Perhaps the most important result concerns the response of the unemployment rate to changes in real wage. It turns out that a shock in real wage increases the unemployment rate in the old EU and decreases it in the transition countries. Changes in the Kaitz index create different responses as well. Although the direction of the unemployment rate's reaction to shocks in other institutional variables is the same, the magnitudes of the responses differ considerably. We also estimate the probability of significant responses; not surprisingly, they too differ considerably.

These conclusions seem to be particularly important regarding future recommendations for EU Labour Market Policy. The dilemma, whether to regulate or deregulate the labour market, becomes even more complicated to solve. A different direction and magnitude of unemployment's reaction to changes in real wages as well as in selected institutional variables favour de-regulation. Employees in CEE countries, however, favour rapid growth of real salaries and look forward to bridging the gap between new and old EU.

The reminder of this chapter is as follows. In the opening section, we present an overview of the findings of empirical studies on identification of institutional variables in the labour market. The third section summarizes the current development in the EU Labour Market Policy. The next section focuses on the statistical properties of the time series employed in our empirical investigations and reports the estimation results. The last section concludes.

2 What do we know about labour market institutions?

For many years, labour economics has enjoyed a vigorous and continuously growing discussion on the role of labour market institutions for the labour market flexibility and performance. Since the late 1990s, economists have been struggling with identification of institutions and their impact on the labour market. Empirical studies have flourished. Dynamic (e.g. Nickell *et al.* 2005 or Amable *et al.* 2007) and static (e.g. Bassanini and Duval 2006 or Baccaro and Rei 2007) framework within the cross-country context has been employed. Concerning the direct effects, Saint-Paul (2004) and Nickell and Layard (1999) provide an overview on theoretical mechanisms. Blanchard and Giavazzi (2003) and Griffith *et al.* (2007) have found a significant impact of product and labour market regulations. The dependence of macroeconomic shocks on labour market institutions and their joint effect on unemployment has also been analysed by Blanchard and Wolfers (2000) and Nickell *et al.* (2005). Even the interdependencies between labour market and financial market institutions have been studied (Wasmer and Weil 2004; Gatti *et al.* 2010). Despite a growing amount of studies, however, the available evidence still remains inconclusive or even contradictory (Blanchard 2006; Lehmann and Muravyev 2012).

The obtained results are far from consistent, showing considerable differences not only in terms of magnitude, but also in terms of direction of the influence. Howell *et al.* (2007) mention three main causes of the inconclusive results: selection of time period, selection of institutional indicators and the specification of models. Whilst the first point is hard to tackle since data limitations restrict the flexibility of choosing the time period, the latter two aspects can be reasonably dealt with (Sachs 2010).

Empiricists are confronted with the problem of finding reliable approximations for institutions. For some institutional categories several indicators capturing some vital aspects of institutions are available. The predominantly used indicators are: employment protection legislation (EPL), amount and duration of replacement rates, union density, bargaining coordination and centralization, labour taxes, product market regulation. Belot and Van Ours (2004) tested the interactions between the tax rate and the replacement rate, and the bargaining centralization with both the union density and the employment protection. Bassanini and Duval (2009) concentrated on the relationships between single institutions and the institutional framework as a whole.

More recently, Sachs (2010, 2011) applied a Bayesian Model Averaging approach to a panel covering 17 OECD countries for a long time span (1982–2005). Using data on 14 institutional indicators of five institutional categories (product market regulation, employment protection, unemployment benefit system, labour tax system, bargaining system), Sachs showed that a number of institutional indicators are robustly linked to the evolution of the unemployment rate. Specifically, the robust factors are the employment protection legislation, the public ownership and the barriers to entry, the payroll tax and the consumption tax rate, the bargaining coordination, as well as the unemployment benefits for the first year, and the fourth and fifth year of unemployment (Sachs 2010).

Studies on labour market institutions concern also the volatility of wages. Abbritti and Weber (2010) investigated the importance of labour market institutions for inflation and unemployment dynamics. Using the New Keynesian framework, they argued that labour market institutions should be divided into institutions causing unemployment rigidities and causing real wage rigidities. The two types of institutions have opposite effects and their interaction is crucial for the dynamics of inflation and unemployment. Within the VAR framework, Abbritti and Weber found that there is a profound difference in the responses of unemployment and inflation to shocks under different constellations of the labour market.

Not surprisingly, the effects of real wages have always been of special importance for applied works. The relationships between real wages, economic growth and output have been analysed, among others, by Prescott (1998) and

Hall and Jones (1999). The impact of real wages on migration has been studied by Hendricks (2002) and Rosenzweig (2010). The link between real wages and inequalities has been shown by Deaton (2010). Finally, Rodrik (1999) offers an example of real wage analysis within the political economy framework.

In the context of wage analysis, the most controversial and frequently discussed issue is the effect of minimum wage on the employment and unemployment rate. Although the conventional textbook labour market model clearly predicts disemployment effects following the introduction of a binding minimum wage (Cahuc and Zylberberg 2004), a theoretical case for positive employment effects has also been formulated (notably by Card and Krueger 1995). In light of this theoretical ambiguity, economists have mobilized a variety of methods (time-series analysis, cross-section and panel data, controlled experiments relying on difference-in-differences estimators, identification of substitution and scale effects, distinction between effects on employment and hours, etc.) in an on-going attempt to measure the underlying employment elasticity. This body of research failed to establish a lasting consensus, with some researchers concluding from extant evidence that employment elasticity is significantly negative (Brown *et al.* 1982; Neumark and Wascher 2004), while others defend the opposite conclusion (Card and Krueger 1995). A reconciliatory position in this debate is the view that any employment effects (be they positive or negative) are probably very small (Kennan 1995; Dolado *et al.* 1996; ILO 2010).[1]

The analyses of labour market institutions predominantly focus on the developed countries. The evidence available for transition countries is much more limited. Cazes and Nesporova (2003) have estimated that the labour market institutions in Central and Eastern European countries during the late 1990s had had a similar impact on the labour market performance as in the developed countries. They have also suggested, however, that the influence of labour market institutions on labour market performance in the group of the Commonwealth of Independent States could be significantly different than in the Central and South-Eastern Europe. Cazes and Nesporova as well as the recent work of Fialova and Schneider (2009) or Lehmann and Muravyev (2012) have relied on standard linear regression models. Empirical studies mostly utilize OECD data. A standard routine is to augment the EU-15 countries by the data from a handful of transition countries (typically, the Czech Republic, Hungary, Poland and the Slovak Republic). Only Lehmann and Muravyev (2011, 2012) have grouped the transition countries and have distinguished between Central European economies (Czech Republic, Estonia, Hungary, Latvia, Lithuania, Poland, the Slovak Republic and Slovenia), South Eastern European economies (Albania, Bosnia and Herzegovina, Bulgaria, Croatia, Macedonia, Montenegro, Romania and Serbia) and the Commonwealth of Independent States (CIS[2]). Lehmann and Muravyev have also presented a comparison between these groups, EU-15, and the US. They have also created a unique dataset covering the European and Central Asian transition countries, which have experienced radical economic and institutional transition during the last two decades. Their econometric analysis implies that institutions matter for labour market outcomes and that deregulation of labour markets improves their performance. The analysis also suggests several significant interactions between different institutions, which is in line with the idea of beneficial effects of reform complementarily and broad reform packages (Lehmann and Muraveyv 2012).

3 EU Labour Market Policy in 2008–2013

The contemporary EU Labour Market Policy has become eclectic. Contrary to the popular beliefs, the policy aims at deregulating the labour law. It is also true, however, that the EU policy tends to unify the European labour markets. The former should result in increased flexibility of labour markets. The latter reflects the attempts to co-ordinate the policy actions. Whether this diverse policy will be successful or not depends on how the policy will adjust to structural differences. An interesting example of overcoming the institutional background offers the system of Country-Specific Recommendations. The Recommendations are meant to tackle specific issues appearing in different parts of the European Union. Problems appear regardless of the institutional background. The solutions, however, depend heavily on institutions.

The economic crisis that first broke out in 2008 has taken a tremendous toll on labour markets across the EU. Unemployment figures have increased, while employment rates continue to fall. It has been observed that the crisis has served to accelerate previously existing structural trends, generating increasing inequality, polarization and atypical employment (Crisis takes its toll: disentangling five years of labour market developments, p. 27). The aim of the EU policy was demonstrating that, the stricter the labour law, the less flexibly the labour market can operate.

However at first, policy action in response to the crisis of 2008–2009 focused on containing the short-term labour market impact of the crisis. EU countries put in place fiscal stimulus measures to sustain aggregated demand and contain excessive job shedding, in line with what was recommended in the European Economic Recovery Plan of November 2008. Temporary measures included employment subsidies and targeted labour cost reductions, the reinforcement of automatic stabilizers, and the implementation of short-time working schemes (Labour Market Developments in Europe 2013, p. 51).

In 2010, in response to what was arguably a crisis of globalization, the EU launched also the Europe 2020 strategy for growth as a successor to its only partially successful Lisbon strategy (Developments in inequality and social protection in Europe, p. 45). The principal aim of this new long-term strategy is to deliver more growth that is simultaneously 'smart' – by means of additional investment in education, research and innovation; 'sustainable' – by, among other things, moving in the direction of a low-carbon economy; and 'inclusive' – by boosting job creation (with 75 per cent the employment rate target for the population aged 20–64) and reducing poverty (European Commission 2010). 'Inclusive growth' is consistent with a long-standing objective of European integration, namely to drive upward convergence of living standards among EU citizens.

The notion underlying this policy mix was that to improve people's chances of finding sufficiently well-paid employment by enabling them to acquire the appropriate skills, in conjunction with a labour market that allows individuals to move across jobs and countries and a social protection system that supports income and increased labour market participation, constituted a recipe for success (European Commission 2010).

In order to ensure that the Europe 2020 strategy delivers on these goals, a system of economic governance has been put in place to coordinate policy actions between the EU and the national levels.

While labour market reforms are adopted at the national level in the Member States, the impetus and initiative for such reforms have their roots in the European Union's management of the financial and economic crisis, followed by the sovereign debt crisis and in its new economic governance programme. At this European level, two main tools can be identified: the Country-Specific Recommendations (CSRs) for most Member States issued by the European Commission under the so-called 'European Semester' and the 'Macro-economic Imbalance Procedure' and the Memorandums of Understanding (MoU) for the programme countries – i.e. those currently in receipt of, or having in the past received, financial assistance from the EU as a bailout to cope with the crisis (i.e. Greece, Ireland, Portugal and Cyprus). Another development that will affect European legislation – in this area and more generally – is the recent introduction by the European Commission of a new Regulatory Fitness and Performance Programme (REFIT) that will have an impact on the entire EU legislative stock and, in particular, the social field (Deregulation of labour law at any price, 2014, pp. 59–60).

Since 2010, the fight against the crisis has been partially phased-out due to fiscal constraints. Smooth re-balancing has become necessary in countries troubled by current account reversals. Reform action becomes increasingly focused on macro-structural aspects of employment protection, automatic stabilizers and the wage setting framework (Labour Market Developments in Europe 2013, p. 51).

Another area where the EU institutions are increasingly active is in wages systems. In principle, the European Union has no competences with respect to wage levels or wage-formation mechanisms. The treaties of Maastricht, Amsterdam and Lisbon exclude the wages from the EU competences. But in the first decade of the new millennium the debate on minimum-wage co-ordination in the EU resurfaced: first, as a result of the EU enlargements and concerns about their impact on low wages and social dumping, and second, in the context of the economic crisis and problem of Europe's competitiveness. The crisis has made wages (both their development and the mechanisms of their formation) one of the central targets of EU policymaking.

With the adoption of the so-called Euro-Plus Pact in March 2011, wages have been officially declared a main adjustment variable for re-addressing economic imbalances and national competitiveness in Europe. The most direct forms of European intervention in national wage policy are to be found in those countries currently dependent on international loans from the EU and the IMF. However, within the new framework of European Economic Governance, the systematic surveillance of national wage developments and the regular recommendations for national wage-setting have become a normal feature of European policy due to minimum wages exerting a strong influence on the national wage structure and the degree of wage dispersion. Indeed, in many European countries – especially those with relatively weak collective bargaining systems – minimum wages have a signalling character for the overall wage developments (Schulten 2012a, p. 1).

The debate on establishing more explicit mechanisms of wage policy coordination, in particular minimum wage levels, is currently re-emerging in European policy and focuses along three axes (Fernandez-Macias and Vacas-Soriano, 2014, p. 93; for an overview of the attempts to co-ordinate the minimum wage at the pan-European level see also Vaughan-Whitehead 2010):

- the mode of regulation (hard law opposed to soft law in EU terminology);
- the extent of co-ordination (levels versus systems with the countries where minimum wages are set by government regulation – the statutory model and countries where minimum wages are set by collective bargaining);
- the definition of target levels (a proportion – 50 per cent or 60 per cent of median or average wages or gross domestic product (GDP) per capita or per worker).

The institutional difficulty in setting common wage policy (different systems and situation on local labour markets) and current minimum wage levels and their distance from the hypothetical common target are very important axes of divergence across Europe.

Apart from wages system, the EU labour reforms concern law and are designed to boost business flexibility, to reduce the alleged complexity and strictness of labour law. The financial and economic crisis was used as a pretext to carry out reforms (Cazes *et al.* 2012; Clauwaert and Schömann 2012; Escande Varniol *et al.* 2012; Lokiec and Robin-Olivier 2012).

Interestingly, in 2011 and 2012, a number of major, wide-ranging reforms of labour market took place not only in countries participating in financial adjustment programmes with structural reform conditionalities (notably Greece, Portugal), but also in countries that had accelerated the pace of reform as a result of rising bond market tensions and capital flights (e.g. Spain, Italy, Slovenia) and with a view to creating the conditions for a competitiveness recovery (e.g. the 2013 reform in France) (Labour Market Developments in Europe 2013, p. 51).

Needed changes in these countries included: reform of public services (EPSU 2012), reform of industrial relations systems and fundamental reforms of individual and collective labour law (including working time, atypical employment, and dismissal protection law, as well as collective bargaining systems) (Clauwaert and Schömann 2012; Schömann 2014, p. 23).

The current EU strategy for a job-rich recovery for the year before includes some priorities like (Labour Market Developments in Europe 2013, p. 57):

- prioritize, and strengthen wherever possible, investment in education, research and innovation, and pay particular attention to maintaining or reinforcing the coverage and effectiveness of employment services and Active Labour Market Policies, such as training for the unemployed and youth guarantee schemes and life-long learning;
- pursue the modernization of social protection systems to ensure their effectiveness, adequacy and sustainability, including by restricting access to early retirement and enabling longer working lives, and by monitoring the impact of unemployment benefits to ensure appropriate eligibility and effective job-seeking requirements;
- substantially reduce the tax burden on labour, notably for the low-paid and in those countries where the tax burden is comparatively high and hampers job creation;
- continue to modernise labour markets by simplifying employment legislation, notably to reduce labour market segmentation, and develop flexible working arrangements;
- monitor the effects of wage-setting systems, in particular indexation mechanisms, and if necessary, amend them.

In particular, the Country-Specific Recommendations agreed for 2013–2014 propose, for example, to create the conditions for increasing labour market participation of underrepresented groups including women (e.g. Austria, Germany, Hungary, Malta, Netherlands, Poland, Slovakia), older workers (e.g. Austria, Belgium, Bulgaria, Finland, France, Luxembourg, Poland), migrant workers (e.g. Austria, Belgium, Sweden) and the low-skilled (e.g. Bulgaria, Sweden among others). Some Member States have been also recommended to shift taxes from labour to less growth distortive tax bases, notably with a view to reduce the tax burden on labour for low-income earners (e.g. Austria, Belgium, the Czech Republic, France, Latvia, Slovakia). A few countries, including Belgium, Luxembourg, Finland, France and Slovenia, were recommended also in 2013 to renew their efforts to ensure that their wage-setting systems – including where appropriate wage indexation or minimum wage – allow for wages to better respond to productivity developments and labour market conditions, so as to support competitiveness and job creation. Another important initiative was the Social Investment Package of February 2013. This Package was grounded on the idea that social policies should empower people from an early age, strengthen their capabilities to cope with risks across the course of life and enhance their opportunities to participate in society and the labour market.

A part of this Social Package is the Youth Employment Package of December 2012. This Package includes a Council Recommendation to introduce Youth Guarantee schemes, a Quality Framework for Traineeships and a European Alliance for Apprenticeships to facilitate school-to-work transition by improving the quality and supply of apprenticeship and traineeships across the EU (Labour Market Developments in Europe 2013, p. 58).

To conclude, all Member States of the EU require substantial structural reforms aiming at improving the resilience of the labour market. The reforms should introduce more internal and external flexibility, and facilitate the transition between jobs. The common pan-European labour market still faces pertinent challenges concerning the support of employment, the mobilization of labour supply and demand, as well as poverty and social exclusion across the Union.

4 Data and empirical strategy

The selection of indicators is closely related to the question of how to specify the model. Considerable regional differences within the European Union may influence both significance and the direction of the response of unemployment to changes in other variables. For our research we have chosen:

- gender gap index
- real wages
- Kaitz index
- union density
- tax wedge.

Union density and tax wedge are the predominantly used indicators as institutional categories in the studies. The gender gap and the Kaitz indices are the new approaches to the analysis of labour market institutions.

Why is gender gap a manifestation of institutional changes? Gender gap is defined as the differences between women and men, especially as reflected in social, political, intellectual, cultural or economic attainments or attitudes. Gender gap may refer to: gender pay gap,[3] income disparity by gender in a purely economic context, workers number gap – the difference between the number of men and women in a profession, or unbalanced sex ratio.

In turn, the significance of the minimum wage is not determined by its absolute value alone but also by its position within each national wage system. A direct comparison of absolute levels of minimum wages is not meaningful if countries differ with respect to the distribution of productivities: in a country with high average productivity, the 'bite' of a relatively low wage floor might be weak; in a low-productivity country, however, the same minimum wage could have a much stronger impact.

A straightforward method to relate the absolute level of the minimum wage to other wages is the so-called Kaitz index (named after its first formulation in 1970 by the American economist Hyman Kaitz) which serves to express the relative value of the statutory minimum wage and is measured statistically by expressing the minimum wage as a percentage of the national average or median wage of the working population (Schulten 2012a, p. 4).

The Kaitz index is thus a measure of the 'bite' of the minimum wage: small values indicate that the wage floor is a long way from the centre of the earnings distribution and its impact therefore potentially low; conversely, a high Kaitz index reveals that the minimum wage is close to the centre of the distribution and that it potentially affects a larger number of employees. It should be noted, however, that the Kaitz index alone does not allow any conclusion to be drawn about whether a given level of the minimum wage is economically desirable or not. This question can only be addressed with additional information such as the structure of wage costs and the productivity of different types of workers (Rycx and Kampelmann, 2012, p. 18). In addition, as Dolado *et al.* point out, the Kaitz index may misrepresent the impact of minimum wages in countries where other institutions such as benefit systems act as effective wage floors (Dolado *et al.*, 1996, p. 325).

European countries are not homogeneous with respect to their minimum wage policies. Indeed, minimum wage systems typically reflect the wider institutional context of national labour markets as well as their historical development. For example many transition countries from Central and Eastern Europe operate systems in which a single wage floor is fixed at the national level. This is contrary to countries with strong traditions of sectoral bargaining like Italy or Sweden where trade unions negotiate different minima for each sector.

In our case we can distinguish between the countries where:

- the minimum wage that applies to most workers and employees is determined through the decision of a governmental agency or collective bargaining at the national level: France, the Netherlands, the UK, Ireland, Spain, Portugal, Poland, the Czech Republic, Hungary, Slovakia, Estonia, Lithuania, Latvia and Slovenia;
- the minimum wage that applies to most workers and employees is determined at the European level, for instance in sector or regional negotiations: Belgium, Greece.

Gender inequality, as well as the level of average and minimum wages, is an important element of institutional structure of the labour market. Defining this structure, we can refer to the 'four levels of Social Analysis' of O.E. Williamson (2000), who treated the institutional framework as exogenous and explored the transaction and transformation costs of various organizational forms (Williamson 2000, pp. 595–612). He distinguished four levels of institutions: level 1 refers to informal institutions (as norms, traditions, culture), level 2 relates to the formal environment (formal rules of the game), level 3 where the institutions of governance (play of the game, rules of transaction) are located and level 4 of resource allocation and employment (conditions of economic decisions).

In the case of labour market analysis, level 2 concerns the legislation conditioning labour market policy (Labour Code, Legal Acts relating to the labour market, social security system, tax system) and labour's market organizations (i.e. unions, organizations of employers, etc.). In turn, level 3 concerns the types of contracts and system of wage bargaining. Level 4 contains determinants of individual decisions of employees and employers as the level of wages, duration of employment, work intensity and activity (Woźniak-Jęchorek 2013, p. 19). Thus the gender gap and Kaitz indices, as well as real wages as institutions, are located in level 4 of institutional structure of the market.

To show gender inequality we have chosen the complex Global Gender Gap Index introduced by the World Economic Forum in 2006. This index examines the gap between men and women in four fundamental categories (sub-indices): economic participation and opportunity (outcomes on salaries, participation levels and access to high-skilled employment), educational attainment (outcomes on access to basic and higher level education), political empowerment (outcomes on representation in decision-making structures) and health and survival (outcomes on life expectancy and sex ratio). We can interpret the score as the percentage of the inequality between women and men that has been closed. In the case of all sub-indices, the highest possible score is 1 (equality) and the lowest possible score is 0 (inequality), thus binding the scores between inequality and equality benchmarks. The equality and inequality benchmarks remain fixed across time, allowing the reader to track progress of an individual country in relation to an ideal standard of equality. It is important also that while many global indices tend to be tied to income levels, the Global Gender Gap Index is disassociated from the income and resource level of an economy; instead it seeks to measure how equitably the available income, resources and opportunities are distributed between women and men.

To calculate the Kaitz index, we used the data from the ILO Minimum Wage Database and National Statistics Offices. The ILO provides detailed information on current levels of minimum wages, including existing sub-minima, and average nominal wages, but the problem was with the complexity of data for the years 2000–2012. We have also employed the OECD Minimum Wage Database and Eurostat, but the coverage of the former database is much broader and includes all 100 ILO member countries.

Other institutional indicators used in our research are union density and tax wedge origin of the OECD Database.

International comparisons of labour union power focus on union membership in relation to the total labour force (union density). We used the data from the OECD and ICTWSS database (Institutional Characteristics of Trade Unions, Wage Setting, State Intervention and Social Pacts, 1960–2010) (Visser 2010). Trade union density corresponds to the ratio of wage and salary earners that are trade union members, divided by the total number of wage and salary earners (from OECD *Labour Force Statistics*). This is the gross density rate defined as total union membership including the unemployed, students and retired workers as a share either of all wage and salary earners in employment or of the civilian labour force, which includes the unemployed. The broader definition shows a more realistic picture of the labour unions' representation in the workforce. However, the higher the number of unionized retirees, the more distorted is the density rate. To avoid this, we can focus on the net union density rate, which is calculated by dividing net union membership (total membership less unemployed and retired) by the number of active wage and salary earners (Lesch 2004, p. 12). For showing a general trend we used the broader definition of gross density rate.

Tax wedge shows the difference between the total labour cost incurred by the employer and the net remuneration of the employee. The measure of the tax wedge on labour is defined as the difference between the salary costs of a single 'average worker' to their employer and the amount of net income ('take home pay') that the worker receives. The taxes included are personal income taxes, compulsory social security contributions paid by both employees and employers, the family benefits they receive in the form of cash transfers as well as the social security contributions and payroll taxes paid by their employers for the few countries that have them. The amount of these taxes is expressed as a percentage of the total labour costs for firms, i.e. the sum of gross earnings, employers' social security contributions and payroll taxes. The 'average worker' is taken to represent a full-time worker in industry (OECD 2007, p. 60).

5 Empirical investigations

In our empirical investigations we use separate panels for old and new EU members. The first group consists of Belgium, France, Greece, Ireland, the Netherlands, Portugal, Spain and the UK. The second group consists of the Czech Republic, Estonia, Hungary, Poland, Latvia, Lithuania and the Slovak Republic. The series are yearly and cover the time span between 2000 and 2011. Notice, however, that the sample size changes and depends primarily on the availability of data. For the old EU members we adjust only one model, skipping France due to the missing observations on gender gap prior to 2006. For the new EU members the entire group is used only for the model with the Kaitz index. The series from Latvia and Lithuania are not available for models with tax wedge and union density. For the latter variable, Hungary is also skipped. Estonian data is missing in the model with the gender gap.

In this section we first summarize the statistical properties of the labour market variables. To ensure stationarity the series is expressed in first differences. We present the descriptive statistics and focus on the kernel densities of the variables. Then we estimate a structural VAR model to perform the impulse-response analysis. The availability of data has influenced the empirical procedure. Instead of estimating one structural model of unemployment with five explanatory variables, we use separate structural vector autoregression models with unemployment rate, real wage and one institutional variable. Again, to ensure stationarity, the SVAR models are estimated for the first differences. The data ordering depicts our assumptions on the instantaneous causality, which goes from the real wage, through the institutional variable, to unemployment rate. Structural factorization is used to perform the impulse-response analysis. Finally, we checked for significance of the estimated values of the response functions. We did not intend, however, to trace out whether the responses of unemployment to shocks in selected variables of interest are significant or not at a pre-specified significance level. Instead, we report the empirical probabilities that the estimated responses significantly differ from zero and compare these probabilities for both groups of countries. We apply the method presented by Lütkepohl (2005) and calculate the probability for the first $k(K-1)$ responses, where K stands for the number of variables, and k is the lag length. Notice that the estimated model has been selected by minimizing the Schwarz criterion and checked for stability. The error bands for impulse-response analysis were obtained analytically.

5.1 Statistical properties of labour market variables

The estimated kernel densities for variables expressed in first differences are presented in Figure 10.1. Additionally, in Table 10.1 we report the descriptive statistics. Whilst the differences in mean value, skewness and kurtosis are rather moderate, standard deviation exposes how heterogeneous the EU labour market is. With the exception of gender gap, the standard deviations estimated for the transition countries are almost two times greater. A large volatility should be therefore considered a stylized fact of the Central European labour market.

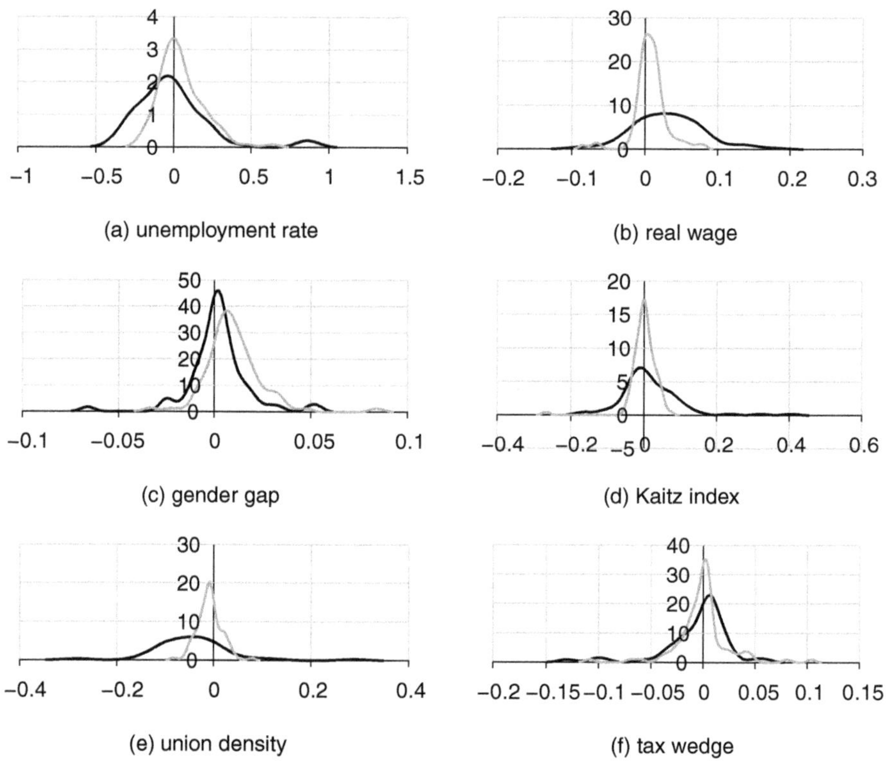

Figure 10.1 Kernel distributions of variables expressed in first differences (source: own estimations on OECD, WEF and ILO data).

Table 10.1 Descriptive statistics of variables expressed in first differences

	Unemployment		*Real wage*		*Gender gap*		*Kaitz index*		*Union density*		*Tax wedge*	
	Old EU	*New EU*	*Old EU*	*New EU*	*Old EU*	*New EU*	*Old EU*	*New EU*	*Old EU*	*New EU*	*Old EU*	*New EU*
Mean	0.050	–0.007	0.008	0.033	0.010	0.002	0.000	0.019	–0.008	–0.042	–0.001	–0.006
Median	0.026	–0.034	0.006	0.030	0.008	0.002	0.000	0.000	–0.008	–0.045	0.001	0.004
Std. dev.	0.146	0.243	0.024	0.048	0.015	0.016	0.037	0.087	0.025	0.084	0.027	0.033
Skewness	1.128	1.679	–0.511	0.360	1.363	–1.743	–4.101	1.622	0.244	0.360	0.059	–1.743
Kurtosis	5.092	7.227	7.452	3.714	9.496	7.406	31.641	8.512	4.159	3.714	8.491	7.406

Source: own estimations on OECD, WEF and ILO data.

A closer look at Figures 10.1a and 10.1b reveals two other distinctive features of the labour markets in the new EU. A small yet negative average change in the unemployment rate estimated for the CEE countries shows that the transition process has not been concluded during the first decade of the twenty-first century. So does the real wage, for which the average yearly change (notice that throughout this chapter we refer to first differences of log-linearized series) is four times larger than in the old EU. The dynamics of both variables indicate that the economic system in transition countries is still searching for a new level of equilibrium with a smaller unemployment rate and a higher real wage.

The other interesting feature is the large kurtosis. Leptokurtic distribution, however, is a common feature of both old EU and new EU economies. The large values of kurtoses are not surprising as the sample covers the largest global crisis since the 1930s and the consecutive post-crisis recovery. The largest value of kurtosis estimated for the Kaitz index in old EU countries, however, cannot be explained by the global crisis. We put it down to a dramatic decline in the Kaitz index observed in Ireland in 2001. Large values of kurtosis have also a more technical consequence, as the fat tails might have influenced the estimation results.

5.2 Impulse-response analysis results

Table 10.2 summarizes the estimated probabilities and the signs of the response values. With the exception of gender gap, which seems to be of special importance for the transition countries, the probabilities do not differ considerably. The most striking, yet expected difference between the old and new EU members, is the direction of the response of unemployment rate to a shock in real wages. For both old and new EU members the probabilities exceed the 0.9 level, but this is where the similarities end. A shock in real wage causes an increase in unemployment rate in the old EU economies. In a sharp contrast to this result, we find out that in CEE countries a shock in real wage generates a negative reaction of

Table 10.2 Summary of the impulse-response analysis

Variables	*Old EU*		*New EU*	
	Probability	*Response*	*Probability*	*Response*
Real wage	0.998	positive	1.000	negative
Gender gap	0.044	positive	0.918	positive
Real wage	0.997	positive	1.000	negative
Kaitz index	0.887	negative	1.000	positive
Real wage	0.990	positive	0.984	negative
Union density	0.965	positive	0.765	positive
Real wage	0.999	positive	0.926	negative
Tax wedge	0.631	positive	0.782	positive

Source: own estimations on OECD, WEF and ILO data.

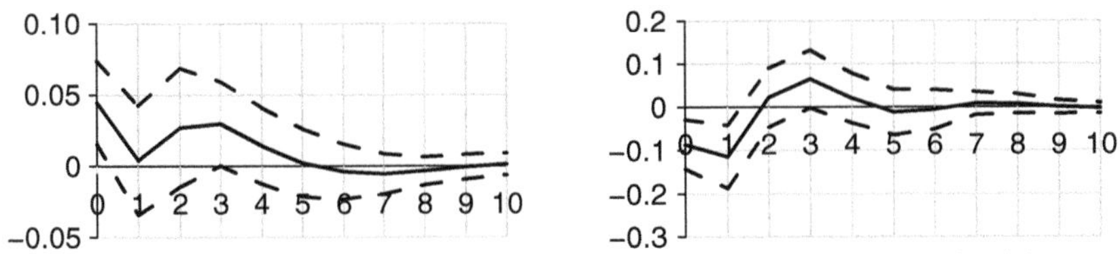

(a) response to shock in gender gap, old EU

(b) response to shock in gender gap, new EU

Figure 10.2 Impulse response analysis results: responses to shocks in real wage (source: own estimations on OECD, WEF and ILO data).

unemployment rate. The response to shock in real wage obtained for a model with union density is presented in Figure 10.2. We also detect a different direction of unemployment responses to a shock in the Kaitz index. In the old EU this shock produces a decrease in the unemployment rate. The opposite effect is observed in the new EU.

Comparing to the old EU countries, the unemployment rate in CEE countries is characterized by a higher level of persistence. The response of unemployment to its own shock is about 20 per cent larger in the new than in the old EU members. In fact, unemployment's elasticity to all shocks in CEE countries exceeds the magnitude of unemployment responses in the old EU members. For instance, a shock in the Kaitz index generates a response (in the absolute value terms) that is more than 70 per cent larger in the transition countries. The responses are depicted in Figure 10.3.

An interesting dynamic feature of the estimated response functions is the pace at which the responses die out. Despite the considerable differences in magnitude, they die out in approximately the same time. Unemployment's return to its initial level of equilibrium is surprisingly long lasting. It takes almost ten years for the responses to a shock in the Kaitz index and union density to die out.

6 Concluding remarks

For the last decade, the largest EU accession has been changing the labour market dynamics in unified Europe. Both new and old EU members have been affected by the accession. Much more profitable job opportunities in the West have attracted employees from transition countries. The new EU members have met new obligations defined as economic stabilization in terms of low inflation rate and full employment. The latter, according to the Europe 2020 Strategy, sets the employment rate at 75 per cent. Without a doubt, a 75 per cent employment rate would effectively bridge the gap between old and new EU countries. A closer look at labour market institutions and their impact on the unemployment rate, however, reveals potential problems for a fast gap bridging.

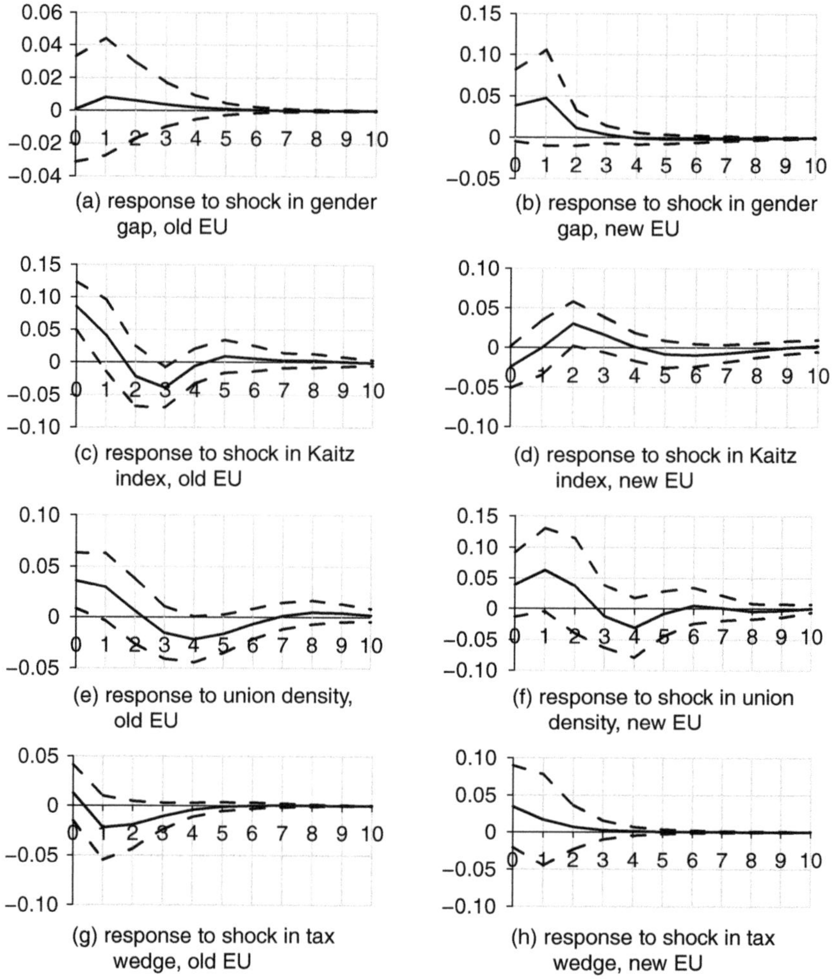

Figure 10.3 Impulse response analysis results: responses to shocks in institutional variables (source: own estimations on OECD, WEF and ILO data).

Transition countries have struggled with several institutional problems slowing down the labour market convergence. Poor infrastructure for family support has caused a low labour activity of women. The minimum wage has generated some additional frictions. The most striking difference, however, has concerned the real wage. Our research shows that changes in real wage are the most important factor affecting the labour market in Europe. Yet, its impact differs in new and old EU countries. A shock in real wage produces negative reaction of unemployment rate in transition countries. Quite the opposite effect is found for the old EU. Another feature that characterizes the differences between the old and new EU labour markets is the persistent unemployment observed in the transition countries. Unemployment's response to its own shock is approximately 20 per cent larger in the new than in the old EU members. Moreover, this pattern is also found for the magnitude of unemployment's reaction to other shocks.

Is the EU labour market able to effectively close the gap between West and East? Our empirical enquires show that decisions regarding the level of regulation are in fact crucial for the European labour market. Imposing regulations at the EU level might be extremely difficult. It may also lead to different results across the continent. A highly diversified institutional background favours country-specific actions. Perhaps the most problematic issue concerns the use of wages as an adjustment variable. Due to the considerable differences in direction of unemployment's reaction to changes in real wages, a common wage policy for old and new EU countries becomes questionable. The same remark applies to minimum wage regulation. According to our empirical results, reduction of the gender gap and the tax wedge is less controversial. EU policy towards gender gap, however, is primarily focused on closing the gap in salaries. Nevertheless, the reduction of both gender gap and tax wedge follows Country-Specific Recommendations. Concerning the institutional differences, this method of conducting a unified labour market policy seems to be most effective.

Notes

1 For recent development in minimum wage discussion in Europe see Vaughan-Whitehead (2010).

2 Until recently, the CIS included 12 out of 15 constituent republics of the former USSR, namely Armenia, Azerbaijan, Belarus, Georgia, Kazakhstan, Kyrgyzstan, Moldova, Russian Federation, Ukraine, Tajikistan, Turkmenistan and Uzbekistan with Georgia officially leaving the organization in August 2009 (Lehmann and Muravyev 2011, p. 3).

3 In the EU the gender pay gap is measured as a percentage of men's earnings and represents the difference between the average gross hourly earnings of male and female employees. Gross earnings are wages or salaries paid directly to an employee before any deductions for income tax and social security contributions are made. In the EU, data on the gender pay gap is based on the methodology of the Structure of Earnings Survey (SES). In the EU, the gender pay gap is referred to officially as the 'unadjusted gender pay gap', as it does not take into account all of the factors that impact the gender pay gap, such as differences in education, labour market experience, hours worked, type of job, etc. Even when these factors are taken into consideration, more than half of the gender pay gap remains unexplained. Using hourly pay as a basis for calculating the gender pay gap can also mask specific differences in pay that go unrecorded, for example, bonus payments and performance-related pay or seasonal payments. According to the Report of European Commission 2013, women in 2011 in the EU, on average, earned around 16 per cent less per hour than men. The gender pay gap varies across Europe. It is below 10 per cent in Slovenia, Poland, Italy, Luxembourg and Romania, but wider than 20 per cent in Austria, the Czech Republic, Estonia, Germany, Greece and Finland. Although the overall gender pay gap has narrowed in the last decade, in some countries the national gender pay gap has actually been widening (Latvia, Portugal) (Tackling the gender pay gap in the European Union 2013, pp. 2–3).

Bibliography

Abbritti, M. and Weber, S., 2010, Labour market institutions and the business cycle: Unemployment rigidities vs. real wage rigidities, Working Paper Series, No. 1183, April, European Central Bank.

Amable, B., Demmou, L. and Gatti, D., 2007, Employment performance and institutions: new answers to an old question, IZA Discussion Papers, No. 2731.

Anspal, S. and Võrk, A., 2007, Labour market institutions and productivity in the new EU member states, PRAXIS Working Papers, No. 27, PRAXIS Centre for Policy Studies.

Ashenfelter, O.C., 2012, Comparing real wages, NBER Working Papers Series, No. 18006.

Aumayr-Pintar, Ch. and Cabrita, J., 2014, Pay outcomes and wage bargaining regimes, in: *Pay in Europe in the 21st Century*, European Foundation for the Improvement of Living and Working Conditions, Eurofound.

Baccaro, L. and Rei, D., 2007, Institutional determinants of unemployment in OECD countries: Does the deregulatory view hold water?, *International Organization*, Vol. 61(3), pp. 527–569.

Baker, D., Glyn, A., Howell, D. and Schmitt, J. 2005, Labour market institutions and unemployment: A critical assessment of the cross-country evidence, chapter 3 of D. Howell (ed.), *Fighting Unemployment: The Limits of Free Market Orthodoxy*, Oxford: Oxford University Press.

Bassanini, A. and Duval, R., 2006, The determinants of unemployment across OECD countries: Reassessing the role of policies and institutions, OECD Economic Department Working Papers, No. 486.

Bassanini, A. and Duval, R., 2009, Unemployment, institutions and reform complementaries: Re-assessing the aggregate evidence for OECD countries, *Oxford Review of Economic Policy*, Vol. 25(1), pp. 40–59.

Belot, M. and van Ours, J.C. 2004, Does the recent success of some OECD countries in lowering their unemployment rate lie in the clever design of their labor market reforms?, *Oxford Economic Papers*, Vol. 56(1), pp. 621–642.

Blanchard, O., 2006, European unemployment: The evolution of facts and ideas, *Economic Policy*, Vol. 21(45), pp. 5–59.

Blanchard, O. and Giavazzi, F., 2003, Macroeconomic effects of regulation and deregulation in goods and labor markets, *Quarterly Journal of Economics*, Vol. 118(3), pp. 879–907.

Blanchard, O. and Wolfers, J., 2000, The role of shocks and institutions in the rise of European unemployment: The aggregate evidence, *Economic Journal*, Vol. 110(462), pp. 1–33.

Boeri, T. and Garibaldi, P., 2005, Are labour markets in the new member states sufficiently flexible for the EMU?, *Journal of Banking & Finance*, Vol. 30(5), pp. 1393–1407.

Boeri, T. and Van Ours, J., 2008, *The Economics of Imperfect Labor Markets*, Princeton: Princeton University Press.

Brown, G., Giiroy, G. and Kohen, A., 1982, The effect of the minimum wage on employment and unemployment, *Journal of Economic Literature*, Vol. 20, pp. 487–528.

Cahuc, P. and Zylberberg, A., 2004, *Labor Economics*, Cambridge: MIT Press.

Card, D. and Krueger, A., 1995, *Myth and Measurement: The New Economics of the Minimum Wage*, Princeton: Princeton University Press.

Cazes, S. and Nesporova, A., 2003, *Labour Markets in Transition: Balancing Flexibility and Security in Central and Eastern Europe*, Geneva: ILO.

Cazes, S., Khatiwada, S. and Malo, M., 2012, Employment protection and collective bargaining: Beyond the deregulation agenda, Employment Sector, Employment Working Paper, No. 133, Geneva: ILO.

Clauwaert, S. and Schömann, I., 2012, The crisis and national labour law reforms: A mapping exercise, Working Paper, No. 2012.04, Brussels: ETUI.

Crisis takes its toll: disentangling five years of labour market developments, 2014, in: *Benchmarking Working Europe 2014*, Brussels: ETUI, pp. 27–43.

Deaton, A., 2010, Price indexes, inequality and the measurement of world poverty, *American Economic Review*, Vol. 100(1), pp. 5–34.

Deregulation of labour law at any price, 2014, in: *Benchmarking Working Europe 2014*, Brussels: ETUI, pp. 59–68.

Developments in inequality and social protection in Europe, 2014, in: *Benchmarking Working Europe 2014*, Brussels: ETUI, pp. 45–57.

Dolado, J., Kramarz, F., Machin, S., Manning, A., Margolis, D. and Teulings, C., 1996, The economic impact of minimum wages in Europe, *Economic Policy*, Vol. 23, pp. 319–370.

Dority, B. and Fuess Jr, S., 2007, Labor market institutions and unemployment: Can earlier findings be replicated?, *Quarterly Journal of Business and Economics*, Vol. 46(4), pp. 23–44.

Dugger, W.M., 1996, Redefining economics: From market allocation to social provisioning. In: C.J. Whalen (ed.), *Political Economy for the 21st Century: Contemporary Views on the Trend of Economics*, Armonk, NY: M.E. Sharpe, pp. 31–44.

Eichhorst, W., Feil, M. and Braun, C., 2008, What have we learned? Assessing labor market institutions and indicators, IZA Discussion Paper, No. 3470.

Elmeskov, J., Martin, J.P and Scarpetta, S., 1998, Key lessons for labour market reforms: Evidence from OECD countries' experiences, *Swedish Economic Policy Review*, Vol. 5(2), pp. 205–252.

EPSU, 2012, Adjustments in the public sector in Europe: scope, effects and policy issues. Available at: www.epsu.org/a/8831.

Escande Varniol, M.-C., Laulom, S. and Mazuyer, E. (eds), 2012, *Quel droit social dans une Europe en crise*, Brussels: Larcier.

European Commission, 2010, Communication from the Commission, Europe 2020: A strategy for smart, sustainable and inclusive growth, COM(2010) 2020 final, 3 March 2010.

Fernandez-Macias, E. and Vacas-Soriano, C., 2014, Minimum wage policies and levels in Europe: An accounting exercise, in: *Pay in Europe in the 21st Century*, European Foundation for the Improvement of Living and Working Conditions, Eurofound.

Fialova, K. and Schneider, O., 2009, Labor market institutions and their effect on labor market performance in the new EU member countries, *Eastern European Economics*, Vol. 47(3), pp. 57–83.

Gatti, D., Rault, C. and Vaubourg, A., 2010, Unemployment and finance: How do financial and labour market factors interact?, William Davidson Institute Working Paper, No. 973.

Griffith, R., Harrison, R. and Macartney, G., 2007, Product market reforms, labour market institutions and unemployment, *Economic Journal*, Vol. 117(518), pp. C124–C166.

Hall, R.E. and Jones, Ch.I, 1999, Why do some countries produce so much more output per worker than others?, *The Quarterly Journal of Economics*, Vol. 114(1), pp. 83–116.

Hausmann, R., Tyson, L.D. and Zahidi, S., 2012, *The Global Gender Gap Report 2012*, Geneva: World Economic Forum.

Hendricks, Z., 2002, How important is human capital for development? Evidence from immigrant earnings, *The American Economic Review*, Vol. 92(1), pp. 198–219.

Hicks, J.R., 1937, Mr. Keynes and the 'Classics': A suggested interpretation, *Econometrica*, Vol. 5(2), pp. 147–159.

Howell, D.R., Baker, D., Glyn, A. and Schmitt, J., 2007, Are protective labor market institutions at the root of unemployment? A critical review of the evidence, *Capitalism and Society*, Vol. 2(1), pp. 1–17.

ILO, 2010, *Global Wage Report 2010/11: Wage Policies in Times of Crisis*, Geneva: International Labour Office.

IMF, 2003, *World Economic Outlook*, Chapter IV, April.

Kampelmann, S., Garnero, A. and Rycx, F., 2013, Minimum wages in Europe: Does the diversity of systems lead to a diversity of outcomes?, Report 128, Brussels: ETUI.

Kennan, J., 1995, The elusive effects of minimum wages, *Journal of Economic Literature*, Vol. 33(4), pp. 1949–1965.

Kuźmiar, S. and Pilc, M., 2013, The role of the labor market institutions for the labor market performance in transition countries. Conference paper, ESPAnet 2013, 5–7 September 2013, Poznań.

Labour Market Developments in Europe 2013, *European Economy* Vol. 6, European Commission.

Layard, R., Nickell, S. and Jackman, R., 2005, *Unemployment: Macroeconomic Performance and the Labour Market*, 2nd edn, Oxford: Oxford University Press.

Lehmann, H. and Muravyev, A., 2011, Labor markets and labor market institutions in transition economies, IZA Discussion Paper No. 5905, August.

Lehmann, H. and Muravyev, A., 2012, Labor market institutions and labor market performance: What can we learn from transition countries?, *Economics of Transition*, Vol. 20(2), pp. 235–269.

Lesch, H., 2004, Trade union density in international comparison, CESifo Forum, No. 4.

Lokiec, P. and Robin-Olivier, S. (eds), 2012, Les réactions du droit du travail à la crise, *Le Droit Ouvrier*, 2.

Lütkepohl, H., 2005, *New Introduction to Multiple Time Series Analysis*, Berlin, Heidelberg: Springer Verlag.

Modigliani, F., 1944, Liquidity preference and the theory of interest and money, *Econometrica*, Vol. 12(1), pp. 45–88.

Muller, A., 2011, Employment protection legislation tested by the economic crisis: A global review of the regulation of collective dismissals for economic reasons. Dialogue in Brief, No. 3, Geneva: ILO.

Neumark, D. and Wascher, W., 2004, Minimum wages, labor market institutions, and youth employment: A cross-national analysis, *Industrial and Labor Relations Review*, Vol. 57(2), pp. 223–248.

Nickell, S., 1997, Unemployment and labour market rigidities: Europe versus North America, *Journal of Economic Perspectives*, Vol. 11(3), pp. 55–74.

Nickell, S. and Layard, R., 1999, Labor market institutions and economic performance, *Handbook of Labour Economics*, Vol. 3(3), pp. 3029–3083.

Nickell, S., Nunziata, L. and Ochel, W., 2005, Unemployment in the OECD since the 1960s: What do we know?, *Economic Journal*, Vol. 115(500), pp. 1–27.

Nicoletti, G. and Scarpetta, S., 2005, Product market reforms and employment in OECD countries, OECD Economics Department Working Papers, No. 472.

OECD, 2006, Reassessing the role of policies and institutions for labour market performance: A quantitative analysis, *OECD Employment Outlook*, Chapter 7.

OECD, 2007, Tax wedge on labour, in: *Society at a Glance 2006: OECD Social Indicators*, Paris: OECD Publishing.

Power, M., 2004, Social provisioning as a starting point for feminist economics, *Feminist Economics*, Vol. 10(3), pp. 3–21.

Prescott, E., 1998, Needed: A theory of total factor productivity, *International Economic Review*, Vol. 39(3), pp. 525–551.

Rodrik, D., 1999, Democracies pay higher wages, *The Quarterly Journal of Economics*, Vol. 114(3), pp. 707–738.

Rosenzweig, M., 2010, Global wage inequality and the international flow of migrants, Economic Growth Center Discussion Paper, No. 983, Yale University.

Rycx, F. and Kampelmann, S., 2012, Who earns minimum wages in Europe? New evidence based on household surveys, Report 124, ETUI (European Trade Union Institute), Brussels.

Sachs, A., 2010, A Bayesian approach to determine the impact of institutions on the unemployment rate, Discussion Paper, No. 10–058, ZEW, Centre for European Economic Research, August.

Sachs, A., 2011, Institutions and unemployment: Do interactions matter?, Discussion Paper, No. 11–057, ZEW, Centre for European Economic Research, September.

Saint-Paul, G., 2004, Why are European countries diverging in their unemployment experience?, *Journal of Economic Perspectives*, Vol. 18(4), pp. 49–68.

Scarpetta, S., 1996, Assessing the role of labour market policies and institutional settings of unemployment: A cross-country study, OECD Economic Studies, No. 26, 1996/1.

Schömann, I., 2014, Labour law reforms in Europe: Adjusting employment protection legislation for the worse?, Working Paper, Vol. 2, Brussels: ETUI.

Schulten, T., 2012a, European minimum wage policy: A concept for wage-led growth and fair wages in Europe, in: Social justice and growth: The role of the minimum wage, *International Journal of Labour Research*, International Labour Organization, Vol. 4(1).

Schulten, T., 2012b, Minimum wages in Europe under austerity, WSI Minimum Wage Report 2012, ETUI Policy Brief, No 5.

Schwab, K., Brende, B., Zahidi, S., Bekhouche, Y., Guinault, A., Soo, A., Hausmann, R. and Tyson, L.D., 2013, The Global Gender Gap Report 2013, Geneva: World Economic Forum.

Tackling the gender pay gap in the European Union, 2013, Luxembourg: European Union.

Vaughan-Whitehead, D., 2010, Towards the EU minimum wage policy?, in: D. Vaughan-Whitehead, *The Minimum Wage Revisited in the Enlarged EU*, Cheltenham: Edward Elgar, pp. 509–530.

Visser, J., 2012, The ICTWSS database: Database on institutional characteristics of trade unions, wage setting, state intervention and social pacts in 34 countries between 1960 and 2012.

Wasmer, E. and Weil, P., 2004, The macroeconomics of labor and credit market imperfections, *American Economic Review*, Vol. 94(4), pp. 944–963.

Williamson, O.E., 2000, The new institutional economics: Taking stock, looking ahead, *Journal of Economic Literature*, Vol. 38, September, pp. 595–613.

Woźniak-Jęchorek, B., 2013, Struktura rynku pracy w świetle ekonomii instytucjonalnej, *Gospodarka Narodowa*, Vol. 9, pp. 5–27.

11 A cultural political economy of crisis recovery

(Trans-)national imaginaries, growth dynamics in the 'BRIC' and the Chinese case

Ngai-Ling Sum

Introduction

In times of crisis, economic and political actors often search for and/or construct objects of 'growth', hope' and 'strength' that may secure recovery. This chapter presents the 'BRIC' (Brazil, Russia, India and China) as one such imagined object, in which much hope has been invested since 11 September 2001. This acronym was coined by Jim O'Neill, at the time Goldman Sachs' Chief Economist, after he watched the televised attack on the World Trade Center. Prompted by this haunting image, he began to envisage a new way of thinking about 'growth' that could transcend national perspectives and look beyond the West. With the onset of the 2007 financial crisis, this imaginary gained fresh popularity and was reinvented through the concerted efforts of diverse national and transnational forces (for example, international investment banks, economic strategists, international organizations, think tanks, national governments and business media corporations). This chapter explores the development of BRIC discourses and practices, considering them as economic and financial imaginaries from a cultural political economy perspective.

The first section poses some key questions from a cultural political economy (CPE) entry-point regarding the construction of economic imaginaries. The second section examines three overlapping stages in the making and remaking by (trans-)national forces of the 'BRIC' quartet as an object of 'hope' and 'growth'. It notes that the national and transnational resonance of this imaginary depends not only on financial and economic developments but also on specific discourses, practices and knowledge technologies. The third section examines how 'BRIC' discourses were recontextualized in the Sinophone world as 'four golden brick countries' to signify 'strength' and 'greatest at last'. It shows how China, as one of these 'golden bricks', sought to showcase its strength following the 2007 financial crisis, in spite of a fall in China's exports and rising unemployment. China introduced a vast stimulus package that has posed tremendous fiscal challenges, especially to its regional-local authorities, which increasingly rely on land as collateral for loans and a source of revenue. This intensified land- and debt-based accumulation, inflated the 'property bubble' and stimulated land clearance/dispossession. Though some measures have been taken to dampen the property market, they have been rather limited and have not halted social unrest. The fourth section summarizes the main lessons of this CPE-inspired analysis of the changing 'BRIC' imaginaries and their relevance to understanding the global-national-local contexts and causes of the unfolding of economic and political tensions in China.

Towards a cultural political economy of imagined recoveries

CPE is a broad theoretical current that combines the 'cultural-linguistic turn' (namely, a concern with sense- and meaning-making) with critical political economy (Sum and Jessop 2013). This chapter adopts CPE to examine the emergence, recontextualization, circulation and sedimentation of the 'BRIC' imaginaries as successive (but overlapping) objects of 'hope'/'strength' from 2001 until 2012. This involved new discourses and what neo-Foucauldians call knowledging technologies (Dean 1999; Miller and Rose 2008). A CPE approach adds to these insights by examining the key discursive networks of individual and institutional actors (for example, international investment banks) involved in producing these imaginaries and exploring their performative role and its limits in changing actually existing economic, political and social relations. It examines not only 'how' knowledge is constructed but also poses 'where', 'who', 'what' and 'why' questions. Specifically, as regards the case studies presented below, it asks: (1) where do a particular economic imaginary, such as BRIC, and its related discursive networks originate; (2) which actors are involved in the discursive networks that construct and promote objects of 'hope'/'strength'; (3) what ideas (for example, in stage two in the development of this imaginary, BRIC consumer power) are selected to recontextualize these objects and their referents; (4) what knowledging technologies are involved in normalizing these imaginaries and their associated subjectivities and identities; (5) how do these ideas enter the policy discourses and everyday practices of the financial and policy worlds; and (6) how are they being negotiated and/or resisted in rebuilding social relations?[1] Answering these questions requires detailed study of the relations among discourse, power and structural materialities.

The construction of hope/strength: three stages in the making of 'BRIC'

'BRIC' discourse is grounded in the notion of 'emerging markets', a term coined in 1981 by a fund manager, Antoine van Agtmael of *Emerging Markets Management*. This notion maps some 'Third World' and post-socialist economies as sites of 'new growth opportunities' with 'high risks' but potentially high returns. 'BRIC' was identified as a promising subset of the 'large emerging markets' with excellent high-growth prospects following China's 2001 WTO entry and 11 September 2001. It was then modified in three overlapping stages, with others,

Table 11.1 The production of 'hope'/'strength': three overlapping stages in the production of 'BRIC' knowledge

Stages	*Major actors/institutions*	*Major discourses and knowledge instruments*	*Knowledging technology*
Stage 1 2001–present 'BRIC' as an investor story	International investment banks (e.g. Goldman Sachs) Chief Economist (e.g. Jim O'Neill) & colleagues; fund managers, sales teams, financial journalists, rating agency, etc.	• 2001 Invented the category in the report on *Building Better Global Economic BRICs* • 2003 Research report on *Dreaming with BRICs: The Path to 2050* • Other reports, books, webtours, indexes, etc. (see Table 11.2)	Technology of identification Technology of investability
Stage 2 2004–present 'BRIC' as an investor-consumer story	Economists, investment consultants, business media (Bloomberg, *The Economist*, CNN, blogs, etc.), international organizations (e.g. World Bank, IMF)	Decoupling theses: • The trans-Atlantic economies are in recession due to the subprime crisis and its fallout. Other regions, especially the BRIC, continue to grow during this downturn – strong consumption • 'Decoupling 2.0' article (*The Economist*)	Technology of identification
Stage 3 Late 2008–present 'BRIC' as an investor-consumer-lender story	International organizations (WB, IMF, G20, BRIC Summit, etc.), national leaders, foreign policy analysts and mass media	• BRIC IMF Bond Programme • Buying IMF Special Drawing Rights (e.g. US$50 billion by China on 04/09/09) • Shifting global economic balance of power (e.g. from G8 to G20 or even G2)	Technology of agency

Source: author's own compilation.

perhaps, to come: (1) investor story, (2) investor-consumer story and (3) investor-consumer-lender story. At each stage a key set of nodal actors was involved in constructing 'hope'/'strength' via the use of knowledging instruments and technologies (see Table 11.1).

First stage of the BRIC construction 2001–present: investor story

Contrary to the fluid origin of most discourses, the BRIC idea has a definite starting point: 11 September 2001. Prompted by the attack on the World Trade Center, Goldman Sachs' Chief Economist, Jim O'Neill, reckoned that globalization would go beyond the northern-western world (Tett 2010). This diagnosis allowed O'Neill and his Goldman Sachs team to imagine new sources of growth based on identifying and bundling some useful 'non-western others' with high growth potentials. By 30 November 2001, these 'others' were presented as the 'BRIC' in Goldman Sachs Global Economic Paper No. 66, which was titled *Building Better Global Economic Brics*. Based on models of GDP growth rates until 2050, this economic quartet was constructed as the new object of 'hope', with 'each set to grow again by more than the G7' (2001: S.03). Whereas China and India were predicted to become dominant global suppliers of manufactured/technological goods and services, Brazil and Russia would grow as suppliers of energy and raw materials.

The creation of BRIC as a new 'growth' and 'hope' object for investors initially received mixed responses. While corporate clients, who were looking for new markets, embraced this construction, banks and investors were more sceptical because the BRICs were deemed vulnerable to 'shocks' from political upheavals and changing commodity prices. Nonetheless, O'Neill's team continued to supply their clients with 'hope' based on expected growth and financial returns. For example, *Dreaming with BRICs: The Path to 2050* (2003), argued that:

> The relative importance of the BRICs as an engine of new demand growth and spending power may shift more dramatically and quickly than expected. Higher growth in these economies could offset the impact of greying populations and slower growth in the advanced economies.
>
> Higher growth may lead to higher returns and increased demand for capital. The weight of the BRICs in investment portfolios could rise sharply. Capital flows might move further in their favour, prompting major currency realignments…
>
> (Wilson and Purushothaman 2003: 2)

On the discursive level, this construction of hope/strength relied on metaphors such as 'engines of growth' that could provide 'higher returns' and attract 'favourable capital flows'. Their growth was extrapolated up to 2050. By then, for example, China's RMB gross domestic product could be 30 per cent larger than US GDP, India's could be four times Japan's, and Brazil and Russia could each be 50 per cent bigger than the UK. References to economic attributes like size and rates of growth can be seen, in neo-Foucauldian terms, as a technology of identification in which the BRIC are singled out, made knowable, and visibilized as the largest, high growth and potentially lucrative 'emerging economies'. This technology, once deployed, was circulated by the Goldman team and other actors such as fund managers and financial sales teams. With China's entry into the WTO in 2001 and continuing consolidation of neoliberal globalization, more and more corporations and financial organizations were seeking new markets and profitable investment sites beyond the core advanced economies. New discursive networks, which included corporate executives, investment bankers, fund managers, and so on, began to appropriate and disseminate the BRIC imaginary as their own object of investment and strategic actions. Moreover, as Tett (2010) records, after the 2003 paper, Goldman economists entered 'briclife' with growing interest from leading clients in this new object of hope and speculative returns.

Goldman sustained this interest by churning out more knowledge products. Between 2001 and 2010, it created 20 such products, ranging from reports, new forecasts, a book, videos and webtours (in different languages) to keep 'briclife' going[2] (see Table 11.2). This Goldman story was occasionally challenged by other economists and investment consultants, who asked why some emerging economies were excluded (for example, South Korea and Turkey) and others included (for example, Russia and Brazil). New acronyms were put forward (for example, BRICK and CRIB) to negotiate its meanings and appeals.

Nonetheless, despite these challenges, with one wag later suggesting that BRIC stood for 'bloody ridiculous investment concept' and another proposing CEMENT to describe 'countries in emerging markets excluded by new terminology', the Goldman construction of the BRICs as objects of 'hope'/'strength' continued to circulate amongst economic strategists, investment consultants and sales teams and attract continuing media attention. Its resonance derived not only from the projection of strength of the individual BRIC group members but also from the purported complementarity and coherence of BRIC as an asset/investment class. Major international banks such as HSBC and other investment banks/hedge funds were bundling stocks/shares/bonds and inventing funds marketed under the BRIC brand. Starting with a few funds and index funds, the market has since grown in terms of offers and funds invested. Their attractiveness as investments was related to the spread of risks, asset allocation and portfolio management, prospective profits and the involvement of legendary stock pickers and fund management by gurus. In neo-Foucauldian terms, this discourse and technology of investability: (1) constructs strength, profitability and confidence of these funds and narrated them as asset choices; (2) directs investor subjects to put their money in these economies; and (3) normalizes BRIC as investment sites.

Armed with these investment products, financial sales teams and other intermediaries marketed them to potential clients, contacting them through advertisements, glossy brochures, financial journalism, phone-calls, home visits, and so

Table 11.2 Major BRIC knowledge products constructed by Goldman Sachs team

Name of the knowledge products	*Nature of product (year/ month)*	*Ways of constructing hope and strength*
Building Better Global Economic BRICs	Report November 2001	• Invented the BRIC category and forecast combined GDP growth rate of 12% in the next ten years
Dreaming with BRICs: The Path to 2050	Report October 2003	• Mapping out BRIC's GDP growth until 2050 • Postulating BRIC economies could be larger than G6 in 40 years' time
How Solid are the BRICs?	Forecast December 2005	• Updating the 2003 forecast • Arguing that BRIC would grow more strongly than previous projections
Web Tour: The BRICs Dream (in English, Arabic, Chinese and Japanese)	Webtours May 2006	• A video on the BRIC • Dreaming about BRIC and the changing world after 9/11 • Contending China would overtake the USA in 2050 • Arguing growth of the middle classes in BRIC and major consumers of cars and energies
India's Urbanization: Emerging Opportunities	Report July 2007	• Framing boom in city life • Identifying investment opportunities in urban infrastructure and fast accumulation of financial assets
BRICS and Beyond	Book November 2007	• Updating the 2001 report • Postulating increase in value of BRIC's equity markets • Moving beyond BRIC to other emerging economies (e.g. N-11)
Interview with Jim O'Neill	Video February 2008	• Maintaining BRIC's share of global GDP as 15% • Advising individual BRIC countries (e.g. India needs more FDI) • Arguing for the sustainability of BRIC • Increasing international role of these countries
Building the World: Mapping Infrastructure Demand	Report April 2008	• Identifying increase demand for infrastructure • Arguing China will be the source of one-half to three-quarters of incremental demand • Intensifying pressure on commodity markets
Ten Things for India to Achieve its 2050 Potential	Report June 2008	• Advising on improvement of governance and the need to control inflation • Promoting the liberalization of financial market • Supporting improvement for agricultural productivity
BRICs Lead the Global Recovery	Report May 2009	• Arguing BRIC can help to led the stabilization of the world economy • Promoting BRIC as one of the driving forces in the export-driven recovery
The BRICs as Drivers of Global Consumption	Report August 2009	• Arguing G3 countries face slow and difficult recovery • Maintaining that BRIC can contribute to global domestic demand through higher consumption
The BRICs Nifty 50: The EM & DM Winners	Report and stock baskets November 2009	• Stating good consumption and infrastructural demand from BRIC • Identifying two BRIC Nifty 50 baskets to help investors to access the BRIC market
BRICs at 8: Strong through the Crisis, Outpacing Forecasts	Video March 2010	• BRIC weathered the global crisis remarkably well • On pace to equal the G7 in size by 2032
The Growth Map: Economic Opportunities of BRICs and Beyond	Book 2012	• A sole-authored book by O'Neill that reviews the economic opportunities of BRICs and beyond

Source: author's own compilation based on materials from Goldman Sachs' Idea Website on BRIC.

Table 11.3 Net inflows of portfolio equity to the BRIC economies 2002–2008 (US$ billion)

Country	*2002*	*2003*	*2004*	*2005*	*2006*	*2007*	*2008*
China	2.2	7.7	10.9	20.3	42.9	18.5	3.7
India	1.0	8.2	9.0	12.1	9.5	35.0	–15.0
Brazil	2.0	3.0	2.1	6.5	7.7	26.2	–7.6
Russia	2.6	0.4	0.2	–0.2	6.1	18.7	–15.0
BRIC	**7.8**	**19.3**	**22.2**	**38.7**	**66.2**	**98.4**	**–33.9**
Developing countries	**5.5**	**24.1**	**40.4**	**68.9**	**104.8**	**135.4**	**–57.1**

Source: adapted from World Bank, *Global Development Finance* 2008 and 2010.

on. Knowledging technology and related investment practices of this kind normalize BRIC as a good site for investment. The inflow of portfolio equity funds to BRIC increased by almost twelvefold between 2002 and 2007. As for the share of BRIC investment inflow compared with its counterpart in development countries, BRIC's share was about two-thirds of total inflow between 2003 and 2007 (see Table 11.3). Within the BRIC group, China was the biggest gainer in 2006 and India in 2007. With the onset of the financial crisis, the credit crunch led to the sharp slowdown of inflow to the BRIC in 2008 with China as the exception of a positive inflow of US$ 3.7 billion. Indeed, at the time of writing (Spring 2014), negative sentiment remains high: while the Dow-Jones index has reached all-time nominal highs, the MSCI BRIC Index was some 37 per cent below its 2007 peak. Even the Shanghai Composite Index has declined 31 per cent since the end of 2009, making it the single worst performer among the BRICs.[3]

Second stage of the BRIC construction 2004–present: investor-consumer story

The BRIC as investor story acquired a consumption dimension from mid-2004. This extension began again with a Goldman Sachs report, *The BRICs and Global Markets: Crude, Cars and Capital* (2004). It identified an 'emerging middle class' in these economies, which would lead to increasing demand for commodities, consumer durables and capital services. This BRIC 'dream' was echoed by economic strategists such as Clyde Prestowitz, whose book, *Three Billion New Capitalists*, projected that, by 2020, 'the annual increase in dollar spending by the BRIC will be twice that of the G6' (2005: 227).

This BRIC-as-consumer story gained more resonance following the visible outbreak and accelerating contagion effects of the North Atlantic financial crisis in 2007–2008. As the crisis intensified and spread, investment and policy communities began to look for new signs of 'hope' and possible objects of recovery. Among other objects (for example, the Green New Deal), the BRIC story was re-articulated to include a consumption dimension (see Table 11.1). Thus stage two attributed a new locomotive role to the BRIC on the grounds that their consumer-led demand would defer recession and create recovery opportunities for recession-hit advanced economies.

This narrative was enthusiastically circulated/negotiated by economists, business media (including Bloomberg, *Newsweek*, *The Wall Street Journal* and CNN) and international organizations such as the IMF under the rubric of the 'decoupling thesis'. This asserted that the BRIC economies could still expand thanks to their own investment and consumption, despite recession in the advanced economies. Bloomberg reported Jim O'Neill as saying that 'the BRIC consumer is going to rescue the world' (Marinis 2008) and 'since October 2007, the Chinese shopper alone has been contributing more to global GDP growth than the American consumer' (Mellor and Lim 2008). The technology of identification was deployed again and the 'BRIC' quartet was redefined as such a 'decoupled' object whose autonomous consumption power could save the world economy from recession. A similar story is now being narrated (again by Jim O'Neill) for a new quartet of large emerging economies: the MINT (Mexico, Indonesia, Nigeria and Turkey) (O'Neill 2013).

This new BRIC story was popularized by networks of top investment advisors and fund managers through business, mass and Internet media (Shinnick 2008; Lordabett.com 2009). For example, Peter Schiff, President of Euro-Pacific Capital Inc, argued in his book, *Little Book of Bull Moves in Bear Markets*:

> I'm rather fond of the word decoupling, in fact, because it fits two of my favorite analogies. The first is that America is no longer the engine of economic growth but the caboose. [The second] When China divorces us, the Chinese will keep 100% of their property and their factories, use their products themselves, and enjoy a dramatically improved lifestyle.
>
> (Schiff 2008: 41)

His position was echoed in many YouTube videos, blogs, articles and news items. Nonetheless the 'decoupling thesis' is also negotiated and contested. First, some financial analysts, economists and international/regional organizations, such as the World Bank and Asia Development Bank, were more cautious. They pointed to a contraction of trade rather than decoupling. For example, in April 2008, citing reduced exports, the World Bank lowered its growth forecast for China to 6.5 per cent. Second, another kind of caution was expressed in June 2008, when the IMF released a study called *Convergence and Decoupling*. This argued that decoupling could co-exist with integration. Globalization since 1985 has stimulated greater trade and financial integration and this, in turn, has led to the tighter coupling of business cycles among countries with similar levels of per capita income. But there was also historical evidence that some (groups of) countries have decoupled from the broader global economy at various stages of their development. A third concern was expressed by the UK-based foreign affairs think tank, Chatham House, in the wake of the collapse of Merrill Lynch and Lehman Brothers in September 2008. In one briefing paper, *Synchronized Dive into Recession*, a Chatham House author argued:

> Will a severe OECD recession engulf the rest of the world? Up to mid-2008, the emerging markets remained strong – 'decoupling' did work. Now the crisis has deepened, no region will remain immune to shock waves.
>
> (Rossi 2008)

In spite (or perhaps because) of these different views and the ambiguity of the '(de-)coupling' arguments, the thesis was still circulated. Indeed, Jim O'Neill himself reinforced it in *Newsweek* in March 2009:

> Who said decoupling was dead? The decoupling idea is that, because the BRICs rely increasingly on domestic demand, they can continue to boom even if their most important export market, the United States, slows dramatically. The idea came into disrepute last fall, when the U.S. market collapse started to spread to the BRICs, but there's now lots of evidence that decoupling is alive and well.
>
> (O'Neill 2009)

This claim was echoed by *The Economist* when it presented 'Decoupling 2.0' in its issue of 21 May 2009. This new version interpreted decoupling as 'a narrower phenomenon, confined to a few of the biggest, and least indebted, emerging economies' such as China, India and Brazil. These economies had strong domestic markets and prudent macroeconomic policies and were also growing trade among themselves. In an interview on 'Decoupling is Happening for Real', Michael Buchanan, Goldman Sachs' Asia-Pacific Economist in Hong Kong, explained:

> For the last couple of months, data have revealed a growing divergence between western economies and those in much of Asia, notably China and India...
>
> One reason for this divergence is that the effects of the financial crisis hit Asia much later. While the American economy began slumping in 2007, Asian economies were doing well until the collapse of Lehman Brothers in September [2008]. What followed was a rush of stimulus measures – rate cuts and government spending programs. In Asia's case, these came soon after things soured for the region; in the United States, they came much later though on a much bigger scale.
>
> In addition, developing Asian economies were in pretty good financial shape when the crisis struck. The last major crisis to hit the region – the financial turmoil of 1997–98 – forced governments in Asia to introduce overhauls that ultimately left them with lower debt levels, more resilient banking and regulatory systems and often large foreign exchange reserves.
>
> (Buchanan 2009)

This creative argument narrowed the BRIC-decoupling thesis to two BRIC members: China and, to a lesser extent, India. The 'new decoupling' thesis

Table 11.4 The central–local government's share of the stimulus package and sources of finance in China 2008–2010

Level of government	*Amount (in trillion RMB)*	*Percentage of total*	*Major sources of finance*
Central government	1.2	29.5	• Direct grants • Interest-rate subsidies
Regional-local governments	2.8	70.5	• Loan-based finance • Policy loans • Local government bonds issued by the central government (around RMB200 billion) • Corporate bonds (RMB130 billion were issued in Q4 2008) • Medium-term notes (RMB25 billion were issued in March 2009) • Bank loans

Sources: Naughton 2009; Window of China 2009.

construed them as 'useful others' with large foreign exchange reserves, buoyant fiscal positions and financial stimulus packages. In November 2009, the World Bank raised its 2010 economic forecast for China's GDP growth to 8.4 per cent. These economies offered 'hope' thanks to their good investment markets, rising middle class consumption and relative large stimulus packages (see Table 11.4). This narrowing of BRIC to China and India was reinforced within the policy circuit by Roger Scher who wrote for the Foreign Policy Blogs Network. He questioned Russia's strength and asked whether Chinese and Indian growth indicated a shift 'From BRIC to BIC … or Even IC??' Others proposed 'BriC' to highlight the position of China (see next section). Again, with the benefit of hindsight, it is clear that the decoupling thesis was overdone at a time of increasing integration of the world market, as reflected in sharp increases in export/GDP ratios and a growing share of intermediate goods in global trade, making it harder for large emerging economies to decouple from global cycles (cf. Achuthan 2012). But this chapter is concerned with the unfolding of the BRIC narrative in real time, not with a cheap and easy retrospective critique.

Third stage of the BRIC construction: investor-consumer-lender story

This revised decoupling thesis survived into stage three, which began in late 2008 (see Table 11.1). As the crisis in advanced economies deepened and the search for 'hope' or objects of recovery continued, attention turned to the geopolitical significance of the BRIC quartet. At this stage, policy makers, international organizations, think tanks, foreign policy analysts, and so on acquired a greater role in the construction of 'hope'. This is exemplified in the statement of Gordon Brown, then UK Prime Minister, who was coordinating an IMF rescue package for the global economy in October 2008:

> China ... has very substantial reserves. There are a number of countries that actually can do quite a lot in the immediate future to make sure that the international community has sufficient resources to support countries that get themselves into difficulties.
>
> (cited in Sanderson 2008)

This plea was reiterated as Brown prepared for the G20 meeting in London in April 2009, when China was expected to contribute US$40 billion to the rescue package. Accompanying these specific policy initiatives, foreign policy rhetoric emphasized the emergence of a 'multipolar world order' and 'comprehensive interdependence' among countries (Renate 2009). These new geopolitical imaginaries became more credible when Russia held the first BRIC Leaders' Summit in Yekaterinburg in June 2009 and Brazil, China, India and South Africa[4] hosted the second, third and fourth summits in April 2010, April 2011, March 2012 and March 2013. These summits operated (partly) as arenas for the BRIC(S) leaders to perform and confirm their collective identity as well as to envisage their future (for example, the establishment of the BRIC Development Bank) despite their differences.

In 2009 the BRIC governments contributed towards a more diversified international monetary system. They were influenced not only by appeals from the G20 but also from Stiglitz's *UN Commission on Reforms of the International and Monetary Systems* and the discussions around the *UN Conference on the Global Financial & Economic Crisis*. The Stiglitz Commission advocated 'Special Drawing Rights' (SDRs) as the new 'global currency' that could increase liquidity as well as SDR-denominated bonds. This new approach was backed at the G20 Summit in April 2009, when the then IMF managing director, Dominique Strauss-Kahn, announced the issuance of US$250 million SDR-denominated bonds. When the IMF Executive Board confirmed this on 1 July 2009, China pledged to buy US$50 billion, and Russia, Brazil and India would each gradually purchase US$10 billion.

This new form of financing marked a change in the significance of the BRIC quartet in the global economy and its governance. As lenders to the IMF, their strength was reconfirmed symbolically via: (1) the developed economies' recognition that they should help solve the crisis by subscribing to these new bonds; (2) their disinclination to commit funds on a long-term basis until the IMF re-allocated the country quotas; and (3) their demand for an increase in their voting shares within the IMF governance structure from 5 to 7 per cent of the total.[5] Despite these signs of 'hope'/'strength', some observers commented that the new SDR bonds would only absorb a small proportion of the BRIC's foreign reserves and, therefore, doubted that the SDR system would ever challenge the role of the dollar (Kelly 2009). It has also been suggested that in March 2013 the fifth BRICS Summit suggested a BRICS Development Bank as a counterweight to the IMF and World Bank but a closer look at its proposed Contingent Reserve Arrangement reveals that its capital, equivalent to US$100 billion, is hardly a challenge to these institutions. It could also be seen as a firewall to insulate the BRICS from a crisis-prone IMF–World Bank system.

The continued reworking and re-articulation of BRIC discourses and practices over these three overlapping stages) has helped to naturalize BRIC as a complex object of 'hope'/'strength'. It offered investment opportunities for frustrated investors, consumer demand to facilitate recovery and growth, and reserves to finance international lending. These alleged strengths signified the BRIC economies' progress from 'emerging markets' to an 'emerging global power'. This discursive shift illustrates what neo-Foucauldians call a technology of agency (Cruikshank 1999) based on the coexistence of participation and control in the international arena. On the one hand, the BRIC were encouraged to participate as 'we' in a new 'multipolar world order'. For example, the BRIC's increasing integration in the G20 not only allowed for their participation but also steers the manner of their engagement. Likewise, they were included into broader 'discussion forums' and actions around crisis-management that would actually facilitate the rebuilding and negotiation of the future neoliberal agendas (for example, the dollar-yuan exchange policy, BRIC as consumers and the dollar's hegemonic role) as opposed to challenging it.

Crisis, BRIC-ing of China and its 2008 stimulus package

The rise of the BRICs has not been a smooth process: it has been contested and negotiated by various (trans-)national actors. For example, some global market strategists and economists asked why some emerging economies were excluded (for example, South Korea) and others included (Russia). Some foreign policy analysts have questioned the coherence of the quartet, leading one to use 'BRIC-a-Brac' to convey their diverse and toothless nature (Drezner 2009).[6] More prosaically, others warned of a potential 'BRIC bubble' because, even if their GDP continued to expand, this might not translate into higher stock market returns (Tasker 2010; Evans-Pritchard 2011).

BRIC-ing of China

In the Sinophone world, the term 'BRIC' is translated as 'bricks' and has been recontextualized, initially in Taiwan and then more widely, as 'the four golden brick countries' (金磚四國). The 'golden bricks' imaginary has been embraced by the financial and official communities within China as a symbol of 'strength' and sign of 'greatness-at-last'. This reinforces China's long-standing construction of 'national strength' under a one-party authoritarian regime. Many headlines in its official newspaper, *The People's Daily*, adopted BRIC-related discourses such as 'Shining, golden "BRIC"' (6 September 2006) and 'BRIC set to build golden brick' (16 June 2009). This 'golden' metaphor helps to signify the strength and pride of the Chinese nation, especially after its long history of foreign invasion and national humiliation. More specifically, this claim to strength is expressed quantitatively in terms of a 'shining BRIC' that can 'protect 8% GDP growth rate'.

The 2007 North Atlantic Financial Crisis reduced the demand from American and European markets for China's exports and increased unemployment. The Chinese central government responded to the crisis proactively to raise its domestic and international profile. It reiterated its 'protection of 8% GDP growth rate' to project strength as well as to justify a vast stimulus package of RMB4 trillion (US$586 billion) to revive its economy from November 2008 onwards.

Concurrently, the US Federal Reserve sought to stimulate its domestic economy by quantitative easing in late November 2008. It purchased US$ 600 billion mortgage-backed securities with the aim of recapitalizing banks and boosting lending at home and abroad. In contrast China aimed to stimulate its economy via loan-based programmes purportedly intended to support ten major industrial sectors (including steel, shipbuilding, electronics and petrochemicals), promote infrastructural projects (for example, high speed rail, electric grid), boost consumer spending, develop the rural economy and encourage education and housing (for details, see Tong and Zhang 2009). To enable these loans, the central government loosened credit policies and abolished credit ceilings for commercial banks. This resort to fiscal and monetary stimulus has intensified the fiscal imbalances between the central–local relationships.

China's stimulus package, 'property bubble' and local government debt

When these stimulus measures were communicated to the ministries and local governments, they were eager to seize this opportunity and get their pet projects approved (Naughton 2009). However, based on fiscal practice since the late 1990s, this vast stimulus package was financed by around one-third from central government funding; the rest was expected to come from regional-local governments, governmental ministries and state-owned enterprises (SOEs) (see Table 11.4). In planning terms, this shortfall can be filled by financial resources coming from a mix of local government bonds issued by the central government, corporate bonds, medium-term notes and bank loans (see Table 11.4). However, as China's bond market is not well developed, local governments seek their own sources of finance. They find this hard because (1) they are expected to channel 60 per cent of their revenue to Beijing; (2) the economic downturn reduced revenue from business taxes; and (3) they have no formal mandate to borrow money. This inevitably resulted in a funding gap. Thus a 2009 National Audit Office survey reported that local governments in 18 provinces were failing to provide the expected level 'matching funds', with the poorest performing province sending only 48 per cent of the amount due (Xi *et al.* 2009).

This chapter illustrates these problems from the intensification of the use of land and real estate as means to generate income and growth. This tactic is possible thanks to the land leasehold market formally established in the late 1970s under Deng Xiao-Ping. Urban land is state-owned but the separation of ownership and land-use rights mean that public and private actors can shape its disposition and utilization. Urban land-use rights could be leased for a fee for fixed periods (for example, 70 years for residential housing) and land-right leases are tradable by auctions. This development encourages local officials to convert rural land, which still belongs to rural 'collectives', into urban land by compensating (at least in principle) village communities.

This enables local governments to commodify land in two main ways: as an instrument for leveraging loans and source of revenue. First, local governments have accumulated land, licences and equity investments. However, because the Budget Law prohibits local authorities from raising funds directly, these assets cannot be translated into cash. Local governments therefore set up related financial vehicles to borrow from state-owned banks (for example, Bank of China, China Construction Bank) at low interest rates. Land, land-use rights and real estate are used as collateral for these loans for infrastructural projects and further land and real estate development. With the easy availability of credit and the close relationship between local governments and state-owned banks, local government borrowing rose five times between 2008 and 2009 from RMB1 trillion (US$146 billion) to an estimate of RMB5 trillion (US$730 billion) by the end of 2009 (Zhang 2010). Concurrently, Bank of China and China Construction Bank reported profit rose of 26 and 15 per cent respectively for 2009 (*Business Week* 2010).

Second, land-use rights sold through auctions and licensing are sold to private and state-owned developers (for example, China Poly Group, China Resource Group and China Merchant Group) for property projects. This generates revenue for local governments and stimulates economic growth. In 2009, the Ministry of Land and Resources reported local governments generated RMB1.6 trillion (US$233 billion), a 60 per cent increase compared with 2008. Of these land sale revenues in 2009, 84 per cent came from property development (*China Daily* 2010). Such practices provide two benefits. First, they are a major source of fiscal revenues for local governments, motivating them to support and be part of real estate development; and, second, state-owned and private property developers (and their local government partners) can earn high profit from selling housing units, especially when property prices are rising and cheap credits are still available from state-controlled banks.

The business press, ordinary media and peer pressures help to reinforce the widely shared view that property ownership is a source of economic security, hedge against inflation, social status, family safety net and personal pride. Given the limited outlets to invest savings, continuously rising property values up to 2013 suggested that real estate offers higher returns; indeed, low interest rates and the absence of a national property tax allowed speculative property to be purchased and held relatively cheaply. Thus real estate came increasingly to be seen as an object of investment, ownership and/or speculation. Such private economic-investment calculation matches the central government's focus on high growth rates, dependency of local governments upon land/real estate for revenue, the drive of real-estate developers for profit, and the inflow of investment funds generated by quantitative easing in the US and Europe. This prompted fears of a 'property bubble'. According to Colliers International, residential prices in 70 large- and medium-sized cities across China rose in 2009, with 50–60 per cent increases in Beijing and Shanghai. Such increases reduce housing affordability with the conventionally calculated income-to-price ratio in Beijing at 1 to 22 (FlorCruz 2009; Powell 2010; Smith 2010). This ratio means that housing prices for a standard property are 22 times the average annual income of families.

This inflationary trend has added a political dimension to the housing question. This was acknowledged by then Premier Wen Jiabao when he remarked on 27 February 2010 that 'property prices have risen too fast' and this 'wild horse' has to be tamed. Central government leaders have attempted to dampen the market (for example, tightening credit, suspending home loans to buyers purchasing their third housing unit, raising deposits for purchase of new land to 50 per cent; arranging for the exit from this sector of state-owned developers whose core business is not property, imposing a property tax on residential housing, and so on). However, while these measures have cooled second- and third-tier cities (e.g. Tianjin and Wuhan), their impact is limited in major cities such as Beijing, Shanghai and Shenzhen.

In addition, such tightening policies have encouraged banks to find other ways to increase their credit (for example, selling off loans to state-owned trusts and asset-management companies and turning loans into investment products and selling them to private investors). These practices in a land- and debt-based mode of accumulation are supported by those with vested interests in the property and easy credit boom. These include profits for foreign investors, jobs and perks for officials, revenue and growth statistics for ministries and local governments, profit/investment for state-owned banks and related investment vehicles as well as state-owned/private property developers, easy credits for infrastructure-related departments and organizations, and, of course, benefits to property owners (on the real estate coalition, see Sum 2011). These benefits come at a price. Over-investment/speculation in real estate and rising rents destabilize the economy and have weakened the socio-economic position of ordinary people especially in terms of affordability of housing, land appropriation and under-compensation in rural towns. In this regard, rising property prices and wealth accumulation co-exist with social unrest related to resettlement compensation, land clearance, affordability of housing, inflationary pressures, living conditions of the post-80 generations, migrant workers and farmers, as well as administrative excesses.

In addition, the tightening of credit since 2011 has meant that public and private sector borrowers are faced with problems in repaying and servicing their loans. According to the National Audit office, local government debt had risen by nearly 70 per cent from June 2010 to US$3 trillion as of June 2013. Lending in the shadow banking system has increased from 12 per cent of GDP in 2009 to

40 per cent in 2014. There is even talk of a China 'Minsky moment' (Durden 2014). This debt problem is compounded by: (1) the first steps in 2014 to scaling down the US$ 85 billion-a-month asset purchase programme of quantitative easing; and (2) an outflow of capital from the BRIC economies following indications of US and European recovery. Consequently easy credit conditions have turned into a search for hard cash. Local governments, (quasi)state-owned and private firms have to face higher interest payments and higher costs of servicing debts. Some private and state-owned firms (e.g. Zhejiang Xingrun Real Estate Co.) encountered serious difficulties in rolling over their debts and declared bankruptcy. This potential 'Minsky moment' in China can be attributed in part to the transfer of debt (or even 'debt crisis') from the US (and UK) via the Eurozone and sovereign debt crises to China. But it also has important endogenous roots in China's strange mix of excess savings and debt-fuelled growth reflected in central–local dynamics. Thus the global imbalances have not been resolved but merely reshuffled, assuming new forms and manifesting themselves in new sites.

Concluding remarks: the search for new imaginaries

This chapter used a CPE approach. It identified three overlapping stages in the construction of the BRIC economies as a (trans-)national object of 'growth'/'hope'/'strength' since 2001. These discursive shifts were not arbitrary but related to major new material conjunctures – the 9/11 attack on the World Trade Center and the financial crisis that has been unfolding since 2007. A CPE approach highlights such discursive-material linkages and examines how diverse actors experiment with discourses and practices that would orient their interpretations and actions in changed structural circumstances. Some of these discourses (such as the 'decoupling thesis') have been negotiated, selected, deepened, sedimented and naturalized as efforts to manage the security and financial crises continued. In addition, a CPE approach would also examine how: (1) these processes have been mediated by discursive networks that include international investment banks, economic strategists, business media, think tanks, international organizations and foreign policy makers; and (2) governmental knowledging technologies of power, such as identification, investability and agency, were deployed to privilege and naturalize the BRIC economies as objects of 'hope'/'strength' relevant for the imagined recovery of the global political economy.

The BRIC imaginary is negotiated and appropriated differently across time and space. For example, China is regarded as unique and, within the Sinophone world, it is recontextualized as one of 'the four golden brick countries' that symbolizes China 'strength' and sign of 'greatness-at-last' through its capacity to 'protect 8% GDP growth rate'. Responding to the 2007 financial crisis, China continued its investment-led strategy by marshalling a vast economic stimulus package that has intensified some deep-rooted national-local economic and political tensions. The stimulus package gave a 'green light' for regional and local authorities to bring forward 'pet projects' on condition that they raised 70 per cent of the requisite funding. Given the key role of land sales and property development in this context, this has come at the price of forced displacement from land, state terror, dispossession of the already vulnerable and increasing inequality. This represents the part of the 'dark side' of China's stimulus package and reveals the limits of an approach that is too often narrated in the (trans-) national arena exclusively in terms of 'hope'/'strength'. Addressing such neglected or marginalized problems is a key part of the CPE approach, which aims to critique hegemonic imaginaries and narratives.

On the global level, some of the worries about the validity of the BRIC imaginary became stronger after 2010, prompting an initially gradual and then accelerating retreat in BRIC portfolio investments. Indeed, in 2013–2014, the anticipation and then the first steps in tapering US quantitative easing and indications of US and European recovery have unsettled investors and governments in the BRIC economies and other emerging markets. Foreign exchange panics led to the depreciation and selling of the Indian rupee, China's Renminbi, the Brazilian Real and the South African Rand. For example, the Brazilian Real devalued by 20 per cent coupled with inflation and social unrest in August 2013. Lord responded by coining the term 'Fragile Five' (Brazil, Indonesia, India, Turkey and South Africa) in August 2013 to denote their vulnerabilities. Åslund of the Peterson Institute for International Economics announced that 'the BRICs party is over' (2013). Even O'Neill was reported as saying that 'If I were to change it, I would just leave the "C"' (Magalhaes 2013) and started to promote a new acronym called MINT (Mexico, Indonesia, Nigeria and Turkey) as the next transnational imaginary to be hyped. In short, from a CPE perspective, imaginaries do not exist in a vacuum but must be related to extra-discursive contexts and changes. The BRIC imaginary captured for a time key trends in the world economy and even helped to create the potential that it identified, not only economically but also politically. But continuing global trends, including the financial and economic repercussions of crisis-management policies in the advanced economies, have increasingly, as some anticipated, turned the BRIC imaginary sour and prompted the search for new imaginaries of hope and strength. They have also prompted the talk of the BRICs economies and states themselves to seek alternatives to the current global order, although these alternatives have yet to be tested.

Notes

1 Sum (2004) elaborates this approach in outlining six and later seven discursive-material moments involved in the remaking of social relations; see also Sum and Jessop (2013: 219–224).
2 For details of these products, search BRIC at www.goldmansachs.com/our-thinking/archive, accessed 8 February 2014.
3 See www.nasdaq.com/article/the-gl.
4 South Africa joined the BRIC summit in 2011 at the invitation of China.
5 In the G20 Pittsburgh Meeting (September 2009), the discussion of IMF governance reform was blocked by European governments – notably France and the UK – because

of worries about losing influence at the IMF. On 25 April 2010, China's voting power in the World Bank increased from 2.78 to 4.42 per cent.
6 The fundamental differences among the BRIC include diverse political systems, and dissimilar views on key policy issues such as free trade and energy pricing.

References

Achuthan, L. (2012) The Yo-Yo Years, Presentation at Bloomberg Sovereign Debt Conference, Frankfurt am Main, 22 March. Available at www.businesscycle.com/pdf/ecri-the-yo-yo-years.pdf, accessed 14 June 2014.

Åslund, A. (2013) Now the Brics Party Is Over, They Must Wind Down the State's Role, *Financial Times*, 27 August. Available at www.ft.com/cms/s/0/0147b43c-040b-11e3-8aab-00144feab7de.html#axzz2slbmgNbH, accessed 8 February 2014.

Buchanan, M. (2009) Decoupling Is Happening for Real, 10 July 2009. www.chartwelletfadvisor.com/etf-newsletters/vol. 06-iss096.pdf, accessed on 21 February 2013 (no longer available on the web).

Business Week (2010) China Construction Bank 2009 Profit Up 15 Percent. 28 March. www.businessweek.com/ap/financialnews/D9EO1OQ00.htm, accessed on 8 February 2014.

China Daily (2010) China's Land Sales Revenue Close to $233 bln in 2009. 2 February. www.chinadaily.com.cn/china/2010-02/02/content_9417378.htm, accessed on 1 March 2014.

Cruikshank, B. (1999) *The Will to Empower*, Ithaca: Cornell University Press.

Dean, M. (1999) *Governmentality: Power and Rule in Modern Society*, Thousand Oaks: Sage.

Drezner, D.J. (2009) BRIC-a-brac, http://drezner.foreignpolicy.com/posts/2009/06/17/bric-a-brac, accessed on 8 February 2014.

Durden, T. (2014) China's 'Minsky Moment" Is Here, Morgan Stanley Finds. www.zerohedge.com/news/2014-03-19/chinas-minsky-moment-here-morgan-stanley-finds, accessed on 28 June 2014.

Evans-Pritchard, A. (2011) Goldman Sachs Shuns the BRIC for Wall Street. www.telegraph.co.uk/finance/economics/8265175/Goldman-Sachs-shuns-the-BRICs-for-Wall-Street.html, accessed 8 February 2014.

FlorCruz, J. (2009) Will the China Property Bubble Pop? www.cnn.com/2009/BUSINESS/12/30/china.property.bubble/index.html, accessed 8 February 2014.

Goldman Sachs (2010) Idea Website on BRIC. http://www2.goldmansachs.com/ideas/brics/index.html, accessed on 8 February 2014.

Kelly, B. (2009) Brazil, Russia, India and China (the BRICs) Throw Down the Gauntlet of the International Monetary System. 28 June. www.eastasiaforum.org/2009/06/28/brazil-russia-india-and-china-the-brics-throw-down-the-gauntlet-on-monetary-system-reform, accessed on 8 February 2014.

Lord, J. (2013) EM Currencies: Fragile Five, *Morgan Stanley Research*, 1 August, p. 15, www.morganstanleyfa.com/public/projectfiles/dce4d168-15f9-4245-9605-e37e-2caf114c.pdf, accessed on 8 February 2014.

Lordabett.com (2009) Why Decoupling Should Benefit International Investors. https://www.lordabbett.com/articles/wp_why_decoupling_should.pdf, accessed on 3 March 2010 (no longer available on the web).

Magalhaes, L. (2013) China Only BRIC Country Currently Worthy of the Title – O'Neill, *Wall Street Journal*, 23 August. http://blogs.wsj.com/moneybeat/2013/08/23/china-only-bric-country-currently-worthy-of-the-title-oneill/, accessed 8 February 2014.

Marinis, A. (2008) BRIC Consumers Can't Hold Off World Recession. www.livemint.com/2008/12/18211911/Bric-consumers-can8217t-hol.html, accessed on 8 February 2014.

Mellor, W. and Lim, L-M. (2008) BRIC Shoppers will 'Rescue World', Goldman Sachs Says. www.bloomberg.com/apps/news?pid=newsarchive&sid=a3aTPjYcw8a8, accessed 8 February 2014.

Miller, P. and Rose, N. (2008) *Governing the Present*, Cambridge: Polity.

Naughton, B. (2009) Understanding Chinese Stimulus Package, *Chinese Leadership Monitor No. 28*, Spring. www.hoover.org/publications/clm/issues/44613157.html, accessed on 8 February 2014.

O'Neill, J. (2009) The New Shopping Superpower. www.newsweek.com/2009/03/20/the-new-shopping-superpower.html, accessed on 8 February 2014.

Powell, B. (2010) China's Property: Bubble, Bubble, Toil and Trouble, *Time*, 22 March. www.time.com/time/magazine/article/0,9171,1971284,00.html, accessed on 8 February 2014.

Renard, T. (2009) A BRIC in the World: Emerging Powers, Europe, and the Coming Order, Royal Institute for International Relations, *Egmont Paper 31*, Brussels: Academia Press.

Rossi, V. (2008) Synchronized Dive into Recession: Focus on Damage Limitation, International Economic Programme, October, IEP BP 08/04. www.chathamhouse.org/sites/default/files/public/Research/International%20Economics/bp1008recession.pdf, on 8 February 2014.

Sanderson, H. (2008) China Wants More Say in Global Financial Bodies, *USA Today*, 29 October. www.usatoday.com/money/economy/2008-10-29-2068576087_x.htm, accessed on 8 February 2014.

Scher, R. (2009) From BRIC to BIC .th.. or Even to IC??, New York: Foreign Policy Association. http://risingpowers.foreignpolicyblogs.com/2009/06/08/from-bric-to-bic%E2%80%A6or-even-ic/, accessed 8 February 2014.

Schiff, P. (2008) *Little Book of Bull Moves in Bear Markets*, Chichester: Wiley.

Schmidt, G. (2010) Erasing our Innovation Deficit. www.washingtonpost.com/wp-dyn/content/article/2010/02/09/AR2010020901191.html, accessed 8 February 2014.

Shinnick, R. (2008) Decoupling Thesis Intact, Seeking Alpha, 10 February. http://seekingalpha.com/article/63886-decoupling-thesis-intact, accessed on 8 February 2014.

Smith, C. (2010) Global Economy's Next Threat: China's Real Estate Bubble. www.dailyfinance.com/story/global-economys-next-threat-chinas-real-estate-bubble/19302329/#, accessed 8 February 2014.

Sum, N.-L. (2004) Discourses, Material Power and (Counter-)Hegemony. www.lancaster.ac.uk/cperc/docs/Sum%20CPERC%20Working%20Paper%202012-01.pdf, accessed on 8 February 2014.

Sum, N.-L. (2011) Financial Crisis, Land-Induced Financialization and the Subalterns in China, in C. Scherrer (ed.) *Social China*, Berlin: Springer-Verlag, 199–208.

Sum, N.-L. and Jessop, B. (2013) *Towards a Cultural Political Economy: Putting Culture in its Place in Political Economy*, Cheltenham: Edward Elgar.

Tasker, P. (2010) Beware the Lure of GDP When Seeking Stocks in Brics. www.ft.com/cms/s/0/18f2c282-ff1b-11de-a677-00144feab49a.html, accessed on 8 February 2014.

Tett, G. (2010) The Story of the Brics. www.ft.com/cms/s/2/112ca932- 00ab-11df-ae8d-00144feabdc0.html, accessed on 8 February 2014.

Tong, S. and Zhang, Y. (2009) China's Responses to the Economic Crisis, EAI Background Brief No. 438, National Singapore University, www.eai.nus.edu.sg/BB438.pdf, accessed on 8 February 2014.

Wilson, D. and Purushothaman, R. (2003) Dreaming with the BRICs: The Path to 2050, Goldman Sachs Global Economic Research Website, Global Economic Paper No. 99. www.goldmansachs.com/japan/ideas/brics/book/99-dreaming.pdf, accessed on 8 February 2014.

Window of China (2009) China Updates Details of Stimulus Fund, 21 May. http://news.xinhuanet.com/english/2009-05/21/content_11415559.htm, accessed on 8 February 2014.

Zhang, M. (2010) CBRC Beefs Up Measures, *Shanghai Daily*, 25 February. www.shanghaidaily.com/Business/finance/CBRC-beefs-up-measures/shdaily.shtml, accessed 8 February 2014.

Index

Page numbers in *italics* denote tables, those in **bold** denote figures.

For Product Safety Concerns and Information please contact our EU representative GPSR@taylorandfrancis.com
Taylor & Francis Verlag GmbH, Kaufingerstraße 24, 80331 München, Germany

www.ingramcontent.com/pod-product-compliance
Ingram Content Group UK Ltd.
Pitfield, Milton Keynes, MK11 3LW, UK
UKHW020158200926
475702UK00004B/523
9781138805590